Do You Know Who I am?

DO YOU KNOW WHO I AM?
A MEMOIR

TIM PIGOTT-SMITH

BLOOMSBURY
LONDON · OXFORD · NEW YORK · NEW DELHI · SYDNEY

Bloomsbury Continuum
An imprint of Bloomsbury Publishing Plc

50 Bedford Square
London
WC1B 3DP
UK

1385 Broadway
New York
NY 10018
USA

www.bloomsbury.com

Bloomsbury, Continuum and the Diana logo are trademarks of Bloomsbury Publishing Plc

First published 2017

British Library Cataloguing-in-Publication Data
A catalogue record for this book is available from the British Library.

Library of Congress Cataloguing-in-Publication data has been applied for.

ISBN: HB: 978-1-4729-3424-6
        ePDF: 978-1-4729-3422-2
        ePub: 978-1-4729-3425-3

2 4 6 8 10 9 7 5 3 1

Typeset by Integra Software Services Pvt. Ltd.
Printed and bound in Great Britain by CPI Group (UK) Ltd, Croydon CR0 4YY

To find out more about our authors and books visit www.bloomsbury.com.
Here you will find extracts, author interviews, details of forthcoming events and the option to sign up for our newsletters.

For Pam and my family, and our old friend
Howard Davies, who died shortly after I delivered this book

CONTENTS

Illustrations   ix

1   A Skeleton in the Cupboard   1

2   Shakespeare's Birthplace   9

3   Shakespeare's School   21

4   The Right Direction   31

5   The Real Thing   41

6   At Last   51

7   The RSC, Stratford   63

8   The RSC, London   71

9   Washington DC   85

10 The Big Apple   93

11 Backwards a Bit   99

12 Sideways   107

12A Upwards a Bit   117

14 The TV Club   127

15 Escape   143

16 Finding Merrick   155

17 Being Merrick   165

18 After Merrick   177

19 Dame Peg   189

20   The Bitter Smell of Success   199

21   Back to the Theatre   211

22   The Black Glove   225

23   Compass   233

24   *The Chief*   247

25   Endgame   255

26   Stepping Stones   267

27   Further Steps   279

28   A King on Broadway   289

29   Do You Know Who I Am?   305

Index   319

ILLUSTRATIONS

1   The author as a young child   2
2   The author as Sir Joseph Surface in *School for
    Scandal* by Richard Brinsley Sheridan, Wyggeston
    Boys School, 1961   12
3   The cast of *The Famous Victories of King Henry V*,
    King Edward VI School, Stratford, 1964,
    (author extreme right)   23
4   The author as Hal in *The Famous Victories of King
    Henry V*   23
5   *Dadadidactics*, an evening of surrealist drama,
    Bristol University, 1965. The author with Ian
    Gardhouse in 'Mort and Levy'   32
6   The author as Pompey in William Shakespeare's
    Antony and Cleopatra, with Patrick Stewart
    (Enobarbus) and Richard Johnson (Antony), Royal
    Shakespeare Company, 1973. Photograph:
    Zoe Dominic   72
7   The author rehearsing *Titus Andronicus* with Colin
    Blakely, Royal Shakespeare Company, 1973   77
8   *This Week* magazine cover featuring John Wood as
    Sherlock Holmes and the author as Dr Watson in
    Sherlock Holmes, Kennedy Center, Washington
    DC, 1974   89
9   The author as Angelo in *Measure for Measure* by
    William Shakespeare, BBC TV, 1979   113
10 The author as Vasques in *'Tis Pity She's a Whore* by
    John Ford, BBC TV, 1980   129
11 The author as Timothy Perkins, *School Play*,
    BBC TV, 1981   131

12 The author as Mr Blenkinsop in *Hannah*,
BBC TV, 1980   133

13 The author as Sir Henry Percy (Hotspur) in William
Shakespeare's *Henry IV Part I*; Hotspur's death
scene, BBC TV, 1979   135

14 From the same scene, *Henry IV Part I*   135

15 The author as a young Captain Hardy in *Aspects
of a Hero*, filmed on the HMS *Victory*, ATV, 1980,
with Kenneth Colley and Michael N. Harbour   149

16 The author playing an older Captain Hardy,
Aspects of a Hero, 1980   151

17 The author playing a very young Hamer
Shawcross in *Fame is the Spur*, BBC TV, 1982   152

18 The author as Ronald Merrick with Art Malik as
Hari Kumar in *The Jewel in the Crown*, ITV, 1984   164

19 Ronald Merrick, *The Jewel in the Crown*   166

20 Rehearsing for *The Jewel in the Crown* on 'Chetak',
India, 1982   168

21 The author as a one-armed Ronald Merrick awaiting
his death   170

22 The author with Christopher Morahan, Dame
Peggy Ashcroft and Jim O'Brien at the BAFTA
awards, 1985   181

23 The author photographed on the first night of
Benefactors by Michael Frayn, Vaudeville Theatre
stage door, 1984   186

24 The author with Dame Peggy Ashcroft at a
reception for *The Jewel in the Crown*, 1985   196

25 The author with Mark Buffery in *Sexual Perversity
in Chicago* by David Mamet, Bristol Old Vic, 1978   203

26 The author in *Bengal Lancer*, a play based on the
book by Francis Yeats-Brown, Leicester Haymarket
and Lyric Hammersmith, 1985   206

27 The author as Francis Crick in *Life Story*,
BBC TV, 1985   212

28 Dame Judi Dench as Sarah Eldridge in *Entertaining Strangers* by David Edgar, National Theatre, Cottesloe, 1987   217

29 The author as Henry Moule in *Entertaining Strangers*   219

30 The author as Iachimo in *Cymbeline* with Peter Woodward as Posthumus, National Theatre, 1986-88   220

31 A villain, a king and a clown – Iachimo, Leontes and Trinculo, publicity image for *Cymbeline*, *A Winter's Tale* and *The Tempest*, National Theatre,1986-1988   220

32 The Bond glove. Handmade by M, alias Dame Judi Dench, on the set of *Quantum of Solace*   231

33 Atahualpa's death scene in *The Royal Hunt of the Sun* by Peter Shaffer, Compass tour, 1989   243

34 The author as John Stafford in *The Chief*, Anglia TV, 1989-91   248

35 Anthony Quayle as Aaron the Moor in William Shakespeare's *Titus Andronicus*, Shakespeare Memorial Theatre, 1959   257

36 The author as Salieri in *Amadeus* by Peter Shaffer, Compass, 1991   261

37 The set for *Hamlet*, Open Air Theatre, Regent's Park, 1994   269

38 Damian Lewis as Hamlet and Pamela Miles as Gertrude in *Hamlet*, Open Air Theatre, Regent's Park, 1994   271

39 The author as Larry Slade in *The Iceman Cometh* by Eugene O'Neill, Almeida, Old Vic and Broadway, 1998-9   277

40 With Kevin Spacey in *The Iceman Cometh*   277

41 The author as King Lear with Bernard Lloyd as Gloucester, *King Lear*, West Yorkshire Playhouse, 2011 283

42 The author as Prospero in *The Tempest*, Bath Theatre Royal, 2012. Photograph: Nobby Clark   287

43 The author with his wife, Pamela Miles   290

44   The author, playing Charles, prepares in his dressing
     room backstage at Wyndham's Theatre in 2015,
     prior to a performance of *King Charles III*, written by
     Mike Bartlett and directed by Rupert Goold.
     Photograph: © Matt Humphrey for Curtain
     Call, 2017   299
45   The author's son Tom with his wife Rachel, on
     their wedding day, 2011   306
46   The author's parents, 1937   308

1

A Skeleton in the Cupboard

Was I born with an audience in my head? Or did one arrive later?

I have a theory that most actors are performing for one of their parents. I believe I am acting for both my parents, but if I had to choose I would have to say I am an actor because of my mother.

In the post-war baby-boom years of a surprise Labour government, the Marshall Plan and the newly formed National Health Service, 900,000 babies per annum were born. My parents were among the optimists who thought this new world was ready for their offspring, so although I was born during the first Age of Austerity, in 1946, my mum and dad weren't far wrong, were they?

My parents lived through two world wars. The world now is a darkening place, with terrorism on the increase, and 40 per cent child poverty in the London Borough of Camden where I live. My generation has survived the atomic threat, witnessed terrifying conflicts in Vietnam, Iraq, Afghanistan and – ongoing – in Syria, but we have not been through anything like the Blitz. My education was provided by the state. I own a house in London. We all live longer. We baby boomers have been pretty lucky.

My mum was a very strong woman, who would, I suspect, have become a professional actress had her circumstances been different. She was the daughter of a lower-middle-class grocer, who had a corner shop in Rugby, the town where I was born. Mum's father was portly, very strict and rather intimidating. I was both in awe of, and very fond of him. A fine gardener and vegetable grower, he kept his tools and seed trays in an air-raid shelter, just past the outside loo, in the small backyard behind his shop.

To those of us born in 1946 the war was still part of everyday life, visible in reminders like Grandpa's Anderson shelter: these shelters had been provided free to people who earned less than £5 a week, and cheap to others. Bomb damage – gaps in rows of houses – rationing coupons and the lack of basic food that rationing indicated, and fuel shortages were the inevitable aftermath of six years of conflict.

The impact of the war was also there, *in*visibly, in tangible national pride that a great cause had been fought for, and a victory over evil achieved. The BBC – the wireless – was the voice of the nation. Friendly bobbies patrolled the streets. The monarchy was cherished, and was, unquestionably, a binding social factor. There was a desire to honour what had nearly been lost – civilised values. There was a sense of national identity. When boycotting South Africa became an issue, many people were angry because they had served alongside South Africans, most notably in the desert war.

Grandpa's air-raid shelter was a low semicircle of strips of corrugated iron, half-buried in the earth, covered with moss and ivy, some seven or eight yards long, and you went down a couple of steps to enter it. It was musty, cobwebbed, eerie, but I spent quite a bit of time down there reading, and, with Grandpa, doing little jobs for him. My favourite job was helping him deliver the groceries. He had a motorbike with a large wooden box on wheels fitted to the front. He would load up the grocery boxes and bags, squeeze me into the corner, and off we would set. The roads were quieter then. Grandpa never wore a helmet – you didn't have to – but he did wear goggles. He also wore a waistcoat, with a watch and chain, and he always sported a cloth cap.

I enjoyed Grandpa's shop, too. Dark-brown shelves displayed tins of corned beef and Spam, cartons of Ovaltine, jars of Bisto. Grandpa had beer on tap, and the locals would come in with their jugs. My first memory of the shop was arriving with my mum, late at night, after a train journey from Southampton and a boat trip from Africa. Dad was working as a journalist on the *East African Standard*, and he was still in Nairobi, completing his contract. Out there we had a bungalow, and a soft-topped Morris which Dad used to drive into the Kenya National Park where we had picnics: why we were not eaten alive I cannot imagine – you would not get into Longleat nowadays in a soft-top car! We had servants, a houseboy and a cook. I don't think Mum and Dad had ever had it so good. Or, to be honest, would have it so good, ever again. I remember it, and they talked about it, with a sort of Empire glow, a post-war colonial moment of reward for the horrors of the war, during which my mum had done some volunteer nursing and Dad was in charge of ground staff at an RAF station near Rugby.

Mum did amateur productions of plays at Nairobi's Donovan Maule Theatre, and my parents gave big parties to which they invited their Indian lawyer, incurring disapproval from some of their friends. The African idyll went sour because I became ill. Aged 4, I developed an abscess in my ear, for which the doctor gave me the then equivalent of penicillin, known as M & B. These drugs, named after the company that made them – May and Bryant – did not work, so they gave me more. And more. Until I was so sick that the doctor told my mother to get me back to England for serious medical attention. Dad left Nairobi not long before the Mau Mau became active.

On the boat home, where the drug regime was continued, I went into a coma. Things looked bad, not to say terminal. The ship's medical team broadcast a message to the effect that a child on board was very sick, and needed the urgent attention of a doctor. A doctor came, asked some questions, took one look at me, and said, 'Stop the drugs.'

It emerged much later that I was allergic to the sulphur in M & B, but by the time my life had been saved, my blood was 96 per cent white. My immune system was shot to bits. This imbalance in my blood was not righted until my teenage years. Consequently, I was a frail child, managing to catch every bug that was around, spending sometimes weeks in bed with flu, developing sinusitis and regularly being injected with courses of penicillin, to which – mercifully – I was not allergic. Penicillin, however, is thick and glutinous. The painful injections went into my backside. They arrived with Dr Doleman three times a day. Bowler-hatted, in a black overcoat, doctor's bag in hand, he would cross the lawn funereally to our flat in Leicester, where we lived when I was nearly 6. When I was 8 my blood count was still so askew that I was admitted to hospital with suspected leukaemia. I was by then so sick of injections that on one occasion it took eight people to hold me down to get the needle in. I did not have leukaemia.

The doctor who saved my life on the boat home from Africa was Dr Leonard Hirsch, a Jew who had got out of Germany before the war. My mother was enduringly grateful for his life-saving moment of inspiration. Blue airmail letters, on flimsy Onion Skin paper, were exchanged with Dr Hirsch two or three times a year. In 1971, I was in Rome, where he lived with his sister in a smart, small apartment. Over tea, he was charming and hospitable. Mum was thrilled that I was able to thank him in person for what he had done, although he humbly appeared disinterested in having saved me. I sensed he did not like the past, with good reason, and he dodged a lot of my questions. Nor was he going to permit any emotion. The most I managed was a sort of hyper-sincere 'thank you' as I shook his hand on leaving.

Along with my coma came an experience that I have never fully understood. I remember, quite clearly, getting out of the top bunk in which I was sleeping on board ship on the way home from Africa and watching my bare feet climb down the bunk ladder. I surmised that there was no one there, which was odd: my sickbed had been attended by the ship's nurses, and of course my anxious mother. I was never alone. But on this occasion I was able to climb out of bed and go, unaccompanied, through the door of our cabin. I entered a long white passage that didn't appear to lead anywhere. I walked barefoot along this unchanging white corridor for some time. The light was increasingly dazzling, blinding. From what I have read of near-death experiences, this is fairly typical. I don't remember leaving the corridor, or turning back, and I am genuinely unsure if my mind really was aware of the declining state of my body, or if it was just a dream. But the images remain clear to me.

There is a photograph of me on board ship, and I look dreadful: wan, gaunt. My mother, who is kneeling, holding me by the ship's rail, looks worse: pale and distraught. Arriving at night in Rugby was strange, too, after the gloomy railway carriage light, the rattling, smelly old train and the cold. Grandpa raised the hinged end of the counter, swung the little door and ushered me into the cosy, fire-lit room behind the shop. When my grandmother saw me, she looked at my mother and said, 'What have you done to him?' I clearly looked as ill and ghostly as I felt.

Grandpa had bought two small terraced houses opposite the shop, in which two of his sons lived – my uncles Roy and Maurice. They paid Grandpa a peppercorn rent, and eventually inherited their homes. Reg, the eldest, was more artistically inclined. All three brothers remained in Rugby, but my mum, and her sister Honor, were ambitious, and both left. My cousin Michael became a master printer and still lives in his father, Roy's, house, opposite Grandpa's old shop, which was recently destroyed by fire.

My Uncle Reg, whom my mother adored, lived in another part of Rugby, and had two daughters, the eldest of whom, Cousin Liz, maintains my contact with the family. Reg had a good job at British Thomson-Houston. Mum and Reg were close because they did amateur operatics together, both of them appearing in *The Yeomen of the Guard*, *The Pirates of Penzance* and *The Gondoliers*. To one of these productions a cub reporter from the *Rugby Advertiser* was sent as a reviewer. He saw my mum and fell in love with her. A couple of years later, in 1937, they were married, and Dad – who had two sisters and a brother – joined a family that was not just large, but, unlike his own, united. Although I discovered that this unity came at a cost.

Grandpa died of bowel cancer in 1963. Gran was devastated, but she went to live in a flat near Roy and Maurice and was quite comfortable. For the last six weeks of her life Gran came to live at our home, which was then in Stratford-upon-Avon, where Mum looked after her. I had left home by this time. Gran told Mum she wanted to see me because she felt guilty about being in my bed. I was really shocked to find her white, pasty and barely conscious, although her hair was combed and tidy. I sat by her bed – *my* bed – held her hand and tried to talk to her. For a fleeting moment she managed to focus on me – it was like a baby whose rolling eyes suddenly fix you: you know that they have, however briefly, actually seen you. Although Gran was unable to speak, struggling to sit up, she squeezed my hand very hard. Then she faded back into some half-world. She died that night, very peacefully: a hard-working, caring wife and mother, and a woman of great personal dignity. I was so numb I managed to help the nurse lay her out.

I was unable to get to Gran's funeral because I was involved in technical rehearsals for a play: time, tide and the theatre wait for no man. Talking to Cousin Liz I discovered the most extraordinary secret about my gran. Over the next 30 years I gave my mother several opportunities to share this confidence with me, but this skeleton was well and truly shut in the family cupboard.

The skeleton was this: when Grandpa married Gran, she already had a child – by another man. In the early 1900s this was seriously frowned upon. Gran had left home as a young girl and gone to London, where she found employment in the theatre, working for Zena Dare, the musical comedy star. She became pregnant and was sent home in disgrace. Was Gran impregnated by a wicked actor? She was pleased that I went to university, but was less happy about my going to drama school. Perhaps this was why.

Eventually I asked my Uncle Maurice, Mum's youngest brother and one surviving sibling, and this is what he told me: Grandpa had married Ada, unaware that she had a baby, Sid, who was being brought up by her Northamptonshire farming family. When Ada and Eddie were married, Gran was pregnant again – with Reg! My gran! The children thought Sid was a distant cousin.

It pains me that my lovely gran spent her life separated from one of her children, and this family skeleton explains a lot about the way my mother developed, denied any ambitions she might have had to become a professional actress.

And I think that is partly why I became an actor. Someone had to do Mum's acting for her!

2

SHAKESPEARE'S BIRTHPLACE

I was 4 when we got home from Africa. Dad was working for the *Rugby Advertiser*, so we lived with Gran and Grandpa until he landed the job of news editor of the *Leicester Mercury*. We moved to a very pleasant flat in the Stoneygate area, and, although my parents could ill afford it, they sent me to a private school, where the teachers thought I was clever and pushed me too hard. I grew to hate it, so, because I sang well, I was brought to London, to audition for Westminster Cathedral Choir School. This would have solved the educational issue, but it meant leaving home. I sabotaged Mum's dream with an uncomfortable, indifferent audition, but I *did* get into the choir of Leicester Cathedral.

The choir was a five-days-a-week commitment – and you only got paid for weddings and funerals. I had just got into the top six on the descant side (a lighter soprano than the opposing altos), when my voice broke. But by then I had spent four years as a Cathedral chorister. I liked the beauty and calm of the Cathedral, the dressing up, the dramatic sermons, the ritual, the sense of history. I still love plainchant: I always enjoyed singing psalms as a choirboy.

Through my teens I went to church regularly with Mum, who was a devout Christian. Churches, temples, synagogues and mosques are the only buildings devoted exclusively to the spirit, and although I abandoned my adolescent faith there is a clear connection between the world of the spirit and that of the theatre. The theatre's roots in Ancient Greece are related to temples, and in this country to churches. The act of people coming together for a play is an act of communion akin to a church service, and the best theatre not only entertains you, it instructs, moves, changes and improves you.

At St John the Baptist Junior School I was very happy. I didn't enjoy work that much, but because I was conscientious and well supported by my parents I did enough to get by, and, with the 11-plus looming, getting by was of some concern. Mum and Dad tutored me using past exam papers. The real problem with the 11-plus was that children who didn't make grammar school were branded failures, and they went to secondary modern schools. England was really class-conscious then, and failure carried a social stigma. There was a *13-* plus, and Dad's newspaper, the *Leicester Mercury*, annually carried the story of some brave kid who made it from their secondary modern into a grammar school. This served merely to demonstrate the fate of those stuck in the failure regime. I was motivated by a desire to avoid such failure, and, to our palpable relief, I passed.

Wyggeston Boys' – over a thousand-strong even in 1957 – was probably the best school in Leicester – a grammar school with public school pretensions. David Attenborough and I occasionally swap memories, because Horace Lacey, the biology teacher who inspired David, taught me, too. It was not Mr Lacey's fault that I was more interested in English than dissecting worms.

As I wheeled my bike up the Great Drive – which was over a hundred yards long – clutching my satchel, with tie tied and compulsory cap on head, I could see, across expansive games fields, the Great Hall, where we held morning assembly. The Hall was large enough to house the senior school (800-plus), and boasted a mighty organ in the gallery. We did school plays here, and the school orchestra gave concerts of a very high standard. Opposite the Great Hall was Headmaster's House, and, next to that, *Headmaster's goldfish bowl*, as the open-air swimming pool was commonly known. Unlucky first-formers were thrown into it, fully clothed: Wyggy had public school pretensions in every way.

I was one of the lucky ones. I knew it, and seized my opportunities with both hands. The education provided by Wyggy was superb – structured, with lots of games, which I enjoyed, although I was still a pretty skinny specimen. The school had been a hospital during the war, and the simple, low buildings thrown up as wards were now primitive classrooms. It summed up the way things were – poor but proud. During my first year, I loved gym and athletics, started learning the violin and sang in house and school choirs. When my voice broke, my extra free time was happily taken up with cricket, which I love, but never had the nerve for; rugby, which I found absolutely thrilling, and was pretty good at, and swimming, at which I was, unfortunately, very good – I was Leicester Junior Schools Breaststroke Champion at the age of 11. I hated training for swimming, and at Wyggy, under the eagle eye of whip-cracking Mrs Herbert, there was a lot. Endless lengths, with a small float under your neck, to exercise your legs. Boring.

At the end of the first year I was considered just clever enough to be put into an express stream – O level in three years instead of four. It was a mistake, but despite my faltering academic development, there was always someone I could look up to. Ed Rayner was a short, stately man, who wore thick glasses, dark suits, waistcoats, ties and polished shoes: he was a committed history teacher. I was third-rate at history, and my efforts must have disappointed Ed, but he was endlessly encouraging. The *real* bond between us was the school play.

In the second form, I auditioned for *The Caucasian Chalk Circle* – Ed was nothing if not ambitious! I was in the running for the role of Grusha, the lead girl. It was between me and one Daryl Runswick, who became a renowned King's Singer, and branched off into jazz, taking up the double bass. *He* landed the role of Grusha, while I became an unlikely mother-in-law and various serving maids.

The play I did with Ed that I most enjoyed was *The School for Scandal*. It was elegantly staged and quite funny – largely because of Simon Hoggart as Mrs Candour. His father, Richard, had joined Leicester University; famous for *The Uses of Literacy* and infamous for his role in the *Lady Chatterley's Lover* trial, he was a key witness in support of Lawrence's racy book.

Sir Joseph Surface in School for Scandal, *Wyggeston Boys School, 1961, in a bad wig, and a costume made by my mum*

I played Sir Joseph. The school magazine said my scene with Sir Oliver Teazle was of a professional standard, but at 15 I had no idea what I was doing. I said the words in the right order, and, as I spoke quite well, it must have sounded better than it felt.

Ed lived near the bottom of the Great Drive and in the mid-eighties we walked up it together. Wyggy had become the Queen Elizabeth Sixth Form College. The Great Hall stood empty and neglected; the organ had been boarded up and secured with a padlocked chain. There was no curtain on the stage where we had performed, and, in the body of the hall, two boys were playing badminton.

Ed led me disconsolately across the drive to Headmaster's House. As boys we had not even been allowed inside the garden gate, which now hung off its hinges, rusted, unpainted. The front door was ajar. Round the walls of the spacious hall were cages containing games kit. Shorts and plimsolls stuck out between the bars, and socks and football boots littered the unpolished, scratched parquet floor. There was an air of desolation, heightened by the tangy odour of the changing room. Ed had tears in his eyes. After a few moments, he said quietly, 'Headmaster used to hold dances here.' It was a fleeting image of a lost beauty. Ed had not long retired, but there was clearly nothing left of the beloved school to which he had given his life. His lovely wife, Pam, died all too young, and although he was well supported by their children he missed her badly. He died last year, in his late eighties. Goodbye, Mr Chips.

The summer before I went to Wyggy I was first taken to Stratford-upon-Avon. Theatre in Leicester in the late fifties was poor, particularly when the old Haymarket closed. A touring company called Century Theatre performed in their caravan auditorium, playing an adventurous repertoire that included O'Casey and Ionesco, but for a mere ten shillings (50p) Leicester's Provincial Coach Company transported you to Stratford's Memorial Theatre, and provided your ticket.

On my first trip in 1956, to see Emlyn Williams as Shylock, I was sitting near the front of the coach, and as we got closer to Stratford I watched the country road with eager anticipation.

Approaching one particular bend, seeing the green bank, the gnarled tree and the clement curve of the road, I could hardly breathe. 'I know this place,' I thought; 'I have been here before.' As the great baseball player Yogi Berra said, 'It felt like déjà-vu, all over again!' Thanks to Provincial, I enjoyed many great productions and actors – a star-studded parade of Olivier, Gielgud, Charles Laughton, Sam Wanamaker, Judi Dench, Peter O'Toole, Peggy Ashcroft, Paul Robeson, Vanessa Redgrave, Christopher Plummer, Dorothy Tutin, Albert Finney and Eric Porter.

Moving to live in Stratford in 1962, when Dad became the editor of the *Stratford-upon-Avon Herald*, was a dream come true. Every week his front page carried a quote from Shakespeare: 'I wish no other herald, no other speaker of my living actions.' My new school was the King Edward VI School. It is more than likely that the Bard was the school's most famous old boy, a connection that was not lost on me.

On our first night of actually living in Stratford, Dad said, 'Let's just go down to the theatre and see what's on.' The Shakespeare season ran from April to October, and for the rest of the year there was opera, ballet, the local amateur operatic society and occasionally plays on tour: that night *The Rehearsal* was playing, a confection of Jean Anouilh's bound for the West End, which made accessible the then popular themes of illusion and reality.

When the play begins, the actors appear in seventeenth-century costume, but when they start to talk about aeroplanes you realise they are not *of* the seventeenth century: they are costumed because they are rehearsing a seventeenth-century play by Marivaux. *The Rehearsal* is clever, somewhat dated in its naivety; great theatre but not, in the end, great writing. The cast was stellar, boasting a flamboyant, red-heeled Robert Hardy (leading actors at the Comédie-Française used to wear red heels), the remarkable Alan Badel and the young Maggie Smith. If this was life in Stratford, then it was certainly for me.

I could not keep away from the theatre, and would often go down to join the queue at five in the morning to get a cheap seat for that evening: it only cost two shillings to stand (10p).

I stood through five separate performances of a plain but lucid *Julius Caesar* featuring Tom Fleming – who went on to become the voice of the nation on royal occasions – as Brutus, and Cyril Cusack as an irascible Cassius. Roy Dotrice was an extravagant, epileptic Caesar. I also stood to see Paul Scofield in Peter Brook's revolutionary *Lear*.

To add to the excitement, Peter Hall was turning the old Memorial Theatre into the Royal Shakespeare Company, and some of the great names I had seen performing became founder members of the RSC – the new face of British theatre. At this time, Olivier was sowing the seeds of the National Theatre in Chichester. But most of provincial England was a very different kettle of fish.

In the history of twentieth-century theatre, my life stands at an interesting point. I am a sort of bridge between a lost past and the present. I do not want that old world – and its actors – to be forgotten. Charlton Heston did not say much that was sensible – although as a former president of the National Rifle Association he was unnecessarily articulate about the right to own a gun – but he did say 'Acting is smoke.' I want to try and capture some of that smoke. To give you an idea of the excitement created by the RSC, you need to know what theatre was like elsewhere in England.

Post-war, there was an amazing, countrywide network of repertory theatres which had begun as a movement in 1912, led by Miss Annie Horniman at the Gaiety Theatre, Manchester. 'Rep' is a demeaning word that is slightly unfair to what was, before film and television, a great source of entertainment for most people. As well as a few great stars, when I started work in 1969, there was still an army of unsung actors who kept repertory alive. As with the well-made play, which became unfashionable in the wake of *Look Back in Anger* in the late 1950s, not everything about the fedora-wearing, loud, devoted ranks of strolling play-ers was so out of date that it needed discarding. These people had phenomenal memories and strong voices. Loud they may have been, on and off the stage, but they could move from drawing-room comedy to Shakespeare, from thriller to farce, from Ibsen to panto with total ease and competence. They fuelled the fire at one-weekly, two-weekly, three-weekly and four-weekly reps in – Bolton, Derby, Lincoln, Margate, Southwold, Frinton, Dundee, Amersham, Liverpool, Horsham, Ipswich, Leatherhead, Colchester, and many other cities.

Companies were built around a leading man and lady, plus character actors and juveniles, and the rehearsal structure was rigid so that, in the limited time available, the entire play was read, blocked (placed on the stage) and rehearsed, allowing sufficient free time for learning. The youngest, least experienced actors would play the small parts; they might have to dress up as a yokel or as an aristocrat, in which case they were contractually obligated to provide their own evening dress! In addition to some stage-managing – responsibilities being related to the size of the company and the play – they would frequently have to act somebody a lot older. Lighting was less sophisticated then and make-up more important. At the age of 19, you might find yourself playing Scrotum, the wrinkled retainer. You needed to know which of the many sticks of Leichner in your make-up kit to apply to your baby face to help you age. If you wanted to wear a moustache or beard, you would have to make your own, steaming open, and straightening, bunches of crêpe hair, fashioning it yourself, and sticking it on with Spirit Gum. Actors had their own substantial make-up kits – sometimes kept in battered old cigar boxes – and an essential ingredient was Crowes Cremine – thick white removal cream.

The book *The Art of Coarse Acting* by Michael Green captures the vulgar aspect of theatre then: how do you do a soliloquy in theatre in the round? You stand in the middle and rotate slowly. If you have been stabbed, and have to lie dead onstage, make sure you are almost entirely concealed behind a sofa, with just your feet sticking out at one end, and the handle of the knife visible above the sofa back.

There were many silly stories in circulation, such as the actor who forgets the knife in the murder scene and is obliged to kick his victim to death, explaining as he does so that his boot is poisoned. Things were much less formal, less structured, and mistakes were made. In one play we did during my first professional year, the telephone failed to ring on cue. The girl running the show unashamedly called out, 'Pring-pring!' loudly from the prompt corner. Five actors leapt at the phone! Audiences were relatively untroubled by such mistakes: they would notice them, be amused by them, but not allow them to spoil their evening. They were happy to go with the flow, and for reward were treated to a fantastic range of work – everything from *The Boy Friend* to *Dance of Death*. Actors gave years of their lives to provide entertainment in return for a meagre wage and an itinerant lifestyle.

This lost world of rep was pilloried in the radio series *Round the Horne*, in the Noël Coward-based characters of Dame Celia Molestrangler and ageing juv Binkie Huckaback. Weekly, they played scenes of suppressed British passion, based on the stiff-upper-lip style of *Brief Encounter*. This world is captured more mundanely in a, possibly apocryphal, story about an actor who ruled the roost at Oldham weekly rep for many years. His name was Hughie Wallingford. Imagine the scene: the play is *Dracula*. The curtain rises and the designer has gone to town: a room of Gothic majesty elicits a round of applause from the audience. Bats (probably umbrellas) flit past upstage windows in the moonlight. Owls hoot. Downstage centre there is a coffin in a green spotlight. The lid of the coffin creaks open, and a hand, with very long black fingernails appears, followed shortly by another. The footlights flicker. There is lightning. A head emerges and, as the actor clambers laboriously out of the coffin, swirling his black cape, there is a clap of thunder. The make-up is staggering – a long black wig, dark rings under the eyes, black lipstick and blood trickling from the corner of the mouth. And a lady in the front row says, 'Eee, look! It's Hughie Wallingford!'

No actor today would go to Crewe to find work, but back then actors, in transit between jobs, often bumped into each other on Sundays at Crewe station, where they had to change trains. As they did so, they exchanged information about jobs, calling from one platform to another: 'Did you know they're doing *Hay Fever* at Liverpool next month?' This lifestyle inevitably bred jokes about actors travelling. One such story involves a leading actor who is desperate to get to his next place of employment, and, finding no trains or buses available, begs a lift on a barge transporting horse manure. The bargee takes him on board extremely unwillingly. As they progress at a snail's pace along the canal, a passing fellow boatman calls out: 'Ahoy, matey! What have you on board?' The bargee replies, 'Shit! And an actor.' The actor turns to the bargee and says, imperiously, 'Do you mind if we discuss the billing?'

To sustain this itinerant world, there developed a network of theatrical digs. These were beyond basic, and some of the landladies were notorious. When I started, Ollie Pingle of Cardiff, a dictatorial woman who offered nylon sheets and a greasy breakfast, was famous. In Leeds, Basil Hartley, a retired actor who worshipped Ivor Novello, ran two enormous houses of 'rooms-to-let' called Novello House and Villa Novello. You had your own gas meter and were advised to turn up with a supply of shillings! Around the walls of the rooms were numerous pictures of Basil's hero, and, one suspected from the way he stroked them, one-time lover.

One actor, whose name did outlive him, was Robert Atkins, who ran the Old Vic from 1921 to 1926. He was less 'rep' and more actor-manager. I saw him onstage once when he was very old, playing a wondrously rich and naughty Falstaff. Atkins founded the Regent's Park Open Air Theatre and later ran the Shakespeare Memorial Theatre; here, stories about him abounded, many of them to told me by Tony Church, a founder member of the RSC and the best Polonius ever to David Warner's Hamlet. Because of a certain dryness of character, Tony was known as 'the Established Church'.

Atkins was famed for his combination of bad language and elegant phraseology. The most frequently quoted anecdote tells of his fury at being informed that, because of his notoriously foul language, he was not going to be asked to read the lesson in Holy

Trinity Church on Shakespeare's birthday, a duty and privilege for the artistic director of the Memorial Theatre. Espying the vicar in the street, just after he had received this humiliating news, Atkins hailed him, 'My good man!' The vicar turned, inquisitively. Atkins boomed across the road, with full voice, 'My dear Vicar, advance me one cogent reason why I shouldn't read the fucking lesson!' Atkins impersonations were accompanied by a wrist-shaking gesture of the right hand – fingers splayed – moving vertically up and down at waist level. The gesture alone told people who you were taking off – you had to do it! To it you added a deep, actory voice, with fruity, extended vowels. In some versions of the 'fucking lesson' story, Atkins expatiates on his theme: 'You can take your church, my good man, and the steeple, *and* the bell – which has a most melodious tone – and shove them up your capacious arse, wherein, I am sure, there is ample room!' Such people are easy to laugh at, but they gave colour and life to the theatre.

It has to be a good thing that theatre has moved on from this ramshackle world, but it is easy to underestimate what a local rep meant to its community. It was a place of valued entertainment, a mark of local pride and a social hub. Audiences went to the theatre regularly before the predominance of television. People did a bit of shopping, then dropped in to the theatre, not just for a cup of tea, but to see what was on. It was cheap, and, although standards varied from the tatty to the surprisingly good, it was something people shared.

The network of repertory theatres has dwindled in the last 40 years. If you ask a young actor today what rep they have done, they might say *Twelfth Night*. To actors of my generation, that is shocking. 'Rep' did not mean one play, it meant a six-month contract at least, during which you would perform a minimum of six plays, possibly 20.

In 1963, work began in Stratford on the play cycle that would dominate the following year, the quatercentenary of Shakespeare's birth, when the eyes of the world turned to his birthplace and the work of its thrilling young theatre company. *The Wars of the Roses* began with *Richard II* – the young David Warner – progressed through *Henry IV* and *V* – the young Ian Holm; on to *Henry VI* – David Warner again – ending with *Richard III* – Ian Holm again. This huge cycle of seven plays was adapted by John Barton, who reduced the three parts of *Henry VI* to two plays, *Henry VI* and *Edward IV*. John had been at Cambridge with Peter Hall – an unlikely meeting between a sophisticated young don and the son of a Suffolk stationmaster that was to shape the British theatre in the latter half of the twentieth century. John was an intellectual star with a profound knowledge of English literature and an in-depth understanding of Shakespeare. The company's co-founder and resident academic, he became its soul. The RSC grew fast, and it was exhilarating to see this simple summer season theatre growing into an ensemble of great stature, with an international reputation.

And it was my local rep.

3

SHAKESPEARE'S SCHOOL

From the school website:

William Shakespeare was educated in what is still known as 'Big School'; from the age of seven, Shakespeare would have been taught Latin, Rhetoric and perhaps Greek. Lessons began with prayers at six o'clock in the morning during summer, and continued until 5 o'clock in the afternoon. In winter, although boys were expected to bring their own candles, the poor light meant a shorter day.

By 1962, things had improved a bit.

That summer, at King Edward's, I won the Edgar Flower Reading Prize. Readers chose one prose piece, had to sight-read a sonnet and you were judged by someone from the theatre. In 1962 it was Tony Church and Patience Collier; in 1963, when I won again, it was the marvellous Donald Sinden, who amused us all with his huge theatrical voice and fruity vowels. But in 1964 it was Dame Peggy Ashcroft, who, as Margaret of Anjou, dominated the season, ageing from 16 in *Henry VI*, to the 80-year-old mad Margaret in *Richard III*. She shook off her years as the young Margaret and was terrifying in the great scene when she taunts the captive York (Donald Sinden) with a paper crown drenched in the blood of York's young son. She was pretty scary, too, as the older, unhinged Margaret, with long, grey hair, haunting the court with her crazed curses. She curled her r's audaciously to give a Frenchness to her character. I can still hear that guttural 'r' –

I had an Edward till a Rrrichard killed him.
I had a husband till a Rrrichard killed him.
Thou hadst an Edward till a Rrrichard killed him.
Thou hadst a Rrrichard til a Rrrichard killed him.

When I heard that Peggy Ashcroft, our greatest actress, was to judge the reading competition I was pretty nervous, so I chose my prose piece from *Richard of Bordeaux* by Gordon Daviot (or Josephine Tey, to give the author her better-known pen-name), which had made John Gielgud a star in 1933. As Gielgud had been a champion of Peggy's I thought this was something she would enjoy hearing again. When it came to the judging, and she got to me, the first thing she said was 'I'm afraid I never liked *Richard of Bordeaux*.' It was killing. I learnt then that you should never try to manipulate your audience: you simply do what you are passionate about.

As our august judge dismissed my prose offering, *and* criticised my sentimental delivery, you can imagine how apprehensive I was about the sonnet. I could not bear the thought of further humiliation at the hands of somebody I practically worshipped. To my astonishment, because of my sonnet reading I was given a first-equal prize. I was stunned. I have never forgotten Dame Peggy's verdict: she said she had 'never heard a sonnet read better'. This was a delicious, heady compliment to an 18-year-old who nursed vague dreams of becoming an actor. The frustration was, although I went through the sonnet afterwards with a fine-tooth comb, I never really worked out *why* she thought I'd I read it well.

When I started at King Edward VI School its ethos seemed stuck, very happily, somewhere in the epoch which produced its most famous son, circa 1570. In the autumn term of 1963 we had a new headmaster, Stephen Pratt. Philip Larkin's poem made 1963 famous, but sexual intercourse wasn't the only thing that began that year! Stephen ushered in a new era. Stratford is a reactionary place, but Stephen's smiling urbanity masked keen political skills. Things began to happen so fast you could feel the school lurching towards the twentieth century.

Hal in The Famous Victories of King Henry V, *King Edward VI School, Stratford, 1964* (me, extreme right)

Stephen was authoritative but not intimidating. He wanted more of us to go to university, and talked to each of us individually. Enthusiastic and expansive, he ushered me into his study and sat me in front of his desk. He swept into his chair, wearing, as always, his gown.

'Well, Pigott-Smith. You're rather keen on the theatre, aren't you?' I was somewhat taken aback. Stephen had only been at the school for six weeks! 'Is that right?'

'Yes, sir ...' Hesitantly, I added, 'but my parents insist I go to university. First, sir.'

'Very wise of them. Well ... you'd better go to Bristol.'

'Bristol, sir?'

'Yes, there is a very good drama department there. It's been up and running for about fifteen years. Perfect for you.'

That was it. As I left, Stephen said, 'Get those applications going then, Pigott-Smith.'

My life suddenly had a sense of purpose. And – Stephen added as a parting shot – 'We'll do a mock interview when we know what's happening.'

True to his word, Stephen summoned me to his office again when my interview with Bristol was imminent. Again he relaxed me, telling me I would be likely to meet Professor Glynne Wickham, the department's founder. He ran through a list of probable questions: Is this the right course for you? Do you know what you want to do with your life beyond university? Then he said, 'Well, Tim, they might ask – Who do you think is the most important dramatist writing in this country today?'

Without hesitation, I said, 'Harold Pinter.' After a weighty, not to say Pinteresque, pause, Stephen prompted – '*If* they ask you that, you should go on to say *why* you think he is our most important writer.'

I felt somehow I had failed a test. Stephen rescued me. 'Can you talk about Pinter now?'

'Yes, sir.'

'Well ...?'

And so I filled him in for about two minutes on why Pinter was my man: how his was a new voice – menacing and comic, how he captured people's need to fulfil themselves, and how they rarely managed to achieve their goals. How he understood the insecurities of the modern post-war world.

I remember that exchange with great clarity because on the terrifying day of the actual interview I was asked that exact question by Glynne Wickham himself, so I opened up immediately with both Pinter barrels! I didn't know then that Pinter's first play, *The Room*, was presented to Glynne as a rough sketch on a piece of toilet paper. Glynne had such faith in it he made sure the play was written in full, and given its first performance in the drama department studio.

Many actors will tell you that one teacher spotted their talent and nurtured it. I am forever in Stephen's debt, because I think that that one answer assured me the offer of a place at Bristol University. As our Latin master used to say, '*Education – e – meaning* out; *and duco,* I lead – *e-duco* – I lead out.' Stephen led me, in the purest sense, towards who I was, who I am. Had it not been for his arrival at KES, I would not be doing what I am today.

Before university, there was the thorny issue of A levels. When my mates heard that Bristol wanted two Bs and an E – paltry grades compared with the array of As demanded of students these days – they laughed and said, 'Well, that's the end of your university career, Tim!' I have an agile, magpie brain, but I was never cut out for purely academic study. Bristol was the ideal solution, but everything hinged on achieving the grades. After the exams, I had to wait most of the summer of 1964 for the results. Dad arranged for me to work in the theatre paint-shop – for 30 bob (£1.50) a week.

The paint-shop was situated opposite the theatre on Waterside, and this little kingdom was ruled by a fabulous character, John Collins, a man so deeply ingrained with paint that no soap could ever remove it. He smelled delicately of size, a glue mixed into stage paint, to fix it. John was short, bespectacled, tousle-haired, gruff, creative and fun. No stranger to the bottle, you had to be cautious sometimes after lunch not to catch him in the wrong mood.

It never affected his work, but he could be cantankerous. I was pretty scared of him, but he had two gorgeous assistants, Roz and Gill, and they guided me through my basic tasks and steered me through the perils of post-lunch John psychology. I cleaned brushes, mixed paint, swept up, made tea, fetched and carried.

The greatest change Peter Hall made in creating the RSC was to insist on a London 'shop window'. This was essential to change the way the company was perceived by a London-centric profession, and a public that was not always willing or able to travel to Stratford-upon-Avon. In 1964, two years after the Aldwych Theatre had become a home where the company tackled contemporary plays, Peter Brook was directing a massive ensemble work by Peter Weiss starring Ian Richardson, Patrick Magee and Glenda Jackson. Sally Jacobs designed this revolutionary play, known as the *Marat-Sade*, set in a lunatic asylum where the inmates are allowed to stage the death of Marat. I had fun applying a light wash and splash to the wooden duckboards that helped create the asylum washrooms.

If I had been diligent and John was in a good mood, I would be allowed to cross the road to the theatre. I loved going through the stage door – being nearer the actors, maybe glimpsing Dame Peggy, David Warner, or passing Ian Holm on his way out. It was exciting to mount the wall ladder to the massive paint-frame, which was suspended way above the stage in the fly tower. Here, we painted the flats which were to house *Marat-Sade*. They were *so* big they had to be base-coated *on* the frame. We then painted bricks on them. Today we would use sheets of plastic brick moulds but then canvas flats were the norm, and a skilled painter like John could make canvas look like brick. Nobody ever questioned it.

One day I was allowed on to the stage itself – to do some touching up to one of the enormous periaktoids, as we called them,* designed by John Bury. I clambered up an A-frame ladder and sat astride the 20-foot-high wall, which sloped gradually up

---

* Actually *periaktoi*, huge mobile, triangular pieces of scenery that originated in Greek theatre.

to about 30 feet! The company used time onstage to rehearse entrances and exits – armies swirling on with drum and colours, marching off with alarums. They came and went as I hotched my way round the mighty triangular structure, dabbing away with my gun-metal paint. Health and Safety would simply not permit it these days, but I was thrilled to be almost part of the action. Here was Talbot with his small defeated army; here was Jack Cade with his mob; and now Northumberland with his rebels. They would wait in the wings for the crew to organise the space, sometimes shifting the periaktoi on which I was working. The drums would kick in, followed by the brass, and then the actors would flood on to the stage. With a mighty thrump of feet and timpani, they would come to a halt, and the first few lines of the scene would ring out. It was beyond exciting to be so close to these larger-than-life people.

The energy steaming off the stage was infectious. The commitment of the company was compelling; their discipline was a revelation, the detail required, the eagerness to contribute and the will to get it right, the repetition to achieve accuracy. The French word for rehearsal is *répétition*.

This was my first sight of Peter Hall at work. I had seen him in the flesh, entering the auditorium on a first night, in black tie, with his film-star wife Leslie Caron on his arm. They seemed impossibly glamorous. But what I glimpsed now was a workman in shirt sleeves, demanding the absolute concentration of his team to achieve exactly the desired effect, cracking the whip in an encouraging way, driving things. Peter was never at his most involved when staging a scene – by which I mean giving the actors moves; he was more interested in content than mechanics. He would allow staging to evolve, making occasional suggestions, relying on the actors to find their own way to the best positions on the stage. But when he wanted armies to surge on, he was a master:

'When you hear the high note, storm on from up left. When *they* get to this point here, I want *you lot* to come on downstage right. When *they* engage in battle – which I want about here – onstage centre left by now – you four need to straggle on from UPstage right. There! Come round the periaktoids. The action will by now have moved centre. Make to join the fray, but – when you see your fellow fighters being driven back – think better of it, and as the fighting moves further downstage right, I want to see you making the decision to run away. OK? Exit upstage left. We'll put the detail in later. Let's give it a try. Stand by musicians. Look lively, now, we are short of time.'

He would later refine things with the help of the fight director, but that basic shape, and an understanding of the movement required to tell a story, was something he was a natural at. So from my perch on top of the set, or from my eyrie on the paint-frame, I would do as little painting as possible and observe.

And it was coming down from the paint-frame one day, having watched her rehearsing, that I bumped into Peggy Ashcroft.

'Hello,' she said. She had last seen me in school uniform, smartly dressed in tie and blazer. Here I was in T-shirt, wearing jeans so thick with paint that they practically stood up by themselves, and paint-bespattered plimsolls, but she seemed to know who I was. 'What are you doing here?'

'I'm working in the paint-shop, Dame Peggy,' I mumbled.

'Jolly good. I thought I saw you on the set the other day.'

'I try to get onstage as often as I can, so that I can watch what's going on.'

'Well, you be careful,' she said in a kind but dismissive way. She was holding her script in her arms, which were folded in front of her, and her cardigan was draped over her shoulders – a characteristic pose. She had a tendency sometimes to lean back very slightly, perhaps in order to observe things better. 'Good to see you.' She smiled and moved on.

I was in heaven. But not for long. I was summoned back to the paint-frame by Roz. I had made a complete hash of about ten lines of bricks. She was furious with me, but between us we covered my wobbly lines and all was well. Roz did not tell John, but my time onstage, and on the frame, was severely restricted after that.

Exam results day arrived. It was also press night for *Richard III*, a humid summer's day. 'A Hard Day's Night' was playing on the record player in the paint-shop where I regularly repainted Eric Porter's shield, which was wrecked nightly by the ball and chain attached to Ian Holm's withered arm. There was an air of rising tension in and around the theatre which mirrored my apprehension.

Results were to be posted on the school notice board at four that afternoon. If I failed to get two Bs and an E for Bristol, I imagined my parents would expect me to find a job. It was a long day. At about ten to four I was allowed to leave the paint-shop and, with pounding heart, I walked up Chapel Lane and joined the crush of boys hovering round the notice board. One of my mates, 'Beeky' Reeks, was near the front.

'How did you do, Beeky?' He turned and looked glumly at me through the mass of hopefuls. 'I'm fine,' he replied, with the very clear implication that I was not. My heart stopped. Then his face broke into a grin. 'Guess what, Piggy? You got two Bs and an E!'

Two Bs and an E!! Hallelujah! I had worked incredibly hard to achieve this result, and was beside myself with relief. I ran home to tell Mum and Dad the good news. Coming from a large, fatherless family in the small town of Builth Wells, Dad had had jobs from the age of 10, leaving school at 16. He was bright, ambitious, articulate and wrote well, so he was snaffled up by the local paper, where he began his lifetime's work of learning newspapers. Deprived even of the chance of university, he wanted me to achieve something he had been denied. He was a lovely bloke, my dad, and I was very happy to fulfil this dream for him.

It was also a good night for the theatre, with huge ovations for Ian Holm as Richard and Dame Peggy. This was the last of the *Wars of the Roses* cycle, and the theatre was able to bask in the glow of a massive triumph. The extended curtain call was not just a response to *Richard III*, it was also a recognition of the company's larger achievement. This cycle of plays delivered something that no other company in the country could even have dreamed of. When Peter Hall inherited Stratford, there was some money in the bank. Peter spent it in order to oblige the government to subsidise the company, or watch it die. Here was complete vindication of his vision, and proof of the value of public subsidy. Theatre was an exciting, optimistic place to be – both a reflection and an engine of social change.

And I was on my way to Bristol University.

4

THE RIGHT DIRECTION

The drama department at Bristol was everything I could have hoped for. I was obsessed by drama, and studied just hard enough to get by. I had countless opportunities to act.

I hero-worshipped Glynne Wickham, or, to give him his full name, Glynne William Gladstone Wickham. This hints at his descent from the nineteenth-century politician, to whom he was a great-grandson. Glynne influenced me profoundly: the way I read and prepare a play – my dedication to text – began with him.

Suavely good-looking, with a long, floppy lock of hair, he was a brilliant academic and, not surprisingly with those genes, a canny politician, who created, virtually single-handed, the university discipline of drama in this country. Bristol was the first drama department: in 1964, there were still only two.

Within academic circles there was scepticism about drama. Glynne convinced the Faculty of Arts that, to be fully understood, drama should be studied differently. He persuaded the doubters that you needed to look at how a play was staged, its historical context and the history of its theatre to fully comprehend it. A drama department is not a drama school, and I am not sure the way drama departments have developed is the right way, but in their defence Bristol produces people who shape the worlds of theatre and film – Matthew Warchus is currently the artistic director of the Old Vic; Adrian Noble was and Greg Doran *is* the artistic director of the RSC; Michael Winterbottom (*Butterfly Kiss*, *24 Hour Party People*, *Wonderland*) and Mick Jackson (*The Bodyguard*, *Volcano*, *LA Story*) are internationally recognised film directors.

Dadadidactics, *an evening of surrealist drama, Bristol University, 1965,*
with Ian Gardhouse in 'Mort and Levy'

Our top-dog teachers were the 'three G's' – Glynne, George Rowell, a sophisticated, suave Englishman who taught Restoration and Victorian drama, and George Brandt, a Jewish émigré who taught modern European drama and film, and we got to know them because we did plays together. In the summer vacations we took up residence at Dartington Hall in Devon, and put on plays in an exciting hothouse atmosphere. Staying in the college, we met our lecturers not just in rehearsal but over meals. Glynne was easy, witty company and so was his charming, attractive wife, Hesel. When you saw Hesel, you took another look at Glynne – not just a clever boy. They used to stay at the Liberal Club in town – of course – and would often materialise in my dressing room after a play.

Glynne's seminal work is called *Early English Stages* in which he explains the development of the Elizabethan – the first professional – stage in this country, tracing its roots from morality plays, manor houses and churches. He also elucidates something fundamental to the nature of drama...

The first written words of drama spoken aloud in this country form part of the Easter service and were uttered in a church, in Latin, in the twelfth century. They are known as the *Quem quaeritis* tropes. A trope is three lines, *Quem quaeritis* means *whom do you seek?* This is the trope roughly translated:

1 *Whom do you seek in the sepulchre, O Christians?*
2 *Jesus Christ, O heavenly ones.*
3 *He is risen.*

That's all there was: England's first written play: the roots of theatre and church are deeply intertwined. Glynne demonstrates how the theme of the risen Lord grew into the DNA of early drama, citing *The Winter's Tale*, one of Shakespeare late works. Listed, somewhat curiously in the First Folio under 'Comedies', this play contains violent jealousy, sexual disgust, the death of an innocent child, the unjust imprisonment of a pregnant queen and a man eaten by a bear. Comedy? Well, *The Winter's Tale* has an *actual* resurrection as its climax, when a statue comes to life. The feel-good factor.

Even Shakespeare's tragedies conclude with a sense of renewal and uplift. *Romeo and Juliet* ends with civic union, a vow that the disaster must never be repeated. *Hamlet* ends with Fortinbras as the new king. At the end of *Lear*, Edmund picks up the reins. The need for hope and a sense of possibility in the future are always there. Resurrection has become part of the idea of the play.

Glynne gave us a series of brilliant lectures in our second year. We could barely wait for the next week's 'episode', and practically ran into class. He was on to the Masque by then, Inigo Jones, the development of indoor theatre at Blackfriars and at Court. He made a sort of mystery of it, leaving each lecture with a cliff-hanger. Sensational teaching.

We loved imitating the clinical coolness of his delivery, the way he rolled 'mmmmn' round his mouth before delivering a punchline, and the witty ease with which he slipped in a Latin phrase as if it was street talk – 'the ... mmmmn ... *fons et origo* of the drama ...' As a lecturer, it was what he said that held your attention, his delivery was unflashy, academic, but onstage he had glamour. He was a star.

I talked to him one day about *Hamlet* and have ever since held to his theory that the play takes place over ten years. In Act One, Hamlet is referred to as the young prince, he is a student – say 20. When Hamlet asks the Gravedigger in Act Five how long he has been digging graves, the Gravedigger tells him that he started work 'that very day young Hamlet was born'. Hamlet feigns ignorance. 'When was that?' he asks. 'Cannot you tell that? Every fool can tell that ...' jibes the Gravedigger, 'I have been Gravedigger here, man and boy, these thirty years'.

So the text tells us that the play lasts ten years. Shakespeare never lies to his audience; his characters might lie, but he never does. The ten-year theory explains certain inconsistencies in the text: Hamlet's weight and fitness shift about; the length of his trip to England is not really accounted for. I long to do a production in which the cast age – change size, lose hair. It would amplify the central action, that Hamlet is very slow in implementing his revenge. It takes him ten years *not* to do it! The text contains everything you need.

Glynne was a very good director. In my second year I did an eighteenth-century *comédie larmoyante* with him, *The Conscious Lovers* by Richard Steele. I was playing one of two juvenile leads, but my character was eccentric, and adopted disguises – a lawyer and a very old man – in order to win the hand of his beloved. Glynne encouraged me to go further with these impersonations. Most actors are character actors, and I was instinctively more at ease behind the disguises my character adopted than as the man himself. Glynne really began my acting education. He had an understanding of language which helped you with phrasing, both for comprehension and drama. He had a wit that easily unlocked the comedy. With this production, Glynne put me (and a couple of others in the cast with acting ambitions) on view. And he made sure we were seen by Nat Brenner, principal of the Bristol Old Vic Theatre School. Glynne shaped my life. Nat was to change it.

I wrote to the school, and Nat invited me for an interview. Nervous, hopeful, I went up to the school, two large Victorian semi-detached houses that had been knocked together, gloriously situated on the edge of the downs. In the tradition of most theatrical workspaces it was a bit run down and ramshackle. Nat lived there with his wife, Joan, and two daughters. He was a short man with wiry grey hair that ran back from a widow's peak and a low, deeply wrinkled forehead. His eyes were large, slightly bloodshot, watery, deep-set, with pouchy rings beneath. He was wearing large spectacles. He had flared nostrils. He wore a cardigan, and kept his cigarettes and lighter in its sagging pockets, into which he would thrust his fists and straighten his arms. His voice was smoky ... he was smoking. He ushered me into the office.

As we chatted, he went through some transfixing cigarette business – tapping the fag, priming his lighter, then putting everything away. Suddenly, he took the packet out, removed a fag and put it straight in his mouth the wrong way round, with the filter tip sticking out. He flicked his lighter and moved the flame tantalisingly close to the filter tip. The moment he looked as though he was actually going to light his cigarette, I said, 'Your cigarette is the wrong way round, Mr Brenner.' He turned it round and lit it as though nothing had happened. But by then, of course, he had an idea of the sort of person I was. We talked about *The Conscious Lovers*, and he asked me what I was after. I said I was hoping to do the one-year post-graduate course, and he offered me a place there and then. And when I had my BA – a 2:2 – under my belt, I took up his offer.

Nat was a man of the theatre, having worked as the stage director at the Bristol Old Vic, as well as having done a fair bit of acting and directing. He had taken over the school when it lacked profile, and had buffed up its reputation, which was now for producing actors who worked. Barbara Leigh-Hunt, Brian Blessed, Patrick Stewart, Stephanie Cole were trained there. Jane Lapotaire had just graduated, and in my years at university I had seen memorable performances from her, Christopher Cazenove, Norman Eschle and Neil Cunningham, alumni of the school now carving careers for themselves. When I arrived in the autumn of 1969, Nicholas Ball and Nicholas Jones were in the year above me.

Nat had a particular love of Russian plays. As a Ukrainian, it was in his blood. He was also a great farceur, and understood the manic intensity required of that genre. He loved recounting famous bits of biz. He had seen Tom Walls, one of the Aldwych farceurs from the twenties, perform, and Nat replicated one of his bits of business for us: he stands, wearing a monocle, holding a cup of tea. Shocked by something, he raises his eyebrows sky high. The monocle falls out of his eye, and into the tea. Absolutely unfazed, he stirs the tea with his monocle. He wipes it on the edge of the cup, shakes it dry and replaces it, as if it were the most normal thing in the world.

When a certain company was mounting the great Ben Travers farce *Plunder*, they were in trouble in rehearsals, and could not quite work out why. Nat had just directed it brilliantly with Peter O'Toole at the Bristol Old Vic: they had been great chums when the young O'Toole did his *Hamlet* there. Someone suggested asking Nat's advice. He looked at the model of the set, and said, 'The staircase is in the wrong place.' And that solved their problems.

The teacher with the greatest reputation was the extraordinary Rudi Shelley. A Viennese Jew, he got out of Austria before the war by the skin of his teeth, but maintained a thick native accent all his life. He had several jokey expressions, which he knew quite well were inaccurate. He would say, secretively to the class, 'between you me and the Post Office', and almost wink at us. 'Oh my God,' he would proclaim, 'close your mouth please; you look like a pregnant codfish.' His posture theory was based on a delicately articulated *min-i-a-ture lemon*. 'You place the lemon between your buttocks. You squeeze the lemon gently – gently! Don't crack nuts there!' This got your lower half in place. Then you had to imagine you were wearing a small bolero jacket, which he exhorted you to raise. Lemon squeezed and bolero up, what Rudi called 'Operation Roller-towel', you were physically primed to start. Rudi had an instinctive understanding of our individual strengths and weaknesses, and he would tease you, annoy you almost, into improving. He was always on at me for using too much energy. Years after I left the school, whenever I met him he would say, 'Tell me, Timmy darling, do you still work too hard?'

We often used to meet in London, and on one occasion when he came up for his birthday a small bunch of ex-students gathered to celebrate. 'How are you, Timmy? What are you doing?' I had on this occasion just taken over the role of Mr Rochester in a West End production of *Jane Eyre*. I had enjoyed only one week's rehearsal, and although I opened with flair, three weeks in, without proper rehearsal, I felt ungrounded and was floundering. I explained to Rudi why I was finding life tricky. 'Oh, Timmy, darling', he said with, tired sympathy, 'you always did need a bit more *fuck-you*!' Well, he was spot on. Lack of time had obliged me to use flair to get the part on, and it was pointless trying to rationalise it now. I just had to go onstage and whack it over. And from that day on, I did. Problem solved.

Nicholas Farrell told me a typical Rudi story. Nick was approaching his final shows at the school, and was feeling very self-conscious about his hands. He went to talk to Rudi.

'I am worried about my hands, Rudi,' he whined.

'Your hands?' said Rudi. 'What about your *feet*?'

The last time I saw Rudi, in 1988, he was in his late eighties, very frail, but still teaching occasionally. I was doing a radio play in Bristol, and was at the school to take a Shakespeare class. I saw Rudi on the way in, on his Zimmer frame. He pointed at the front steps, up which he had to be carried. 'I hate those steps,' he said bitterly. After class, a three-hour morning session, I met him again and asked what he had been teaching. Rudi looked at me gleefully and said, 'Consonants!' Three hours! On consonants! But I can guarantee that his students that day never forgot what he told them. And if they were lucky, they would have had Rudi on vowels, too. 'Hit your consonants, ducky. Open your vowels!'

He taught a very pragmatic Stanislavsky-based, character-led approach, giving us simple exercises of being alone onstage, as well as teaching us posture for Jacobean or Restoration plays. He would give us a passage to learn – he liked *The White Devil*. If you asked when he wanted you to learn it, he would say, 'For yesterday, ducky.' Lines learnt, we would work out how, for example, to get up from a chair centre stage, and get to the exit – how to leave the stage. You don't want to deliver a punchline and then have to walk three yards to get off. This is partly instinctive, but also craft. Rudi taught practical stagecraft.

Elderly, other-worldly, Kathleen Stafford taught voice and poetry. Good, solid, old-fashioned stuff. Rib-reserve breathing, diaphragmatic control; find the golden word and the point of the verse structure – the end of the line is a springboard into the next. The old rules are the best. If you know what they are, you can break them. But you remain ignorant of them at your peril.

Singing was taught by John Oxley, still alive, in his nineties. He was renowned for his use of Handel's 'Ombra mai fu'. John would stand in front of you, place one hand flat on his head, and literally draw the long O of the opening 'O-o-o-o-mbra', with his fingers, out through the top of his head. 'Head-tone, Piggy!' he would cry. 'Head-tone!' He refused to believe that people could not sing, and he taught one of our year, who was completely tone deaf, to sing a scale by recognising the vibrations in his chest.

There was a memorial for Nat Brenner at the Theatre Royal in 1990. At the end of the first half we gathered onstage to sing 'Ombra mai fu' – pretty much the school hymn. John strode down the centre aisle and conducted us from the floor of the stalls. So deeply ingrained was this wonderful aria that, 20 years later, not one of us needed the music.

5

THE REAL THING

Acting courses in those days generally lasted two years: the basics of posture and voice can be learnt in that time. You will never teach someone who cannot act *how* to act, however long the course. Three years is too long, and in today's unsympathetic financial climate it militates against poorer students. The one-year post-grad course that six of us were doing in 1967 was cutting it fine, but at least mine was paid for by Warwickshire County Council.

We did a lot of ballet-based movement, and when it came to performing we wore the black leotards, with black polo-neck sweaters in which we did our ballet. It was dressed in this unfortunate fashion that I again encountered Peggy Ashcroft. In 1968, she was still with the RSC, playing Mrs Alving in Ibsen's *Ghosts* at the Bristol Hippodrome, another memorable performance which I saw twice.

The main exercise in our first term was to perform the late-fifteenth-century morality play *Everyman*. This offered a whole range of parts: Friendship, played by Christopher Biggins, Envy and Death. I was lucky enough to be Everyman. We performed such one-off exercises in a dingy basement rehearsal room, without lights or sound. Our small audience sat either side of some carefully arranged rostra with the top removed from one of them so that there was a permanent grave in the middle of the 'set'. It was simple, but effective. Everyman is constantly being reminded that death awaits him, and it was useful, just in spatial terms, that we had to avoid the grave throughout. Death was able to straddle it.

We had good rehearsals and were looking forward to the performance. We were gathering outside the rehearsal room when Nat announced that we had a special guest, and down the stairs he led Dame Peggy. She smiled warmly as she passed, at a bunch of dumbstruck students about to perform a simple play in the most unsophisticated of surroundings to the greatest actress of the day. There is no more exposing costume than black tights. What *do* you do with your hands? Wring them? When Death stood astride the grave, his legs were quivering with fear. We got through without error, but it must have been a dull hour. We were presented en masse to Dame Peggy afterwards, and she smiled knowingly at me, although I wasn't sure that she actually remembered me. How Nat had persuaded her, in her sixtieth year, while on tour, which is tiring anyway, to give up most of a morning to watch some students struggling through a very old play I cannot imagine. It is a mark of her love of young people – she was always more interested in the future than the past – that she gave her time so generously. She penned Nat an elegant note of thanks which he shared with us the following week.

I was slightly envious of one of my fellow students, my friend Simon Cadell, who had theatre in his blood. His grandmother, Jean Cadell, was a well-established actress whom you can see as Mrs Pearce in the Leslie Howard/Wendy Hiller film of *Pygmalion*. Simon revealed himself, in the first weeks at drama school, to be a young actor with an old head on his shoulders. His Berowne, in *Love's Labours Lost*, in a similarly bare production to our *Everyman*, used a heavily pared-down script, and the same unhelpful costume, but Simon's performance was full of dazzling comic invention. I shall never forget the great scene when the king and his fellow students reveal themselves to the audience as traitors to their vows – they have all fallen in love, but cannot bring themselves to admit it to each other, so they express their misgivings one by one, in soliloquy. Berowne talks to the audience first, and then takes cover, so that he can overhear the others.

I have seen Berownes hide behind a bush or climb a tree to hide. In the absence of any kind of set, Simon 'hid' by pretending to be a piece of garden sculpture, a Cupid, with his bow, poised elegantly on one leg. He had to maintain a steely stillness for a long time, but, being centre stage, he was ideally placed to share with the audience his views on what his fellow students were saying to us. He did a heavenly double take and a couple of brilliant slow burns – a burn is a very slow take. When he was on the brink of being found out, being intensely scrutinised by the others – is this *really* a piece of garden statuary? – he engineered a magic piece of business. Simon's face was asymmetrical, and his mouth turned down towards the right; it was made for comedy, and from it he produced a long, slow spurt of water, as though someone had suddenly switched on a garden fountain. This was sophisticated stuff. I had not yet encountered a real actor like this. Simon was in a league apart, and if required he could also 'tear a passion to tatters'.

I got to know Simon's parents quite well when I stayed with them in the Highgate house where they brought up three children and an enormous hound, Pompey. Simon's mother, Gill, was a handsome woman who had also been an actress. His father was an agent. Their house was built in 1666, the year of the Great Fire, and by chance my wife, Pam, and I bought it in 1998. It was a Tardis of a place, and from the top back room you could see right across London. This room was beamed, as was the top *front* room, which Simon's dad used as his office. When Simon told me that his dad was an agent I said, 'Oh dear.' I thought he meant a travelling salesman. He was, I discovered, a *theatrical* agent, with such august clients as Donald Sinden, Frances de la Tour and Tom Kempinski, author of *Duet for One*. Simon's sister Selina is a superb actress, and an excellent director. I met her on the bathroom landing when she was 13.

This was my first real acquaintance with theatre people. As an only child from an ordered house, the noise and kerfuffle of the Cadell family swept me off my feet. They were loud, slightly larger than life, and they lived, ate and breathed theatre. They gave, and those of them still alive still give, the theatre unquestioned dignity. I used to find it a bit hard then to take acting completely seriously. Although it was my passion, it sometimes seemed to me a trivial profession. When I was with the Cadells it never crossed my mind that acting was anything other than a very serious and important profession. We are cynical in this country and don't honour our artists in the way that, for example, the French do. Because of the actor's natural extravagance of nature, we underestimate the intensity with which most performers approach their work. My slight intellectual distance came from my university background, and it took me some years to shake off this snooty way of coping with the fear of failure.

The Cadells taught me about 'the business'. I had no idea what a casting director was, what *Spotlight* was, what *Contacts* was – what an *agent* was! My naivety amused them, but they could see I was sincere, and they never made me feel foolish, sharing their background with huge generosity. Simon was one of the few students at the school with whom I found I could talk. I still had more in common with some of my younger friends from university, like Allan Corduner – they were used to talking, discussing, dissecting, which is what I liked to do. Simon was ahead of us all, though – he had been thinking about the art and craft of acting for as long as he could think.

On one occasion when I was staying with the Cadells, Gill said to me, 'You must see *Dear Octopus* with Cicely Courtneidge and Jack Hulbert. You will never have a chance to see anything like it again. It's the end of an era. Do go!' I went, and saw a piece of theatrical history.

Dear Octopus was a stock family drama, which allowed two treasured old stars – and in this case, a famous theatrical couple – to ply their saccharine trade, being amusing, touching, sweetly insightful, loving, reassuring and terribly, terribly British. Written in 1938 by Dodie Smith, it was made into a film in 1943, in which, by coincidence, Simon's grandmother Jean had a small part. This 1967 stage revival featured Richard Todd, a film star best known for *Robin Hood* and *The Dam Busters*. Here, he bolstered a standard West End package. It was never going to light a fuse, but in the wake of *Look Back in Anger*, which blew the old order apart in 1956, as Gill suggested, it was something of a rarity, the last survivor of a type of play that had been overtaken by Jimmy Porter, John Osborne's anti-hero.

In the late sixties, the West End was still dominated by the traditional play, but Terence Rattigan, William Douglas-Home and Noël Coward were being shoved heartlessly aside to make way for Harold Pinter, Joe Orton, Ann Jellicoe, Peter Shaffer, Tom Stoppard, John Arden – new, challenging, not comforting voices. *West Side Story* had taken British theatre-goers by storm, and musicals, with few exceptions, came from America. Generally, the West End boasted two or three farces – one of them at the Whitehall Theatre (now the Trafalgar Studios), where Brian Rix had been dropping his vicar's trousers and tripping on his own heel for years; there were thrillers on offer; you might well enjoy a revival at the Mermaid, run by Bernard Miles. There was always high comedy. *No Sex Please, We're British* was probably the last of the sexy farces, running for six or seven years – naughty, titillating fare; Ray Cooney wrote and directed many such pleasurable, unchallenging confections. *Dear Octopus* was set in the world pilloried by the critic Kenneth Tynan as 'Loneshire', and, until the social change that was affecting the country found a dramatic voice, such work had been dominant.

The theatre where *Dear Octopus* was playing, the Strand (now the Novello), was packed with an older, middle-class, very well-dressed, completely white audience, who simply devoured their beloved Cicely and Jack. The curtain rose and fell, as in the good old days. I went to a matinee, and tea was served at the interval, so the second act was punctuated by the gentle clink of china. The actors all had actors' voices, speaking exquisitely. It was superb theatre of its kind – entertaining and brilliantly crafted – but it was the end of an era and the play was out of date, trite and shallow. There was, I would bet my life, not one person in the house who would have exchanged their tickets for a play by John Osborne, Samuel Beckett, or even Ibsen with Dame Peggy, playing less than a hundred yards away at the RSC's London home, the Aldwych. With dangerous writing now mainstream, it was becoming harder for the *Dear Octopus* audience to enjoy what theatre had to offer.

There are no skills required to be a critic, and although Tynan worked successfully within Olivier's National Theatre he learnt the hard way that it is not that easy to mount a successful show – his review *Oh! Calcutta!* was a tawdry affair. He *was* active in getting rid of censorship, and in 1968 nudity hit the stage in *Hair*. Until then, every play bound for performance had to pass across the Lord Chamberlain's desk.

When *Krapp's Last Tape* was in rehearsal at the Royal Court, the Lord Chamberlain demanded to see the director Donald McWhinnie, who was informed that there was one speech in the play which was too close to the bone. McWhinnie had no idea which speech the censor had in mind. It turned out to be the punt sequence: in one of his recorded memories, Krapp describes a woman lying in his punt; as he poles along, his shadow falls over her, and the punt – *drifted in amongst the reeds and stuck*. McWhinnie was informed that the sexual innuendo was too much for the Lord Chamberlain. Disingenuously he explained, 'It's just what it says, your honour' (or your lordship or whatever you call a Lord Chamberlain), 'he is punting along, and his shadow falls on the girl, and, because he is distracted, the punt drifts into the reeds.'

The Lord Chamberlain was not convinced. 'Oh, for God's sake,' he cried, 'he's about to roger the girl!'

Which, of course, he is. And which McWhinnie well knew, but he continued to play dumb.

'Goodness me', he said innocently, 'do you really imagine people will think that?'

By suggesting that it was the Lord Chamberlain's dirty mind that had read something into the passage, he got away with it, and the play went ahead, uncensored!

The use of double meaning was an essentially British way of evading the censor. Max Miller, the great music hall comedian, used to offer innuendo, and then accuse his audience of having a dirty mind. His most famous joke involved meeting a naked girl on a narrow mountain ledge. 'I didn't know,' Miller proclaimed innocently, 'whether to block her passage or toss myself off.' And when the audience laughed he would say, in mock shock, 'Ooooh, you are awful.' Ambiguity was the lifeblood of comedy under censorship. Earlier in the twentieth century, Marie Lloyd, another great music hall star, was regularly in trouble for overstepping the mark, so she asked the police to attend a performance in which she placed two chests of drawers upstage, either side of a door, through which she entered cradling a kitten. Her line was: 'You can look at me between the drawers, but you can't touch my little pussy.' The police could indeed not touch her. Anywhere. She was the forerunner of Mrs Slocombe in *Are You Being Served?*

In the sixties, times changed fast. By the end of a full-frontal decade, Edward Albee had lacerated us, Tennessee Williams had dissected the souls of the disaffected and the lost, and Arthur Miller was giving voice to suburban anguish and anger. La MaMa was opening up theatrical form, while the daring Peter Brook, who had burnt a butterfly onstage in bringing us the Vietnam War, now created a play about an African tribe, *The Ik*, at the Round House. Snoo Wilson, Howard Brenton and Howard Barker were rummaging around in comic, political darkness, John Arden was mounting mighty, exciting, but increasingly incomprehensible political allegories, whilst N. F. Simpson had whole-heartedly embraced absurdism. Charles Marowitz ran a successful experimental theatre in central London. Even Olivier had taken on Ionesco with *Rhinoceros* at the Royal Court. David Hare joined the fray in 1970, although he always managed to appeal to the centre ground. It would be many years before the revival of Rattigan – with whom Hare has not a little in common – revealed that not all well-made plays were worthless, and that real craft and good structure are not to be sneezed at; but in those heady experimental days, the old school of writing was doomed.

Simon Cadell and I went together to see Dame Peggy playing Mrs Alving in *Ghosts* at the Aldwych. I had never been backstage to visit a star, but it was second nature to Simon. He was three years younger than me, going straight to drama school from Bedales, although he was 18 going on 30. After the performance, as we waited in the downstairs corridor outside Dame Peggy's dressing room, Simon revealed, quite without any sense of this being exceptional news, that she was his godmother! When we were ushered into the inner sanctum, amazingly, Peggy remembered me. 'We meet again,' she said. Simon was completely at home, saying all the right things with practised ease. I felt self-conscious.

I worked purposefully at drama school, but my one-year course was passing with frightening speed. Then fate intervened. Fate ... and Nat Brenner. I had arrived at university in 1964, with a cartilage tear in my right knee from playing rugby. After a trial, I was picked for the university second team, but the damaged knee flared up every time I played, so by the end of my first term, reckoning that if I was going to be an actor it would be a good idea if I could walk, I reluctantly hung up my boots.

Halfway through my year at the school I was involved in a comic dance routine, a fight, between me – pretty big – and a very small guy. The joke was that the small guy threw me about. The last move required me to somersault. It was fun. As I completed the somersault one day, there was a noise like a rifle crack. My right knee was locked at right angles. It stayed at right angles for the remaining six weeks of my second term. In the vacation, I had a meniscectomy – they slice into your knee and clean up the cartilage. I spent a week in bed, then did some rudimentary physiotherapy, and with a sore knee that was slow to mend I entered my last term at the school, knowing I was not ready to leave. All I could do to save my dream was to work.

At about half past eight one night I was going through my role in the final shows and exercising in a downstairs studio, which at that late hour was deserted, when I realised there was another figure in the dimly lit room. Embarrassed, I stopped, and discovered to my horror that it was Nat! He was doing his evening rounds. I feared he had come to ask me to leave the school.

'What are you up to?' he asked

'I'm trying to make up for lost time, Nat,' I replied.

Yes', he breathed ominously, in his dusky, nicotine tones. His implication was clear. My fears were confirmed, and dejectedly I started getting my gear together. 'You need to do another year, don't you?' said Nat. A statement as much as a question.

'Well, yes, I do,' I replied, taken aback. 'But, Nat, I have had Warwickshire County Council support for four years. I'll never get a grant.'

'I'll give you a scholarship,' he said. 'That'll cover the fees. And I'll write to your authority about maintenance.'

I was speechless.

Nat was as good as his word and just over a year later I completed the two-year course. And I had no debt! Had it not been for that late-night conversation with Nat, I would not be acting now. That day, that man, changed my life. And I have never ceased to be grateful to him. I have thought latterly that it was not a bad deal for the county either – I have given back in tax many times more than the maintenance grant that took me nearer my goal. How lucky I was, compared with students today.

In August 1969, I became a professional actor.

6

At Last

The actors' union was a closed shop in 1969. You couldn't get a job without an Equity contract. You couldn't join Equity without a job. But with the offer of contracts in our hot little hands, six young actors from the Bristol Old Vic Theatre School – four men and two women – were made provisional Equity members, and given a start by our alma mater. Nat Brenner was a socialist and a union man and had trained us well. Those were the days.

Three of our colleagues went to Salisbury, five to the Belgrade in Coventry, where they were joined by Leigh Lawson. David Suchet (RADA) went to Chester, Nickolas Grace (Central) to Frinton. A young actor stood a good chance of working, although acting has always been an unforgiving profession, and even then the drop-out rate in the first year was 40 per cent.

The Bristol Old Vic was four-weekly rep. In rep, you learnt from people playing the leads. During our year, we watched quality actors like Julian Glover, Chris Harris and Stephen Moore. Barbara Leigh-Hunt was a stunning Lady Macbeth. In her programme biog, Barbara listed every play she had ever been in, and her career started with three years in weekly rep at Colwyn Bay!

It eventually became impossible to sustain such companies as BOV financially, and it is much harder for young actors today to find work. Moreover, there is nowhere left where they can get the sort of experience we had, although Tom Morris, the current artistic director, is encouraging stronger relationships with the school, and has recently staged a *King Lear* in 2016, using students to emphasise the generational conflict in the play. Increasingly, though, I hear of drama school graduates looking for jobs with (for example) sympathetic law firms that will have them back when any acting job is over. The way we grew into being actors is not the only way to create professionals, but it was a productive one, and better than spending half the year in an office, waiting for your agent not to call. Take the six of us who started together in 1969. Simon Cadell had just won an Olivier when, tragically, he died at the age of 46. Then there is me and Jeremy Irons. Not a bad advert for the class of '69 at the Bristol Old Vic Theatre School and Repertory Theatre.

We were paid £11 10s (£11.50) a week, and as we spent 70–75 hours per week in the theatre it was possible to save money because you simply didn't have time to spend it. A pie and a pint would cost you 3s 6d – (17½p). Our stage-management duties included making props, tea, sweeping the stage, shifting furniture – and we played small parts. The one time we worked really hard was on 'get-out night', when we helped dismantle the set of the closing show and put up the new one. I would be back to my room (£2.3s per week) between three or four in the morning, and return to the theatre by nine on Sunday morning, in order to start technical rehearsals on the next play.

Our first play was Shaw's *Major Barbara* directed by Val May, with Eleanor Bron eloquent in the title role, and the formidable Sonia Dresdel as Lady Undershaft. Simon was playing Stephen Undershaft. I was playing Snobby Price, one of Major Barbara's Salvation Army converts. Jeremy Irons was playing the butler. We still laugh about his first professional note from our director. Like all of us, he wanted to make his mark, and decided to make his butler very old. The make-up was transforming and on his first entrance an unrecognisable Jeremy opened a pair of double doors, very slowly. Short of breath, he shuffled into the room, *very* slowly. He turned ... slowly. And closed the doors – *extremely* slowly. He turned to face front again, *vee-eeery* slowly, and said, without any noticeable increase in pace, 'M'lady, Lord Undershaft ish below.' When told to bring Lord Undershaft up,

Jeremy repeated the process. Unhurriedly. At the company notes session afterwards, the director said, 'Jeremy – excellent character, but the play is very slow till you come on ... and then it stops!'

In *Macbeth*, Jeremy was again transformed into a superb, dark, haunting Old Seaton. I played the Bleeding Sergeant, a Lord and a soldier, all three looking very different. For audiences, one of the delights of the old rep system was seeing actors change. The march of naturalism makes that acceptance harder. It's a good thing really, but it's a shame, because adopting differing characters, apart from being fun for the audience, is the essence of acting. 'I didn't know it was you!' was the greatest compliment. Or maybe, 'Which one were you?' although that question has its aggravating downside.

When Stephen Moore was whisked out of *One for the Pot*, moving to the West End in a surprise hit starring Prunella Scales, I was asked to take over his part in the Christmas offering – a Rix farce. The main figure (a superb Chris Harris) plays identical twins, and with the deft use of doubles, as the action hots up, it is very clever and very funny. I was the stooge, Charlie Barnett: eight days' rehearsal, while still playing a smaller part, and on! I started well, went through a very bad patch, and then got hold of it again towards the end. My reward was that in *As You Like It*, my last play at BOV, I played Charles the wrestler and Amiens. Wigs and nose-putty were liberally deployed to aid this great double! I played my guitar, Jeremy played the recorder. Julian Slade wrote the romantic music. The season ended reprising *The School for Scandal* for a tour of the West Country. Paid fun.

I was offered a renewed contract, but I needed to leave Bristol. Three of our original six stayed on. One of the older actors knew I was leaving for London and helped me with my audition speeches. In town, I did the rounds with a speech from Anouilh's *Ring Round the Moon*, and a bit of Berowne – 'Oh we have made a vow to study, lords...' You routinely did a Shakespeare and a modern piece. I sometimes used to do one of Luther's sermons (from Osborne's play), which developed into a fit: as Luther wrestled with his God and his constipation, it provided a justifiable excuse for some obvious acting. I wish I had chosen *Luther* for the Royal Court, but I opted for the Anouilh, which ended with my jumping on to a chair for the last couple of lines. On that occasion, in front of Tony Richardson, Jane Howell and John Dexter, I missed the leap up, kicked the chair across the stage and fell flat on my face. I was not offered work. Nor was Simon, whom I joined in a nearby café after *his* offering. I asked him what he had done. 'Well, I thought I would give them something they had never seen before,' said Simon, wryly. He had chosen the Keats sonnet 'Bright Star'! I was impressed. 'That *is* different,' I said. 'How did it go?' Simon smiled that lopsided smile of his, and, hardly able to contain his laughter, said, 'I was halfway through – thought it was going rather well actually – when John Dexter crossed his legs, turned away and yawned!'

One day my agent sent me up for Prospect Theatre. Prospect ranked third in the national pecking order, after the RSC and the National. I took my guitar along, and Toby Robertson, the charming eccentric in charge – who needed a small-part actor who could sing – liked me. It was encouraging to join such an august company for my second job. In 1970 I played Balthasar in *Much Ado About Nothing*. It was for a big national tour, and there was a very good company: John Neville was Benedict, Sylvia Syms played Beatrice; Timothy West, John Castle, Julian Glover, Brian Pringle and Clifford Rose were in support, and an amazing older actor, John Byron, played Leonato.

John had been a ballet dancer and, back in 1947, he was the first television Hamlet. I once watched him practising an entrance. Starting from the spot where he wanted to end up, centre stage, he backed his way to the foot of the stairs, and then moved forward again, working out which foot to end on when he hit his mark. Back and forth. Back and forth. *Then* he worked it backwards from the bottom of the staircase to the top, finding out which foot to *start* on. Having plotted it, he repeated it until he was confident. In performance he used to sweep on, never looking down at the stairs, and always ended up on his mark!

His approach was in stark contrast to that of John Neville. On one occasion John came in to rehearsal with Brian Pringle (Dogberry), direct from the club where they had spent the night drinking. How he was able to perform at all without rehearsing properly, let alone with such ease and brilliance, was beyond me, but he appeared entirely disinterested, throughout rehearsal. On the first night, he charmed the birds off the trees with a brilliant virtuoso display of effortless wit. I had never seen anything like it. And, indeed, never saw anything like it ever again. It was the end of an era, when that kind of actor just did supremely ... what he did.

John had been the artistic director of the new Nottingham Playhouse. He was famous for confronting his board which contained a butcher: John said he didn't tell the butcher what meat to sell, and resented being told by the butcher what plays to put on. By great chance I saw him in *The Importance of Being Earnest*. I happened to be in Nottingham: John was playing Jack Worthing, Michael Crawford was Algy, Helen Ryan was Gwendolen, June Ritchie (then a film star) was Cecily and Patience Collier was Lady Bracknell. Rep. Unforgettable.

Playing Margaret in *Much Ado About Nothing* was Pamela Miles, who caught my eye on the first day of rehearsals. In 1972, she became my wife. Lucky me. She still is my wife – very lucky me. She is a fantastic actress, a truly exceptional human being, a great mother, and she still makes me laugh. I cannot believe how fortunate I was to marry her. I believe that as an actor you can only ever be what you are as a human being. If I am anything at all as a human being, I owe it to Pam. I learnt a lot about acting from her, too: *Stop thinking, Just do it!*

Much Ado was set in Mexico, an idea that emanated from John Neville's then relationship with a black woman. Had Toby Robertson been more courageous, and risked casting more black actors, it might have been a remarkable piece of theatre, way ahead of its time. But he got cold feet, and in spite of the fact that designs were fixed in Mexico he cast Sylvia Syms as Beatrice. It was ... wayward. Towards the end of the tour, Tim West, speaking of my relationship with Pam, said, 'Well, at least *something* good has come out of this!'

Prospect asked me to audition for a national and European tour of *Hamlet* starring Ian McKellen. Ian had scored a massive success for Prospect with his double bill of Shakespeare's *Richard II* and Marlowe's *Edward II*, and his *Hamlet* was awaited with great anticipation. For my audition, I offered Hamlet's great soliloquy 'O what a rogue and peasant slave'. To my surprise, Ian was in the auditorium with the directorial team, which included John David, with whom I had worked at BOV, because he was directing *Man of the World*, the play that would tour in tandem with *Hamlet*. As I launched into 'O what a rogue ...' I realised that my choice of piece was deeply unsuitable, and must have looked plain arrogant. However, John, and Bob Chetwyn, the director of *Hamlet*, liked me enough to offer me the roles of Bernardo, a couple of messengers, and the lovely parts of the First Player and the Player King. I was also to understudy Claudius. Bob Chetwyn had directed Orton and Stoppard, *There's a Girl in My Soup* and a famous *Country Wife* with Maggie Smith. He had worked with Ian McKellen, back in rep at Ipswich, and here they were, teaming up again.

In the last week of the sell-out 14-week tour, we were playing in the Theater an der Wien, where Beethoven lived in a small room high above the stage, and wrote *Fidelio*. One sunny spring afternoon, a gang of us took advantage of the warm weather and met up by an open-air swimming-pool in the woods just outside Vienna. We had not been there long when a new arrival said, 'What about Ronny, eh?' Ronald Lewis was the handsome, one-time film star playing Claudius. I needed no reminding that I was understudying him, nor did it escape my mind that we had only had one understudy rehearsal – of the *first* scene – in the first *week* of the tour – over three months before! Understudying then was pretty much the responsibility of the understudy. I had played Claudius at school at the age of 17, so the text was pretty firmly in my memory, and I had sort of made sure I knew the lines, by listening regularly to them on the tannoy, but I had no idea if I could get through the play. In addition, I was much too young, and very different from the charming stud that Ronny delivered.

We were given to understand by our informant that in Rome, where we had performed before Vienna, Ronny had met an old girlfriend, had gone on something of a bender and had not recovered sufficiently to perform that night. This was not the day of the mobile phone. We had no easy way of contacting stage management, and didn't know if this was true.

After about an hour in the sun, during which we thought the guy with the news was pulling our legs, mine in particular, I nodded to Nick Grace, who was playing the Player Queen, and we met up in the middle of the pool.

'What d'you reckon, Gracie? He's having us on, isn't he?'

'Well, I thought he was, until he said there was a rehearsal at three o'clock. That sounds a bit real, doesn't it?'

'How come he knows, and none of us have been informed?'

'That's not really the point, Timmo.'

It wasn't. In case there was any substance in this nonsense, we decided I had better go to the theatre.

When I arrived, the principals were already there, and I was on as Claudius in four and a half hours. This was some test of nerve, but we did at least have time to go through the play. I knew the moves, and carried the book, and was reasonably confident until the big plotting scene in Act Four, when Claudius and Laertes work out how to murder Hamlet. The terrifying discovery I made that afternoon was that in Act Four, when you think you are on the home straight, Claudius has to pick the play up by the scruff of the neck and drive it.

Actors are fantastically supportive. Ian was warm and business-like, Sue Fleetwood, playing Ophelia was fun, as always; Jimmy Cairncross, who had only just taken over the role of Polonius, was divine, but Faith Brook, who was a remarkable, alcoholic Gertrude, was exacting, and, on occasion, literally pushed me into position. 'Not there. There!' she would say, and move me perhaps a foot, to precisely where she wanted me on the stage. She was firm, rather than unpleasant, and I didn't mind because I admired and liked her: she knew exactly what she wanted and was not about to allow some incompetent to endanger her performance.

Rehearsals over, I decided I would use the beard I wore as the First Player to give me more age, checked Ronny's costume, tried the crown on and retired to the dressing room, which I shared with Jimmy Cairncross. Such experiences tell you a lot about yourself. I am pretty highly strung, and in those days I used to think too much. I was also likely to get into a stew over a minor detail. Julian Curry, playing Horatio, used to say to me, 'Stop fretting, Piggers.' I was a fretter.

This situation was new to me, but I knew for sure that if I started fretting now I would fall at the first fence. The only way I could survive was to hold my nerve. As I studied the text, I did some slow breathing and Jimmy taught me an exercise that he had learnt from Ralph Richardson. If you sit with your hands on your knees, palms turned upwards, almost in a yoga position, and just breathe for five minutes, it is very calming. It helped reduce *my* apprehension, but not the strain in the building, which was tangible, because with me playing Claudius, two other actors were covering my roles. I sat and ran through the lines as the hour of my doom drew closer.

In the theatre there is an institution known as 'The Half'. If the curtain goes up at 7.30 'The Half' is called at 6.55. The quarter is at 7.10, the five at 7.20, and on 'Beginners', at 7.25, the company gathers in the wings for curtain up. 'The Half' is a legal institution, part of an agreement between the management and the ticket-buying public. If an actor is not in the building by 'The Half', the management have time to activate systems to ensure that the paying public see a show. If an actor is consistently late, serious words are spoken, threats are made, salary deducted, and on occasion I have known a strong company manager put the understudy on, so that when the actor *does* turn up, at, say, 7.20 p.m., someone else is playing his part! Mobile phones now make it possible to call or text – 'I'm stuck in traffic, but I will be there!' – but, actually, in this regard actors are impressively disciplined: 99.9 per cent of the time actors observe 'The Half' religiously.

About to go on as Claudius, I was holding myself together. As Beginners was called, Jimmy turned to me.

'You are going to be splendid, dear boy. You are a very fine young actor, and you are going to be superb in this role.' Hogwash, of course, but wonderfully reassuring when you are not sure if you will get through the first speech! Then Jimmy added, 'You know our scene – "He's going to his mother's closet?"'

'Yes?'

'Well, that is just before your soliloquy.' (Claudius has a fine confessional speech – 'O my offence is rank'.)

Jimmy pointed out that the prayer stool from which Claudius delivered the soliloquy was downstage right – what we used to call 'OP' – the side of the stage opposite the prompt corner. Jimmy's implicit point was that I could not possibly be further from the prompter, and therefore not brilliantly placed should I need her services during this exposed, and exposing speech.

'I was wondering,' he went on ... 'when I exit, I could, if you wish, be very close to you with the book, and feed you the lines, in the unlikely event you will need them.' This from an actor who was giving only his third performance as Polonius. 'Would that be helpful or distracting?' Jimmy was a dear man, and I could have hugged him.

'That would be just brilliant, Jimmy. Thank you.'

By that point in the play I wasn't exactly flying, but to every-one's surprise I was more than holding my own. Jimmy and I played our 'little scene', and as I took my place on the prayer stool to begin the soliloquy I saw him sit down in a chair – which he must have positioned earlier – as close to the proscenium arch as was possible – about 6 feet away from me. From inside his costume he took a copy of the play, then his spectacles, and sat there, waiting to prompt me. It gave me such a boost of confidence to see his kindness and support that I just knew I could make it.

And so we reached the major scene in Act Four, plotting with Laertes: this was where I thought I might fall apart. Ophelia's funeral and the duel scene are relatively easy – they are not so long, so complex psychologically, and do not require sustained concentration. *This* scene was the real test. I had asked the stage management to write the lines out, on the message that is delivered to Claudius at the beginning of the scene.

Stuart Wilson, playing Laertes, was aware that my lines were to be in the message, and this gave him some small hope that I might struggle through it. When I actually had the message in my hand I knew that if I started reading it I would end up reading it. I folded it up and put it down. Stuart went white, and his knees almost literally buckled beneath him. I was feeling surprisingly daring by this point, and was determined to get through it, which I did. I recall taking a couple of corners on two wheels, and noticing Stuart break into a sweat, but I made it. Julian Curry told me afterwards that it was actually a very exciting night, because there was some confluence between an ill-prepared, ambitious young actor, playing the part of the vulnerably ambitious Claudius.

I remember that night in Vienna in blurred slow motion, with *some* complete blanks, but I achieved much more than the basic requirement of keeping the curtain up. I didn't know that plans were afoot to transfer the play to the West End. Stuart had never enjoyed playing Laertes, so my Claudius served unwittingly as an audition, and when we came to the Cambridge Theatre, in the autumn of 1971, I made my West End debut as Laertes, the First Player/Player King, and got to share a dressing room for another four months with Jimmy Cairncross, who became a lifelong friend.

Jimmy hated the term 'gay', claiming he was a good old-fashioned homosexual. His long-term partner, David Dodimead, sadly died quite young, and Jimmy moved homewards for his final years, retiring to Edinburgh to live with his sister Dorothy. He worked occasionally at the Lyceum or Pitlochry, loving the odd outing to tread the boards. He was much respected, and often used to teach, or speak at functions. He passed away aged 93.

So here I was in my first long run of a play in the West End, two years after leaving drama school. I had done a year of breathless repertory at Bristol – including two Shakespeares, a Shaw, a Sheridan, a Rix farce, *Oh! What a Lovely War*, a schools tour, and a West Country tour. I had toured for Prospect with *Much Ado*, and done a fringe production of an Edward Bond play at the Oval House. Then *Hamlet*. Now the West End. And, boy, did I learn fast. On press night, our caustic assistant director sent me a card in which he had written, not the usual blandishments and clichés – 'A warm hand on your opening' – but the rather brutal 'Grasp the nettle, and something may come of it!'

I discovered what a nettle Laertes is. Frustratingly, his first scene, admonishing Ophelia, is his best. From then on, it's downhill: there's a lot of shouting and fighting in the second half of the play, but it is unsympathetic, and taxing! I played the first scene well, establishing a slightly snotty brother/father tone in my relationship with Sue Fleetwood as Ophelia. This was the area in which Bob wanted the character to work – a man of fundamentally patrician nature who saw women as inferior, but was not without tenderness towards his sister. Although I played the later stuff quite effectively, and achieved, I think, a genuine emotionality in my response to Ophelia's madness – Sue was at her best in that scene, so it wasn't difficult – I was always reaching up to the part, I never controlled it from above. As the run went on, I found myself doing more and more to get it to work. Not only did I not succeed, I exhausted both myself and my voice.

The play was deemed a success by enough people to keep it running healthily at the Cambridge – a difficult theatre because it was off the beaten path; Covent Garden was still a fruit market in 1971. The production, however, was criticised for being cold, and the multi-mirrored design, by Michael Annals, was deemed bleak. Although Ian did some spine-tingling stuff in the big scene with Ophelia, 'You jig, you amble and you lisp, and nickname God's creatures, and make your wantonness your ignorance' – filling it with sexual disgust – the women seemed to come out of the evening better. There was a wonderful moment in Act Four, when Gertrude, clearly the worse for drink, sat with the mad Ophelia at her feet and they wove wild flowers, crazily, happily in each other's hair.

Ian was well received, cementing his position as the most exciting actor of his generation, but although it wasn't a massive hit, it was good enough to be recorded on video. However, in spite of my double – and the Players' stuff all worked well, particularly the play scene – I was not noticed, and when you are not noticed in a West End run it's pure anonymous slog. When I emerged into the real world, I felt as though I had to start again.

7

THE RSC, STRATFORD

I did an uninspired audition for the RSC and they offered me small parts, nothing like the level of roles I had been playing. As it was an essential ambition of mine to join the company, I felt I should accept and get it out of my system. So in 1972 I went back to Stratford, my home town, to be with the RSC. Trevor Nunn was the artistic director now. I was familiar with Trevor's work because, when in the early sixties he'd turned down Peter Hall's offer of being an assistant, he worked as a director at the new Belgrade Civic Theatre in Coventry. Peter asked him again in 1964 – to come as a director – and he said, 'Yes.' In 1969 he became the artistic director.

This, incidentally, tells you quite a lot about Peter. Michael Rudman, an Associate Director at the National, said of him, with a touch of cruelty, that his greatest gift to the theatre was his temperament. Well, he gave the theatre a great deal more than that, but Rudman's point remains: Peter never appeared to be threatened by anyone. At the National, he dealt brutally with Jonathan Miller, and in a Byzantine way with Michael Blakemore. He was top dog, and gave little quarter to people who opposed him. I once had a stand-up row with Peter during which he called me a 'cunt', but when the dust had settled there was never a moment's retribution. He knew that, at his own invitation, the director, Peter Gill, had built an independent, occasionally subversive empire at the National Theatre Studio, but he didn't care. Hall's successor, Richard Eyre, fired Gill.

Regional theatre was vibrant in the sixties. The Labour Minister for the Arts, Jennie Lee, was a committed advocate of subsidy, and, as a continued part of rebuilding after the war, theatres sprouted up: John Neville's Nottingham Playhouse, Chichester and the Victoria, Stoke-on-Trent, where Peter Cheeseman abolished dress codes: regular middle-class theatregoers might find themselves next to somebody who had come straight from work and was wearing overalls. Birmingham already had the old Rep, where its great founder, Sir Barry Jackson, nurtured actors like Paul Scofield, Derek Jacobi, Elizabeth Spriggs and Albert Finney. Derek Godfrey opened Coventry's Belgrade, a spanking new theatre that locals were proud of, in a fabulous *Cyrano de Bergerac*.

Trevor's work at the Belgrade was compelling: you just knew there was a new kid on the block. His production of Brecht's *The Caucasian Chalk Circle* had a whirl and dynamism that swept you off your feet. The wonderful David Waller played Azdak, and, when Trevor moved to Stratford, Waller became a stalwart of the company. Having at one time given up acting to work in the travel industry, he brought the feel of an ordinary man to his work. This was the growing fashion. Waller played Bottom in Peter Brook's iconic *A Midsummer Night's Dream*, where the sense of an artisan out of his depth was cemented by Waller's ability to be the man in the street.

When Trevor arrived at the RSC, he brought his dynamism with him. An impecunious *Revenger's Tragedy* provided the platform for him, his designer, Christopher Morley, and a mustard-keen company led by Ian Richardson, to defy budgetary restrictions with a rich, free inventiveness. The young Alan Howard was electrifying as an unpredictable Lussurioso. Norman Rodway was deliciously vile and creepy as Spurio, savouring in particular the wicked line 'Old dad, dead?' The production was a massive hit.

Trevor's *King Lear*, starring Eric Porter, alongside many of the *Revenger's* actors, was equally original, full of swirling movement, quoting from Bergman and Eisenstein. With canine physicality Alan Howard was astonishing as Edgar, suggesting how close to Hamlet the part is. David Waller was a blunt, funny Kent, Sue Fleetwood a terrifying Regan. I stood through this production five times. I could not get enough of it.

By 1972 Trevor had been the artistic director for three years, and his mounting of *Coriolanus, Julius Caesar, Antony and Cleopatra* and *Titus Andronicus* – in one season, as *The Romans* – suggested he was picking up a gauntlet thrown down by Peter Hall almost a decade earlier with the *Wars of the Roses* cycle. Trevor was to direct all four plays, with the assistance of Euan Smith and Buzz Goodbody. The company was over 50-strong, led by John Wood, Patrick Stewart, Colin Blakely, Janet Suzman, Margaret Tyzack, Corin Redgrave and Richard Johnson – a film star at the time – as Mark Antony. His self-coined nickname was Golden Bollocks.

I was excited and proud to be coming back home, joining the company, re-entering the stage door of my dreams as an actor. I was to play Aufidius's lieutenant in *Coriolanus*, Metellus Cimber and Dardanius in *Caesar*, Proculeius in *Antony and Cleo*, and I can't remember what in *Titus*. I was also understudying Coriolanus, and later in the season when the original understudy, Clem McCallin, was diagnosed with leukaemia, I took over the understudy of Antony in *Antony and Cleo*. Days when Richard Johnson went off with the local hunt, waiting nervously to see if he had survived, were no fun at all.

There was one problem. The social and sexual revolutions of the sixties had not reached Stratford-upon-Avon. In 1971 I was living with Pam in London – it was called living in sin then, and I simply did not have the nerve to tell my mother. I was completely in love with Pam, and clear that I wanted her to be my wife. Pam swears that I did not propose to her properly. Apparently I just said, 'Well, if we're going to get through the next year when I am in Stratford, we'd better get married.' However inadequate the proposal, we decided we would get married the following year although we had been together then for less than 18 months. The decision was harder for Pam than for me but the date was set for the end of April 1972.

Pam's mum was a lovely, very pretty woman to whom she was devoted, who had suffered unfairly, and from a young age, from cancer and strokes. Poor health restricted her movement, so wherever we were going to marry, poor Connie, sadly, could not be there. This fact, and my intense schedule, persuaded us to have the wedding in Stratford, *and* on a Sunday. Trevor assured me that there was no way we would be working on a Sunday, although, in addition to performing *Coriolanus*, we would by then be previewing *Julius Caesar*.

Initially, we thought my mum's idea, that we should hold the ceremony in my old school chapel, was a good one. The Guild Chapel is a thirteenth-century gem attached to the school, where we held morning assembly. Our art master, Mr Puddephat, unearthed some frescoes on the chapel walls which are still visible but very faded. John Shakespeare, William's father, a town councillor, had been tasked with the post-Reformation job of whitewashing over these Catholic, and therefore unacceptable, paintings. Ironically, this act of vandalism preserved them for a later age.

We knew ours was only the second marriage to take place in the Guild Chapel. What we did not realise was, that, because marriages there were almost without precedent, it was considered a unique, very special place in Stratford to be married. The chapel held warm associations for me, and Pam had always liked it, but nothing could have been further from our minds than a glitzy wedding. My mum fought every detail of the way we wanted the ceremony to be. It was misery. This fearsome side of Mum's nature made her a brilliant mother. She was intensely protective and immensely supportive – deeply involved in my life – *too* involved – something I put down to my near-death as a child.

Nevertheless, Pam and I had a wonderful wedding day. She looked fantastic. I cracked up as she walked towards me down the aisle, and could barely speak the responses. We recorded the service for Pam's mum, but when her dad came to play it he pressed the record button, thereby erasing the service and recording himself collecting the tea things. We spent the night at a hotel in the Cotswolds. Next day I was back at work.

We lived in a tiny rented cottage at Alveston, just outside Stratford. Three days after our wedding, early in the morning, we were disturbed by stones being lobbed at our bedroom window. Dad! I remember 'Vincent' by Don McLean was playing on the radio. Dad had been contacted by an old school friend of mine who was now working as an estate agent. I had asked Martin to keep his eye open for something for me, and here was Dad with a message that a small house at the bottom of the market was for sale for the enormous price of £4,750. Pam and I just had the £500 deposit between us; we got our first mortgage and our first house. We now live in a small house in Hampstead, made possible by getting into the market before property prices began to rise uncontrollably.

Later that year, Pam joined the company, to play a small part in *The Comedy of Errors*, the fifth play of the *Romans* season. The part was beneath her, but it meant we could be together, so three months after our marriage we moved into our first home. It was a red-brick, end-of-terrace, two-bedroom house that boasted 50 yards of narrow garden out the back. We learnt the first of many lessons in doing houses up, and we did this well.

So here we were, in the middle of our first RSC season, married, with a house. And I was happy with the company, too. We were able to work on voice with the great Cicely Berry, and the work was good – even if the small parts were undemanding. By the autumn we were moving on to *Antony and Cleopatra*, but something in the aura was wrong. The productions were superb – *Julius Caesar* had some stunning stuff in it, and Janet Suzman was a fine Cleopatra – but the productions did not seem to ignite public interest. Brutus, in the famous tent scene, remarks –

> There is a tide in the affairs of men
> Which taken at the flood leads on to fortune.
> Omitted, all the voyage of their life
> Is bound in shallows and in miseries.

Shakespeare knew it all. There is a superb biography of Donald Wolfit by Ronald Harwood, his one-time dresser, which is subtitled *His Life and Work in the Unfashionable Theatre.*

Harwood's play *The Dresser* provides a portrait of Wolfit, an independent-minded star who did not want to dance to anyone else's tune, who toured with his own company for years, most famously as Lear and Tamburlaine. You can catch him in *Beckett* or *Lawrence of Arabia* on the television, and even in small cinematic roles you can sense his power. He played often in the West End, and on one occasion – in *Malatesta*, a religious play – he appeared opposite a similarly strong-minded actor, Ernest Milton. I think they were both playing cardinals. By constantly trying to achieve a better position on the stage they found themselves working their way towards the back: one review said that 'they upstaged each other to the greater glory of God'. You get the picture. The real point is, he was unfashionable. And fashion is profoundly influential in the theatre.

Our *Romans* season, which concluded with a towering performance of Titus Andronicus from the mighty Colin Blakely, just did not 'catch the tide'. The National Theatre, based at the Old Vic under Olivier at that time, could do no wrong. Up by the Avon, we slaved away in our authentic leather sandals, togas and armour, but the quality of our work was not properly recognised – who knows why? *Titus* suffered the same fate, although it marked promotion for me.

Patrick Stewart enjoyed justified personal success that season with his Aufidius, Cassius and particularly his Enobarbus. By the time we reached *Titus*, he was exhausted, and asked if he might sit that play out. A few of us were auditioned, and I was asked to take over the small part of Bassianus, Lavinia's husband. He only has two scenes before he is savagely murdered and thrown into a pit. It was a nice reward at the end of a tiring and sadly frustrating season. It was not until I did *A & C* at the National 14 years later that I came across a better production of that play: *Coriolanus* was powerful, *Caesar* and *Titus* superb, but ... we missed the tide.

Ian Hogg, playing Coriolanus, did not have a comfortable season. He is an electrifying actor with a dangerous, scary physicality: Patrick Stewart used to ring his wife every night after the big Coriolanus/Aufidius fight, just to let her know he had survived! At the end of rehearsals, in the spring of 1972, when we left London for Stratford, Ian's performance was stunning, but technical rehearsals of the play involved endless experiments with the hydraulic set that served all four plays: this process lasted 12 days, morning, noon and night. Sunday included. Four previews were cancelled. We began our dress rehearsal at 10.30 one Friday night. It was a bad start.

During that 12-day technical, Ian's performance was lost: although areas of his work remained excitingly intact, he never managed to draw the part together. I watched him striving painfully to get back to where he had been, but the harder he tried the worse it got. Next year, all the plays transferred to the Aldwych, with one or two small cast changes, and one big one, although none of us knew that Ian was going to be replaced, until we read in the paper that Coriolanus was to be played by someone else. This was also how Ian found out he had been fired. He was not told. His agent was not told. He was cast aside and suffered a loss of confidence that lasted ten years. It was cruel treatment of a good servant of the company.

Before I re-joined the RSC, I managed to fit in a superb televisation by Trevor Nunn of *A & C* at Elstree and *The Screens* by Genet at Bristol. When I left BOV in 1970, at the end of my first year as a professional actor, the Theatre Royal was closed for refurbishment. Built in 1766, it is one of the most beautiful theatres in the world. It is intimate: lovely to play. Nat Brenner used to tell us students, 'If you can't do it at the Bristol Old Vic, you can't do it!' Gem that it was, it was desperately in need of modernisation. Everything around the shell of the auditorium was torn down and replaced. When I returned in 1973 I was performing in the new studio.

It was a terrible production of a strange play, but the cast was quite something: Tom Chadbon, Paul Moriarty, Bill Hoyland and John Nettles among the men; the three ladies were Charlotte Cornwell, Kate Nelligan and Diana Quick. Years later, Diana reminded me that I had described this trio as 'the sound of ambition clanking down the corridor'. All these extremely gifted girls became famous: Charlotte in a television series called *Rock Follies*; Diana through *Brideshead Revisited*; Kate Nelligan powered her way swiftly to the top of the theatre tree, playing leads for David Hare and peach parts at the National. She was beautiful, with a mellow voice and soft consonants. She had it all. She moved to America – I think she was Canadian by birth – and to my surprise I didn't hear of her for years. During this time, when she had fallen off my radar, I asked the celebrated New York agent Robbie Lantz what had become of her. 'Tim,' he said laconically, 'the boat may not leave on time, but it does go more than once.' Sure enough, the next year Kate was nominated for an Oscar. The boat may not leave on time, but it does indeed go more than once.

8

THE RSC, LONDON

When *The Romans* came to the Aldwych, in 1973, I was promoted, to Pompey in *Antony and Cleopatra* and Lucius in *Titus Andronicus*. I was still understudying Coriolanus, now played by Nicol Williamson, a mercurial, temperamental actor famous for leaving the stage mid-performance if he was unhappy. When we were introduced, he poked me gently in the chest and said, with a wicked smile, 'Pigott-Smith, eh? You-oo *will* go on!'

Michael Blakemore was doing small parts when Olivier played Coriolanus (1959). Talking with Sir Laurence, Michael commented, 'Great play.' Olivier disagreed. 'Uh-huh,' he said. 'Great *text*.' This is an acting insight into a difficult play that can be loud and impressive but hard to humanise. It is difficult to catch the audience's minds and even harder to engage their feelings. You have to find ways of raising it above the level of 'text'. Olivier did two things: he was funny in the part, and, based on pictures of Mussolini's grisly demise, he created a stunning death fall.

He was standing at the very front of a platform, some 20 feet above the stage. He hurled the final insult, 'Boy!', at Aufidius with a spine-tingling inflection, and, contemptuously, turned his back. Then someone pushed him, and he fell backwards into space. The entire audience lurched forward, gasping, as if to catch him. Two Volscis grabbed his feet, so he was hanging upside down. It is the most exciting thing I have ever seen in a theatre. Aufidius approached and stabbed him in the heart. I can still hear the dagger going through Olivier's leather tunic.

Pompey in Antony and Cleopatra, *with Patrick Stewart (Enobarbus) and Richard Johnson (Antony), Royal Shakespeare Company, 1973*

Our Coriolanus – Nicol – was electric. Rehearsals and previews went well. Nicol was not the greatest fighter, so the first, warring, third of the play could have been better. The second third requires big lungs and an aggressive political mind: Nicol bit words off savagely, with huge arrogance. The last third of the play, when Coriolanus is sent to his death by his mother, Volumnia, demands emotional power, and here he was at his finest.

On press night, Nicol was off colour. He blew the fighting, and, unusually, gabbled the political stuff. I thought we were dead. But at the end of the Volumnia scene he held a much longer pause than usual! He was close to the audience – downstage left: he looked straight out front, allowing his face to crumple slowly into tears. Then, with broken voice, 'Oh mother, mother, what have you done?' The fact that he could not fight was forgotten. The mess of the political section was history, and Nicol went on to enjoy a huge personal success in the part. That one piece of magic – lifting the play above the level of 'text' – swung the evening. It was quite something.

As threatened, I *did* go on. I had had no rehearsal but I knew the part backwards. Word came through on a Friday lunchtime that Nicol could not play the next day's matinee. I was called to the theatre to practise the fights, which I had also learnt but never rehearsed. We played *Julius Caesar* that night, and next morning we ran *Coriolanus*.

I was in the Number One dressing room, next door to Maggie Tyzack – our vituperative Volumnia – with whom I had a great relationship, and she nursed me through to curtain up, doing voice exercises, calling out loudly through the wall from her adjacent dressing room, 'Pataka pataka pataka, Niminy piminy Niminy piminy, oooooh oooooh oooooh!'

A groan went up when it was announced that Nicol was not playing, but I just threw myself at it; and made it nine-tenths of the way, failing to pull the threads together in the death scene when I followed my sudden instinct that Coriolanus would go laughing contemptuously to his death – it wasn't disastrous, but it did not quite come off. However, as when I had gone on for Claudius in

Ian McKellen's *Hamlet*, I had more than kept the curtain up, and the house and the company were very appreciative at the call. I gave a good enough account of the role for Trevor Nunn to give me notes. He was a director who was at his strongest when he could see the play entire, his overview was extraordinary: he talked with great clarity about what I had done, and where I should go next with the part. I could only remember flashes of it, and this is not good acting: you must recall the whole thing so you can sift through it afterwards.

Saturday night was *Julius Caesar*, and, by Monday, Nicol had recovered. There were rumours, as he had been up in Scotland for a football match, that he was not really ill. But when he turned up he was white, suffering from a very evident head cold. In the scene where Coriolanus talks to the young patricians, he served pink champagne! You can occasionally catch Nicol now on television in films like *The Bofors Gun*, and one I love, *The Reckoning*. He came back to London many years later with a one-man show about the great American actor Lionel Barrymore. After the first night he went to a jazz club and sang into the small hours. His marriage had broken up and I believe he was drinking again. When he went into the theatre on the second night he was distinctly the worse for wear. In the course of the show, the story goes, he abused the audience, then, taking the blame on himself, apologised for his inadequate performance, left the stage, left the theatre and left the country. He was never one to do things by halves. Sadly, he died not long after, in 2011, probably from burning the candle at both ends, although he had oesophageal cancer.

As I had to be based in London, Pam and I rented out our little house in Stratford. One of Pam's oldest friends is Penelope Keith, who had a large house in Putney, with a granny flat at the top. We lived there, for £5 per week. Pam was working steadily. In 1973 she went down to Cardiff to the Welsh National Theatre Studio, and gave a stunning performance in D. H. Lawrence's *The Daughter-in-Law*. She went on to do several plays for the Welsh National Theatre, including a vicious Regan in *King Lear*.

Meanwhile, we *Romans* slaved away at the Aldwych, and again this outstanding work never quite caught fire. By the time we got to *Titus*, the company was shattered, and disheartened.

Trevor had a dream that *Titus* would begin with a huge empty black box, and into that box would come a shelf, lowered from the flies, bearing Titus, his *warrior* sons, coffins containing his *dead* sons, Tamara with her *vile* sons, Aaron, slaves and prisoners in chains. Alf Davies, the technical manager at the Aldwych, said, 'It'll crack the grid, Trev.' In other words, the ancient stage machinery would not bear the weight. For that entrance I was wearing: regulation T-shirt, linen trousers and knee-high leather sandals. Over this I had a very heavy – it almost felt like canvas – shift. Then a leather tunic. Then full armour, and on top of that a cape. On top of the cape, I had a lion skin. I was also wearing a leonine wig, and had to carry one corner of a coffin. Multiply that by 20. By the time you got on stage you were a puddle in human form.

Undaunted, we entered technicals and on the Monday morning, as predicted, we cracked the grid. By the end of the week the pressure had, not surprisingly, got too much for Trevor and the poor man had a breakdown: I think it was shingles. On Friday, the day of the first preview, after four slow days of tech we had still not properly rehearsed, staged or lit the final act – and of all Shakespeare's plays, the last act of *Titus* is the hardest, containing, notoriously, the moment when Tamara, eating a piece of pie, is told that the meat she is savouring is that of her two dead sons. Although it is possible to embrace *some* laughter from the audience because it is so ghoulish, it is also easy to be laughed *at*.

On Friday, the morning of the first preview, John Wood, playing Saturninus, had a car crash. He was not injured and turned up just in time to make his rather silly contribution, but the whole venture just seemed fated. Associate director Terry Hands came to the rescue, and although he'd had nothing to do with the production, cleverly staged the last act so we could at least open on time; we had no time for a dress run. Patrick Stewart had taken over the role of Aaron the Moor, and he conceived the part in very broad terms – looking for the macabre humour of the play – black as your hat, with a frizzy fright wig. This performance, like John's, made it hard to anchor the play with reliable gravity.

Colin Blakely, our amazing Titus, was superhuman. He simply ignored the chaos around him, and, like the lionheart he was, provided a magnificent example of – what can I call it? – *survival in spite of*. He was towering. As Lucius, I spent a good deal of time onstage with him, and I learnt masses – acting is an osmotic process. He didn't worry much about where he was on the stage, he just did it. His imagination was simple and powerful, taking the bull by the horns, delivering directly, without frills, and his total commitment carried you along. My admiration for him, before I worked with him, was enormous, but now it knew no bounds. The press, however, didn't go for it. One critic described Colin as 'Angry – one of the seven dwarves'. I was apoplectic: this was a great performance. It seems shocking now that actors blacked up and were likened to dwarves – a mountain of political incorrectness, but that's the way it was.

Years later, I talked to Colin about it; he had been so upset by the response that he turned to Olivier. 'How did ya start, baby?' Olivier asked. Colin described the magnificent opening procession and music, ending with a long crescendoing blare on the buccinas, on which he rode into his own clarion call, 'HAAAAAAAIIIIIIIL ROME!!!' Olivier shrugged and said, 'Well that's where you went wrong,' and added, 'I started very old and very tired.' Clever old dog; get audience sympathy from the off!

One of the assistant directors on *The Romans* was Buzz Goodbody, who has become something of a legend. An attractive woman in her twenties with pale skin and short, light brown, big hair, she wore jeans and long, full shirts that she did not tuck in. When impersonating her, you made circles with your fingers in front of your eyes (her large round specs) and chewed – she invariably chewed gum. I picture her in a chair behind Trevor, leaning forward, earnest, intent, observing. And chewing.

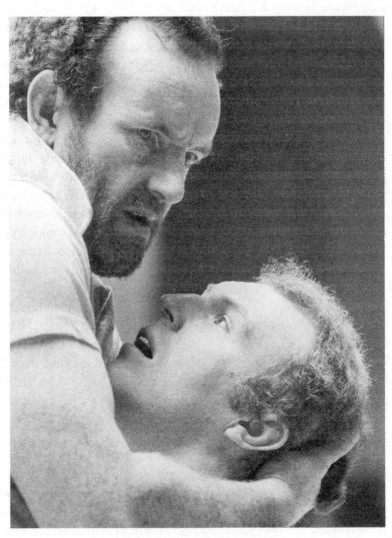

Titus Andronicus *in rehearsal with Colin Blakely, Royal*
Shakespeare Company, 1973

She came to the fore at a National Union of Students Drama Festival, where her production of Dostoyevsky's *Notes from the Underground* was feted, and the RSC snaffled her up. In spite of – maybe because of – her Roedean schooling, she was a Marxist feminist who challenged male authority. Theatres then were nearly all run by men. Joan Littlewood, who ran the Theatre Royal, Stratford East, and is probably best known for *Oh! What a Lovely War*, was the exception that proved the rule, and she retired in 1975, just as Buzz appeared to be finding her feet. Always defending the female minority, Buzz made a special effort to be nice to Pam.

Subversive Buzz may have been, but you never got the feeling she was about to lead a coup. As an assistant, she was very professional and supportive to Trevor, always toeing the party line, which is important – the last thing you need from an assistant is another view. Trevor gave her scenes to rehearse on her own, which he would then look at and comment on. Playing Pompey in *Antony and Cleo*, I was forcing myself not to *think* too much, so Buzz's thematic approach – 'What does Pompey mean in the play?' – represented a university approach that I was trying to move away from. I was good as Pompey; indeed, at one notes session Trevor said he could not imagine it ever being played better, but I couldn't work out why, and just had to go for it with blind faith. This worked until my belief ran out. When I was floundering, Buzz centred me: I could fall back on her notion of what Pompey represents – an old-fashioned sense of honour.

No one in the *Romans* company got to know her intimately. She was not standoffish, and would happily down a pint in the pub, but she was private. Two years of *The Romans* (1972–3) must have been frustrating – dogsbodying throughout technicals, delivering notes, apologising for changes, explaining delays, telling us the call had been altered, asking us to do more overtime. Importantly, she was kind. She never complained and she never passed the buck, which must have been tempting. Buzz was just there. Always there. Chewing. I have one memory of her being close to tears when it got too much for her. Word went round that Buzz was feeling down. Everyone was particularly nice to her: you couldn't help but be concerned for someone who spent all her time thinking about other people.

Before the Swan opened in 1986 there was only one playing space in Stratford – the main theatre that replaced the old building which burnt down in 1926. In the Theatre Gardens in Stratford is a small Victorian folly, a circular building with the feel of a neglected church – the Little Round House. In the years prior to the *Romans* season, it became a focus for the company's untapped creative juices. The actor Martin Bax (related to the composer Arnold Bax) got permission to use it: he cleaned out cobwebs, birds' nests, bird shit, removed whatever bits and bobs the company had stored there, cadged some basic lighting equipment and began to schedule events. As a performance space the Little Round House was crude: in the round, obviously, with two or three rows of concrete seating. You could create an end-on auditorium, using stacked chairs for the audience, although there were no opportunities for scenery. It was adaptable and atmospheric, and actors like Martin channelled their creativity into it. He screened late-night movies, organised concerts and put on plays – which started when the main theatre show was over – late! During the *Romans* season, I remember Heathcote Williams' *The Local Stigmatic*, and a fun evening of excerpts from Shakespeare. I directed *Next Time I'll Sing to You*, James Saunders' haunting play, and Pam played Lizzie.

In spite of the necessarily late curtain, this strange space was always full, and although it could be nervy – for there is nothing quite so testing as playing exclusively to your peers, who happen to be sitting inches away from you – it was genuinely ... buzzy.

In 1974, Buzz was given the means to formalise this creative waste into The Other Place (TOP). The aim was to get plays on for as little money as possible: the very lack of resources was to be a spur. Jerzy Grotowski's *Towards a Poor Theatre* advocated a raw, committed, spiritual approach that transcended the need for money, and it was influential, but, more than anything, TOP exemplified Peter Brook's theories as set out in his 1968 book *The Empty Space*: a desire for a leaner, starker style, contrasting the larger production values required in big theatres. The hut halfway up Southern Lane that housed the hire wardrobe was given over to the RSC's exciting new venture. The first production I saw there was Buzz's *King Lear* with Tony Church, and it was riveting. The bare space intensified the experience, which was not interrupted by scene changes – there was *no* scenery to change. As there were no distractions there was nothing between the audience and the play.

In 1975 Buzz directed *Hamlet* at TOP, starring Ben Kingsley. Pam and I saw an early performance. The only light in the battlement scenes was provided by the guards holding torches. This exciting minimalism was new, and it placed attention firmly on the actors. The impact was profound. It ranks as one of the best *Hamlets* I have seen, and I have seen more than I can remember. Buzz's *Hamlet* had a level of passion that is rare, and sometimes accompanies the early days of a new venture.

As Pam and I walked down the street afterwards, reeling from the power of the play, we bumped into Buzz and chatted with her. She told us she had just been awarded an academic bursary about which she was really enthusiastic, and we learnt later that she had a new boyfriend. Her life seemed rich and full of hope. Which is why, driving through London a couple of days later, Pam and I were stopped in our tracks by an *Evening Standard* billboard, proclaiming 'RSC director takes her own life'.

Suicide is always shocking, but this seemed so utterly illogical. We stopped the car and sat there, disbelieving. Buzz was riding a wave, and at the crest of it she had cut the thread. No one seemed able to fathom why this talented, likeable woman, with life opening up before her, had made such an irreversible choice. We were all agreed that if she had been feeling suicidal, working on *Hamlet* was hardly likely to ease her pain.

'If it be now, 'tis not to come. If it be yet to come, 'twill not be now. If it be not now yet it will come.'

To make up for lack of money, productions had to be ingenious, and creative, and TOP, Buzz's legacy, became central to the growth of the RSC, expanding to the point at which it was necessary to find a larger home. More formal buildings were created and budgets got bigger. In 2001, there was insufficient money to fund TOP productions, and it had to be closed.

In March 2016, TOP opened again, run, fittingly, by a woman, the gifted Erica Whyman. It is again a vital force within the RSC, though I very much doubt that the bottom philosophical brick in the wall, the Empty Space of Buzz's thinking, is still in place. And I wonder how many of the young people who work there now are aware of the contribution made by Buzz Goodbody.

At the end of the Aldwych season I felt again that my work had gone unnoticed, but Trevor needed a money-spinner and had approached Frank Dunlop who suggested *Sherlock Holmes*, something of a departure for the RSC. Frank worked with Olivier at the Old Vic and the *Young* Vic was his idea, providing a burst of irreverent theatrical energy, mixing the classical with the accessible – at what was nicknamed, because of Frank's surname, the Cycle Factory.

Sherlock Holmes was written by a Victorian American actor-manager, William Gillette. He played Holmes and is credited with inventing the meerschaum pipe, the downward curve of the pipe allowing the audience to see his face clearly. In the nineteenth century, stage popularity was limiting, in the same way that nowadays an actor who has spent 20 years in *EastEnders* might have difficulty persuading audiences to take him seriously as Macbeth. Audiences would not take Gillette as anything else, so he got stuck with Holmes, playing it into his eighties. When he toured England in 1911, his page-boy at 221b, Billy, was the young Charlie Chaplin.

The winter of 1973–4 was harsh. The trades unions were rampant, the government could not govern and the country reached a low point with the three-day working week. People needed diversion, and here, from the RSC, was entertainment with the imprimatur of class. The company boasted the ideal Holmes in John Wood, and Philip Locke was the perfect foil as a mad-haired Professor Moriarty. Frank, to my surprise, asked me to play Dr Watson, trying to capture the notion of Holmes and

Watson being young men about town. This was true to Conan Doyle, but I was 26 and John was in his forties, so it didn't quite work: I made John look too old, and appeared callow by his side. It also emerged that unless I provided the audience with a Watson they recognised, stuffier, older, they felt they hadn't seen him. So gradually my caddish young Watson moved towards the more familiar stock figure.

Gillette's play is a melodrama, featuring Moriarty's underground HQ, Holmes's famous rooms at 221b Baker Street and a great action scene in the gasworks – with Holmes using a cunning subterfuge to escape Moriarty and his villainous crew. Carl Toms' revolving set was superb. Around it, fog swirled, newspaper sellers shouted the latest headlines and violin music – delicately spoofing the James Bond theme – gave authentic atmosphere and a witty modern twist. John was a breathtaking Holmes. Frank's production was spectacular. After the unsympathetic response to *The Romans*, suddenly we were in the spotlight. We had great reviews; not me – it took me a couple of months to get the balance right – but we played to packed houses and soon it was rumoured that we might transfer to Broadway.

Before I leave *Sherlock Holmes* at the Aldwych, a story. The last act took place in Watson's Kensington surgery. With the revolve still turning, I appeared upstage centre through double doors, and, as the revolve came to a standstill, sat at my desk, stage right, in front of a large bay window. During a late preview, the revolve stopped, but the 30-foot flat behind me, did not.

I was unaware of the impending disaster: the flat fell forwards, completely engulfing me. The audience gasped because it looked as though I had been crushed. In fact, the bay window saved me: the side came to rest on the desk just beside my elbow, and the lintel brushed my wig. I was safe within the cavity of the bay. After the show, the company manager was hugely apologetic, and said, 'Thank God you're all right. You could have been killed.' It was pretty dramatic, but that's not the story.

When the stage crew had righted the flat, which was hanging out into the auditorium, I could see that a small table in front

of my desk was in pieces. An upright chair was likewise match-
wood. We couldn't play the scene with the stage in this mess, so I
called for the butler – which got a laugh. Sid Livingstone entered
imperiously and remarked, 'A trifle windy out tonight, sir', which
got another big laugh. I replied, 'Yes, Parsons. We should never
have moved to Kensington!' – which got a round. During these
ad libs, and the applause, I piled broken furniture into Sid's arms
and helped him offstage. We had recovered and were ready to
carry on with the *author's* words. That is the story, but it is not
the point.

In the audience that night was a teenager, with whom I was
chatting, 25 years later, about ad libs. Not connecting me with
Watson, he recounted my story – with our 'off the cuff' lines
word perfect. This 'teenager' was an American theatre addict,
whose mum had brought him to London to see theatre at its best,
and his name is Kevin Spacey.

Coincidence rules our lives.

9

WASHINGTON DC

Frank auditioned Pam for the part of Thérèse, the French maid, and at the end of 1974 we faced the prospect of being on Broadway together. Hard to believe. But during the Aldwych run of *Sherlock Holmes*, things were afoot.

I not only admired Ian McKellen as an actor, he was a fantastic role model. In Aberdeen, towards the end of our *Hamlet* tour, I was in my dressing room during a rare lull when there was a knock on the door: it was Ian. I was surprised, but realised we were in Act Four when Shakespeare gives Hamlet a break, too. Nevertheless, my dressing room was on the top floor and Ian had come a long way. I assumed there was a problem.

He asked me if I had enjoyed the tour, and then enquired – as we were nearing the end of it – if I had considered my next move. I said that I had always wanted to join the RSC. He said that was exactly the right thing for me to do, and wished me luck. Then he said, 'And you must work on your chest voice. Your head voice is very strong, and clear. Get that chest going.' Ian had climbed three floors, during his break, to talk to me about my future and my vocal technique. He was dead right, too: the chest needed work. Nerves often pushed my voice up into my head, and sometimes, my throat. What you really want is a voice that comes out of your stomach! My voice has improved gradually and I pride myself now on being a good leading man. I simply follow the example Ian set me.

That was *before* Claudius in Vienna, and Laertes in the West End. Then our ways parted. Now, in 1974, Ian got in touch to say he had been scheduled to play Posthumus in *Cymbeline* for the RSC, but it wasn't going to work. They were looking for a replacement, and was I interested? The prospect of playing such a fascinating leading role for the RSC was the stuff of my dreams. I was grateful to Ian, and contacted the casting department. Head of casting was Maurice Daniels, known as Doris Manuals. His assistant, to whom I spoke, as she was based in London where I was playing Dr Watson, was Genista McIntosh, now Baroness McIntosh of Hudnall, who went on to a stellar career as a theatre CEO. The main issue was that if I played Posthumus I would have to go back and forth between Stratford and the Aldwych, where *Sherlock Holmes* was now scheduled to run right through the summer. Quite rightly, the RSC was milking its surprise cash cow.

I had to meet John Barton, the director of *Cymbeline*. If *he* didn't want me, there was no point. John had two reputations – for being ultra-academic and wildly eccentric. He was married to a *real* academic, Anne Righter, who was trying to cure him of his alarming habit of chewing razor blades, which he kept loose in his pocket. I was summoned to his flat in De Walden Court, central London, which felt like a Cambridge study – brown, dusty, ashy, untidy, book-filled. John was a donnish, striking-looking man, with a good head of dark hair, dusty glasses which he wore on the end of his nose, deep creases under his eyes, an unkempt beard and tobacco-stained teeth. We talked about *Cymbeline* – the play, the part – and he asked me to do a bit for him. I chose the soliloquy at the end of Act Two, full of jealousy and angst. He gave me a couple of notes. I did it again, and he asked me to do the job, providing the schedules could be organised. They were. I did. And I was reunited with my old friend Sue Fleetwood, who was playing Imogen. Iachimo was in the hands of Ian Richardson.

I found John very warm and easy when we met, and he turned out to be the cleverest, kindest director. Sometimes he would give you a technical note like, 'I think you are mis-stressing the fifth line of "Yea, bloody cloth". Could you look at that?' And on another occasion, when I had a solo call with him to work through all of Posthumus's soliloquies, he said to me sweetly, as he finished eating a bowl of spaghetti which had taken a good deal of his attention during my efforts, 'You know that bit about the German boar...?' I knew very well which bit he meant. 'You know that... thing you do?' I knew very well what 'thing' I did – I considered it rather daring. 'Don't do it, please,' he said, gently. 'I go off you.' He was a delicious combination of the coolly analytical and the warm, the simple, the humane.

His famed eccentricities emerged during rehearsals. John had a propensity for falling over things. If you were working in a large empty room, in the middle of which was a chair, you could guarantee that John would fall backwards over it. Once, when he was giving notes, he walked backwards off the stage and fell into the auditorium. We shrieked with concern, but John recovered, did not appear hurt, clambered back up and carried on with his notes as though absolutely nothing had happened. My favourite story revolves around his drinking tea, which he liked in a glass, pint beer mug. One day, he took a sip of tea, swung back on the rear legs of his chair and put the mug down on the floor. When the front legs of the chair came to ground, one of them landed *in* his tea. When he wanted more tea, try as he might, he could not get the mug off the floor, but he was far too preoccupied with his notes to understand that his chair leg was in his tea mug. Someone had to point it out to him: he then looked bemused, as though this had been done *to* him, somewhat unkindly. He retrieved the mug, but did not for a moment stop giving notes.

There is a story that, after the last performance of *Othello* in Japan, on the plane journey home, John sought out Brewster Mason, the giant of a man who had played Othello. John snuggled into the seat next to him, took out his notebook and said, 'Just a few thoughts on last night, Brew.' Brewster pointed out that the play was over, and there was therefore no reason to give him further notes. Rather surprised, John replied, 'That's not really the point, is it?'

One day, John wanted to give *me* notes. We were on the motorway. He was driving. Removing both hands from the steering wheel to take the notes out of his pocket, he spread the notebook in front of him on the steering wheel, and went through them methodically. He was a thinker, a dreamer, an idealist, not really of this world. His *Richard II*, with Ian Richardson and Richard Pascoe alternating Richard and Bolingbroke, has never been equalled. I learnt masses from him in the rehearsal room, and just as much from his sonnet classes. He is rightly revered as a teacher.

John developed his theories about *Cymbeline* with his wife, Anne Righter, whose book *Shakespeare and the Idea of the Play* is well worth a read. He cut the play extravagantly, which it needs. John Napier's designs caught the play's fairy-tale tone, and the whole improbable yarn was relayed from a huge book held by the magician/sorcerer – naughtily played by Jeffrey Dench, Judi's brother. The plot became as clear as a child's fable. Instead of the complicated battles that can muddle Act Four, Jeff simply read the stage directions from his story-book, so the fighting happened quickly, and the complex narrative was easily conveyed. John was a genius at Shakespearean pastiche. When the stage directions were not clear enough, on the spot, he created the line 'The two armies met, and bathed egregiously in each other's gore'.

So ... with Posthumus in Stratford and Dr Watson at the Aldwych, I spent the spring and summer of 1974 commuting to and from our home, and in September we flew to America. This was exciting: our first time in the States, but there was an added tingle factor. We were in Washington, home of the recent Watergate scandal. One of our American investors was an oil magnate who threw a party for us at the Watergate complex, just so we could see inside the building where the burglary that started the whole thing off was committed.

We played six weeks at the Eisenhower Theater in the Kennedy Center, during which the play settled, as we discovered how much more 'out front' you had to be. In the first scene with Holmes,

OCT. 5 1974

This Week

in the nation's capital

John Wood stars as "Sherlock Holmes" and Tim Pigott-Smith plays Doctor Watson in the Royal Shakespeare Company's production of the famous detective story now at the Kennedy Center. Tickets can be purchased on Instant Charge by calling 254-3080 and using any major credit card.

This Week *magazine cover for* Sherlock Holmes, *Kennedy Center, Washington DC, 1974*

Watson provides fodder for Holmes's deductive powers. The mighty sleuth asks a baffled doctor:

> How do I know that you've opened a consulting room and resumed the practice of medicine? How do I know that you have a most clumsy and careless servant girl and that you've moved your dressing-table to the other side of your room?

> WATSON: Holmes, if you'd lived a few centuries ago, they'd have burned you alive.

Watson is astounded by this reasoning, but Holmes explains ... Watson smells of iodoform, and has a black mark – from nitrate of silver – on one finger, revealing that he is again in practice. He has scratches on his polished shoes that expose the new, and clumsy, servant girl. And as Watson's face used to be badly shaved on one side, but is now badly shaved on the *other*, he cannot have moved the window, the light source, he must have moved his dressing table! In the theatre this was all so deliciously absurd it provided good comedy. At the end of Holmes's explanation, I had the line *'Of course!'* which in England was *so* silly it regularly earned an effortless round. In Washington I learnt that if I was even going to get a titter I had to face front, say it very slowly, intensely, and at the same time punch the air with my fist. We had to find a different, much broader way to signal the comedy. This was dangerous because the production worked at its best, and its funniest, when you took it deadly seriously.

Whatever the limitations of our opening at the Eisenhower, we played to packed, contented houses. We spent a wonderful fall in Washington, driving out into the lush Virginia countryside every weekend. I was obsessed by the American Civil War at that time, and we visited Gettysburg, Harpers Ferry and the site of the Battle of Bull Run, first confrontation of the war. We drove Skyline Drive, through Virginia and were stunned by the autumn glory of the Shenandoah Valley. We went to Monticello, Thomas Jefferson's house. We used our time well and really enjoyed ourselves.

We were warned in no uncertain manner *not to stray into H Street*. H Street was just behind the White House, which, of course, we *did* visit. Harry Towb and I shared a dressing room and a ridiculous joke about a grand piano, and I wanted to find some balsa wood so that I could make him a miniature grand piano for the fast-approaching press night in New York. I went out looking for a craft shop and was so preoccupied in my search that I didn't realise, until I left the shop, balsa wood in hand, that I was in the dreaded H Street. I suddenly understood why people had warned us to keep out. In the gutter, on the other side of the road, a black man was lying unconscious. There was blood on the kerb. There were an alarming number of needles strewn about, and some black chicks with skirts just below their armpits. The real shock was, not that such a place existed, but that it existed within a stone's throw of the White House.

Some people in Charlottesville, whose names we had been given, wrote to us at the theatre, keen for us to visit. Dr and Mrs James Camp III – for that was their name – made their money from paper mills. We were enchanted by the drive down through verdant stud country and fields of beautiful horses. The Camps' house was stunning, gloriously situated in woodland – blazing copper and gold in the October sun – with a sensational view over the valley below. Their wealth was self-evident. We were met by Mrs Camp who was welcoming and warm. We were surprised to hear the depth of her Southern tones. Grace was said before brunch – with hominy grits – a strangely secular grace which included a sweet prayer for the success of our play in New York. Dr James III himself appeared, wearing a floor-length red silk dressing gown: camp by name, and ever so slightly camp by nature. It was past noon, and this late entrance in pyjamas and gown posed more questions than it answered, although he too was a kind and considerate host. Many years later, he came out.

That afternoon, impeccably dressed, he showed us round the extremely impressive, very well-funded university campus, where he worked as a doctor. And that evening he and his wife took us to dinner at what we realised – too late – was a segregated club. We were shocked but did not want to offend such immense generosity, and left with promises that we would meet up in New York, where they were coming to see the play again.

The company was not transported to New York by plane, as scheduled, but by coach – a pretty battered old coach, too. Our producers were clearly, and somewhat ominously, not wasting money on us. But, rattling and complaining, we got there. New York was a shock to the system after the wide, slow avenues of Washington. We found a duplex on 46th Street, between Ninth and Tenth Avenues. The area has been gentrified now, but then it really was Hell's Kitchen, and at first it was scary, an echo of H Street – drugs and hookers. At the end of the block was a playground, a wire cage, where reputedly they had filmed bits of *West Side Story*.

On the street outside our apartment, Pam and I waited one day for a cab. The guy who picked us up was a true New Yorker.

'What the fuck are people like you doin' in a street like this?' he demanded.

We did not know how to respond. 'Er ... we live here.'

'Oh, my God!' He was in shock. 'Where ya goin'?' he demanded.

'Sutton Place South,' we replied.

'That's more like it!' he cried. 'That's where the zillionaires live! Jump in!'

We were living in New York and playing on Broadway!

10

THE BIG APPLE

Just off our dodgy street was a surprise courtyard that would not have looked out of place in old Siena. With warm, sepia-tinted stone arches, Clinton Court was a haven, our home. It was reputed to be haunted, but we never felt anything other than safe as houses there. We were two blocks west, easy walking distance, of our theatre the Broadhurst. Opened in 1917, a joint venture between actor-manager George Broadhurst and the Shuberts, the most powerful theatrical Broadway dynasty, it was a gem. It had some history, too: Humphrey Bogart had played there, Leslie Howard, Elia Kazan, Clifford Odets, Helen Hayes, too.

When you enter an English theatre you usually come in from the back, and, like most things in England, it is influenced by class. The Royal Box holds pride of place, and stage-side boxes offer moneyed people the chance to be seen as well as to see the actors on stage. Because of the nature of New York land lots, and the fire regulations, it made more sense to build New York theatres not as we do, long and thin, but sideways on to the street, shallow and wide. Because the stage is wider, you can get more people close to it. The Broadhurst was, I think, still owned by the Shubert family in the seventies, although our producer was Jimmy Nederlander, who had some kind of a relationship with the RSC at the Aldwych. We were tended by Nell Nugent and Liz McCann, charming management Rottweilers. In the end, on Broadway, most things come down to money. Failure is costly.

There is a frightening story of one producer who closed a show at the interval on opening night because he could see it was going nowhere, expensively. Failure with our *Sherlock Holmes*, and we would be on the next boat home; and, given the penurious attitude of our producers in bussing us to New York, none of us would have been surprised if we had been sent home steerage. In 1974, the potential for triumph or virtual extradition was in the hands of the reviewer of the *New York Times*, Clive Barnes. As we neared opening night, tensions rose tangibly.

We had performed this play now for almost a year, and after six weeks in Washington, we were acting it well for American audiences. However, the day before we opened on Broadway we were called to a company meeting where Frank Dunlop, looking uncomfortable and harassed, announced that we were going to make cuts. There was a groan of mild protest. We had had weeks when this work could have been done, but with one final preview left we would have a new version of our play. Cuts, at such a stage, are usually agreed by mutual consent. Not on this occasion. Frank said tersely that we did not have time to argue, and here were the cuts. I lost nothing, but the 12-year-old Cockney lad playing Billy the page-boy had one short scene of gorgeous stuff, virtually his whole part, thrown into the bin. The company – and Frank – were unhappy with this style of work, but this was Broadway.

That night we were a little unsteady, but, annoyingly, running-time came off, and Frank, and the Rottweilers behind him, were visibly relieved. Company morale suffered, but the play did go over better. D-day was upon us. I had never known such a pressured press night. The adrenalin in an actor's system on press night was once found to be the equivalent of two car crashes. There was enough tension around that night for a motorway pile-up, in spite of the fact that we already had three first nights of this play under our belts.

The show went well, and we made our way slowly across the road to the legendary Sardi's for the party. Tradition held that reviews were brought by courier, direct to Sardi's from the newspapers' headquarters, and read aloud to the assembled guests, among whom was Ethel Merman. Sadly, I did not meet her. I heard her, but did not meet her. At about two in the morning, the notices arrived. Nell and Liz read them out, tears with dollar signs in them rolling down their cheeks. It was obscene. By the time we got champagne, which was kept in boxes behind the bar until we were assured of good notices, we had gone off the whole thing.

If you are in a hit in NY, stars come. They really come. On the first Saturday night after opening, word got round that Sammy Davis Jr was in. Actually, you could *see* he was in, leaning out of a box, laughing and clapping. He came round afterwards, sweetly introducing himself as he shook our hands. 'Hi!' he said, smiling, 'Sammy Davis Jr.' Who else, I wonder?

We were informed that the next evening – Sunday – at six o'clock – a coach would be at the stage door to take us to Hackensack in New Jersey, where SDJ was performing in a 3,000-seater amphitheatre. Unlike the beaten-up old bus that had brought us from Washington, champagne was served on this luxury coach. And we had great seats in the theatre for a two-hour solo show packed to the rafters. SDJ did impersonations of Holmes and Moriarty, and really plugged *Sherlock Holmes*. He sang, he told stories, he danced. He was phenomenal. I shall never forget 'Mr Bojangles', a brilliantly danced and sung vignette of an old negro hoofer. I see SDJ still, shoe-shuffling, tapping, high-kicking his way through 'Mr Bojangles', *as* he sang it. Extraordinary. By strange coincidence, the man the song was based on, the original Mr Bojangles, had trodden the same boards as us at the Broadhurst.

We went backstage afterwards – the whole coachload of us – to say thank you. 'Don't go!' cried SDJ. 'I've taken a suite at the Holiday Inn.' The coach took us there. SDJ joined us. He had arranged a buffet! He spoke to everyone. 'Doctor Watson!' (and in mock-English), 'Great stuff, Doc! A-aaand,' turning to Pam, 'the French maid, magnifique!' and kissed his fingers 'Mmmmwwwah!' In spite of the fact that he was wearing a bandage over one eye – his glass eye had been troubling him and the socket was infected – he chatted to everyone till two in the morning. His generosity, both of time and spirit – not to mention money – remains unrivalled. I have never, ever, encountered it, or heard of anything like it since.

Our wigs and moustaches were cared for by Tiv Davenport, who was strangely harsh on SDJ, insisting that he had always wanted to be white, and this was just another expression of his longing. Tiv was not the only American on our team to express such cynicism. We were shocked because this sort of thing never happens in England. To us it was an act of exceptional generosity.

John Wood was not a popular leading man; stories about his unpleasant behaviour dominated company conversations. This one will give you an idea why. On our last night the curtain fell and John asked us all to stay onstage. With some apprehension, we lingered. He made a surprisingly gracious speech, thanking us, and saying he would miss us, but his final words were, 'I'd like to thank you all for turning a middle-aged character actor into a star. And if I have the chance some day, I'll do the same for you.' Verbatim. We were speechless. Philip Locke broke the deadlock, moving elegantly forward, taking John's hand, placing his other hand on top of it and shaking it slowly, as he said with laboured sincerity, 'Thank you so much, John.' John, of course, missed the point.

I was working with Adrian Noble in 2012 when he mentioned that he had been to John's memorial. 'There was no one there!' he said, with genuine astonishment. Adrian directed John in *The Master Builder* and *King Lear*, and word was that he had mellowed, but you couldn't get *in* to Denis Quilley's memorial. The crowd spilled out of St Paul's Covent Garden into the court-yard in front of the church: people adored him. I have a very short list of actors I do not want to work with. John – until he died a few years ago – was at the top of it. It is tragic that such a remarkable actor should have been so flawed a human being, because at his best – Brutus, Holmes, Henry Carr in *Travesties*, Spooner in *No Man's Land* – John was astounding, an electrifying combination of intellect and instinct. One of Olivier's maxims, which I adopted, was 'Never get hurt in the same place twice', and in the years after *Sherlock Holmes* I turned down radio plays to avoid working with John. With his death, my list of people to avoid stands now at two, whose names, as they are alive, I will not disclose. But actually, only to have encountered three avoidable people in nearly 50 years is not bad. And behaviour like John's is now, mercifully, very, very rare. But for stories of unpleasant actors, and how to deal with them, Tiv's Tale takes some beating.

Tiv was a 50ish NY gay guy, with a very beautiful, very gay moustache. He and I were talking one night about actors we had worked with who were unpleasant, a conversation provoked by some vile act of John's. Tiv had worked on a movie with Kirk Douglas, who, he said, treated him appallingly: abusing him, and berating his work on a daily basis. Tiv got so fed up with this he decided to get his own back. In the movie – sadly I can't remember its name – Douglas had to wear a moustache. I sensed that these whiskers, and their application, was the main source of tension between him and Tiv, and I suspect that Tiv's own spectacular, home-grown appendage made matters worse. So, fed up with being abused, Tiv implemented his wicked revenge, and this it was: he did not tell KD until the movie was over that the moustache Tiv stuck on him, for at least two-thirds of the film, was made from Tiv's own pubic hair. As revenge goes, that is an out and out winner. Don't upset the make-up man!

And so we came home to our little house in Stratford. Neither of us thought we would ever work again. For the next few months there was very little work about. We decided that, much as we liked our Stratford house, we had to move. On a purely practical level, Pam and I worked out that if we did not live in London we would spend far too much time and money travelling. And less time together. We were also thinking about having a child. Both of us were adamant that we would not start a family until we had a foot in London. So we set about looking, and prepared to sell.

We sold easily, and, in July 1975, moved to Greenwich, to a very small, Victorian, terraced, two-bedroom house, with kitchen and bathroom downstairs at the back. Nineteen seventy-five was a hot summer. We had some savings from New York, and as there was still precious little work around we drew benefit and did the house up. We were a bit more ambitious this time. Pam was always brilliant at curtains and soft furnishings and I was learning DIY fast – poverty can be a great motivator. I did some tongue and grooving in the bathroom – it was fashionable then – built some cupboards in the kitchen, and even plumbed in a washbasin to our bedroom. I learnt to plumb because when I installed the first batten for the tongue and grooving I worked out exactly where the rising main went, and put the first nail straight into it. If you ever do that, don't take the nail out! The only plumber I managed to contact could not come for three weeks, so ... 32p later – that was all it cost – I learnt plumbing.

The only thing I have ever really lost sleep over is money. At this time, I lost quite a lot. This was the closest I have ever been to leaving my chosen profession, but somehow we got by, partly because of help from the state. If it had not been for unemployment benefit I might have had to get another job. It is impossibly hard for actors, in these harsh and shameful days, to get state support. It is quite simply wrong not to help people in genuine need. I seem to recall I got about £8 a week, which didn't even cover our mortgage but it helped. Neither of us liked claiming benefit; actors prefer to work. We could *not* get decent jobs, but we had made it to town, and we had a sweet house.

And we had a child on the way.

11

Backwards a Bit

Work often comes in roundabout ways ...

Penny Keith was – and still is – very generous to us. We had rented the granny flat at the top of her house, and if she was entertaining she always invited us to join her classy chums downstairs. Jeremy Brett was often there. On hearing we were Broadway-bound, he exclaimed, after his usual extravagant fashion, 'Tim and Pam *DAR*lings, I will give you a number to ring. You MUST meet these people. They are part of old New York. You will ad*ORE* them!'

When *Sherlock Holmes* was up and running in New York, I called the number Jeremy had given us, and made myself known to Arnold. He was courteous, immensely proper, and in a cultivated East Coast accent said he would see us next week after the play, at the foot of the stairs from the dressing rooms, adding – 'I know the Broadhurst.'

He was unmistakable: a short, immaculately dressed man, with dapper moustache, wearing neatly buttoned overcoat, silk scarf and a bowler. Arnold shook our hands warmly saying, 'How charming to meet you both. We loved the play.' Turning to the woman by his side he said, 'I'd like you to meet my great friend, Maureen O'Sullivan.' We were rooted to the spot. Maureen O'Sullivan was one of the biggest celebrities of the thirties. Mia Farrow's mother, she was a huge international star, and still a very striking woman. Dressed in fur (this was 1974), she was sweet, generous and disarmingly normal. Whoever Arnold was, he was clearly well connected.

His surname was Weissberger, and he was a showbiz lawyer who had made his name as Orson Welles's attorney. In the wake of Welles's great film *Citizen Kane*, based on the life of William Randolph Hearst, Arnold famously established the precedent that a person cannot copyright his own life. He had represented Marlene Dietrich, and was a great personal friend of John Gielgud's. He lived with Milton Goldman, a boisterous character, who was an august theatrical agent.

When the cabbie who took us to 'where the zillionaires live' dropped us off, it was at Arnold and Milton's in Sutton Place South, one of the most prestigious residential addresses in New York – Arthur Miller had lived there with Marilyn Monroe. Arnold and Milton had an impeccably appointed apartment, sporting five original Magrittes and a Christmas card from the Queen! We never quite worked out if that was a joke, but the whole place was jaw-dropping.

Arnold was a man of the sweetest, most unassuming nature. He and Milton came to London every summer, to see theatre. They stayed at the Savoy, and threw parties in their riverside suite. At the first one we attended, in our barren summer of 1975, there were a few theatrical royals, including Sir Michael Redgrave, who was frail. At one point, he flopped down into the sofa behind which I was standing, and his head fell back, hitting my elbow quite hard. I almost lost my drink, and turned round to discover that I had very nearly concussed a great actor and knight of the realm. Pam and I also met the casting director who ruled British film, the respected, almost feared, Maude Spector.

Maude was much less terrifying than her name, chatting easily to us for some time. Feeling we should not trap her – two out-of-work actors talking to the queen of film casting – we made to move on. As we were edging away, she said, 'Tim, can you come and see me tomorrow?' I replied that my availability was currently my greatest asset. 'I'll call your agent in the morning,' she said. 'Nothing for you, I am afraid, my dear,' she said kindly to Pam, 'this is boy's stuff.'

Rolf Kruger, my first agent, who was a fine, straight-talking man, rang mid-morning and arranged for me to go and meet Maude and the producer of *Aces High*, the film she was casting, later that day. When they want you, they don't hang about. As the great Groucho Marx observed, 'The contrary is also true!' – when they *don't* want you, you can't get near them!

Aces High was a cracking adaptation of the enduringly success-ful First World War stage play *Journey's End* by R. C. Sherriff, transposed to the Royal Flying Corps, so the cameras could soar off into the skies, not get bogged down in clichéd mud. It was to be directed by Jack Gold, a very successful director, probably best known for the great TV film he had just made about Quentin Crisp, starring John Hurt, *The Naked Civil Servant*. Maude had me in mind for a two-day part, which she and the producer offered me on the spot, subject to Jack's approval. I did not meet Jack till my first day's shooting.

So … thanks to Arnold … I was making a feature film.

On my first day I had to enter a room and say one line – simple stuff. Except that *in* the room were Malcolm McDowell, then a big name; the great American star Ray Milland; and one of my cinematic heroes, Trevor Howard, as well as Richard Johnston (I didn't call him Golden Bollocks that day!). It didn't help that Peter Firth, Simon Ward and Christopher Plummer were wandering around outside. I imagined I would fail to open the door on time, trip over the cables and stumble over my lines. *Pull yourself together, Pigott-Smith, you went on for Claudius, and Coriolanus. You have played on Broadway!! You can handle this.* In the event I survived my first appearance in a big movie that was well received, but I did discover a different kind of fear.

Fear is something actors learn to live with, but this was raw terror. I had to turn up – without any rehearsal – stand and deliver. *Aces High* was a big movie – the sheer scale of the venture was unfamiliar and intimidating. Big movies involve hundreds of people, armies of caravans, wagons for food, wagons for loos, trailers for the assistant directors, animals, cars, planes, props men, gaffers, grips, stand-ins, extras – supporting artists – make-up people, dressers, best boys. It is always daunting.

Oliver Stone's *Alexander*, in 2004, is the biggest film I have been in to date. I started with ten days in Morocco, and three months later – in the meantime having rehearsed, performed and closed a play at the National Theatre – I rejoined the movie for its last two weeks in Thailand. In the interim, the budget was rumoured to have increased by $100,000,000! On my first appearance I had to deliver a six-line speech, which, owing to a bureaucratic balls-up, was handed to me 20 minutes before shooting. The first day on any picture is nerve-racking, but on this day, before me on the set, were all the main principals – ten to 15 leading actors, behind whom were ranged 500 extras, and behind them an army of 1,500, just passing by. They had been so busy arranging all *that*, they had forgotten to give the only speaking actor his lines. You can't survive something like that, without cold fear getting hold of your guts.

Fear can afflict an actor at any moment. The French call it *le claque*. I call it 'the parrot'. You can be sailing along quite merrily, and a parrot will fly down and circle your head, squawking, 'You're in trouble!' The parrot lands on your shoulder and talks to you: 'You haven't got a clue what you're doing, have you?' he will parrot. 'Call, yourself an actor? Geoff Boycott's mum could do better with a stick of rhubarb. You are in trouble, son. This time … you are *not going to get through it*.' If the parrot finishes that sentence, you are doomed. His voice will get louder and louder, until it drowns the voices of the other actors, destroys any sense of the scene, play, film – whatever – and leaves you floundering. There is only one thing to do: you turn to the parrot, and say, quite firmly, 'Fuck off.' I have seen fear strike the most surprising people, onstage and on screen. I once smelled another actor's fear because he did not know his lines. Sweat breaks out instantly on the brow and top lip. The heart pounds and rises in your chest. It's HELL!

I have only once had trouble with lines. I was performing a major role (in *King Charles III*, at the Almeida), eight times a week, and I simply did not have long enough to learn the enormous part I was rehearsing at the same time – George in Albee's *Who's Afraid of Virginia Woolf?*. I had to fight the parrot. At one point in rehearsal, the parrot won. I just knew I wasn't going to be ready by first preview. I broke down completely, and wept. It was torture. Not just for me, but for the other actors. If you sense insecurity in another actor, *you* cannot act.

The winter of 1975 did not bring much change – bits of radio, the odd day's work: it was hard, a blank, although it was good to have time to prepare our new London home for our baby. One thing that did happen during this lull was my introduction to the world of the voiceover. I have never liked the notion of doing commercials, and have only ever done one – to sort out a tax issue when I had been doing too much badly paid theatre! The voiceover, however, did not worry me in the same way.

I called in to Rolf one afternoon and he asked me to ring a commercials producer about doing the voice for an advert. I was in Covent Garden, so I found a phone box. The producer needed someone who could get through a slab of text very fast, so, armed with a pencil and a pocket full of coins, I rang him back and wrote the words down on the *Yellow Pages*. The producer said, 'OK. I'll say "when" and you start. You've got twenty-nine seconds.' I read it through. There was an ominous silence. 'Oh dear,' he said miserably, 'thirty-two seconds.' I asked if I could have another shot at it. 'No one can do it!' he sighed pessimistically, but he let me try. I fed in more coins, and set off at the speed of light. I finished. There was a silence, and then he more or less whooped with delight, 'twenty-eight seconds! Great. You've got the job!'

I did the ad for a couple of years, and one day I learnt why it was that actors were so keen to do voiceovers. In 1977 I was driving to Nottingham, where I was playing Orsino in *Twelfth Night*, when the big end on our Beetle went. It was going to cost £360 to put right – seven or eight weeks' wages. I did not have the money.

Just after this disaster, a letter arrived containing a cheque for £365. I called Rolf, and asked what it was for. He explained that it was my 'residuals payment' for the voiceover. 'What's a residuals payment?' I asked. Rolf explained, as to a 2-year-old child, that it was a sort of commercials repeat fee. This was wondrous news. Once I had made it into voiceovers, we were never hard up again. And we no longer needed to claim benefit.

'All you need to be an actor,' Olivier said, 'are the eyes of an angel and the voice of a god.' I have always responded to the quality of a voice, whether it be a singer or a speaker, and always worked quite hard at my own voice, because it is a fundamental acting tool. Golden Bollocks had a wonderful rich bass voice. O'Toole had an electrifying razor of a voice. Richard Burton had a sensational voice, dark and furry. I treasured an old spool-to-spool tape-recording of *Under Milk Wood*, by Dylan Thomas, that I had taken direct from my transistor radio. I played it until the tape fell apart, by which time I knew the entire piece by heart. The hairs on the back of my neck still stand up when I listen to Burton reading *The Ancient Mariner*. Perhaps the greatest voice of all was Paul Scofield's. His recordings of Eliot's *The Waste Land* and *The Four Quartets* are sheer magic. He is an orchestra, strings, brass, woodwind, percussion, deep, high, light, strong, camp, smooth, rasping, funny, grave.

Scofield was astounding in *Timon of Athens*. It is a strange, unfinished play, but through the mud some diamonds shine. One such gem is the great soliloquy, when Timon leaves Athens:

Let me look back upon thee, O thou wall
That girdlest in those wolves, dive in the earth
And fence not Athens!

Timon's disgust with his fellow men has got too much for him, and he takes himself into exile. Scofield began this speech with a tone of tortured regret.

As the speech progresses, its violent misanthropy limits your acting options, and at some point you simply have to start cursing. Sco, as he was affectionately known, got to within about ten lines of the end of the speech, drew *in* his mounting anger, and began again, very low, very quiet, vitriolic. Line by line, he raised the note *and* the volume, so that by the end of the speech, he was at full pitch, and right at the top of his vocal register. He built to:

And grant as Timon grows, his hate may grow
To the whole race of mankind.

And he positively screamed the final syllable – *Aaa-men!* It was vocal virtuosity of the highest order, and, more importantly, gave the most bloodcurdling impression of inconsolable hatred. Spine-tingling. It would probably sound oratorical today, over-blown – the deadening hand of naturalism has diminished the power of that tool in the actor's armoury.

12

SIDEWAYS

In April 1976 our son, Tom, was born. His head first appeared – in an air of growing panic – with the cord round his neck. Neither of the young nurses was equipped to deal with this emergency, but by some miracle a midwife (who everyone thought had gone home) suddenly reappeared. She took Tom's head, pushed it back in, untwisted the cord and he shot out like a bar of soap. Not for the squeamish. Mind-blowing. I said to Pam, who had not made a sound, 'Well, you're not going through that again.'

Margaret Tyzack, a good friend from RSC days, lived nearby and during Pam's pregnancy her father died – in six shocking weeks, of pancreatic cancer – almost as Maggie did years later. This sudden tragedy left Maggie's mother, in particular, shattered. We named our amazing little boy Tom Edward, only to discover that they were Maggie's father's names! Both of them! Maggie's mum, Doris, helped us look after Tom, and in some small way this extraordinary coincidence helped her come to terms with the loss of *her* Tom.

Mid-1976, Desmond Davis asked to meet me; he had been on my radar for years because he directed one of my favourite films, *The Girl with Green Eyes*, starring Rita Tushingham, a typical sixties, black and white movie made by Woodfall, a ground-breaking British company. This gritty, moving love story was directed with unusual sensitivity.

Des had served a long apprenticeship – he was clapper boy on *The African Queen* – and worked his way up to camera operator on Woodfall's early movies, *A Taste of Honey* ('Tush' again),

The Loneliness of the Long Distance Runner (which launched Tom Courtenay) and *Tom Jones* (which spread Albert Finney's fame) – all sixties movies which I loved.

A young cameraman who worked for him when he was directing said to me, 'Des can do anything with a camera.' Well, he learnt the hard way, beginning as a sergeant cameraman with the Army Film and Photo Unit. He experienced some pretty terrifying war scenarios, filming the British surrender in Singapore, Javanese civilian prison camps and British soldiers liberated from the Japanese POW camps.

One of the things that is less present in the profession now is the influence of people who have worked in the real world, and not spent all their time in 'the business'. When I started, a lot of actors had done National Service. For instance, my friend Bernie Lloyd did 18 months in Hong Kong. Compulsory enlistment at 18 ended in 1960, so I just missed it. When you were working with people who had seen active service, you knew that they were bringing real – and not always pleasant – experiences to their work. They were generally unwilling to talk about their previous lives – it was years before Des told me about his war work. Very recently, he sent me a piece he had written about his time in north Jakarta, where warehouses with vital supplies were being plundered. Wire barricades were erected, and warnings – trespassers will be shot ...

> We waited. Then voices and the rustle of leaves. Whispers
> and the metallic ping of wire-cutters. I set the exposure
> on my camera as the Sgt signalled to us and shouted
> 'Stop or we fire!' Figures melted into the jungle as we
> ran forward. But not all. Someone was still trying to get
> through the wire. The Sgt nodded to one of the squaddies
> who levelled his rifle and fired. Shrouded by leaves, it
> was not a clear shot. I ran forward with the platoon, my
> camera running and tracking down close on to a figure
> that lay on the ground by broken strands of wire. The face
> of a 7-year-old boy filled the frame. His dead eyes stared

into mine. I switched off the camera and stood up. The squaddie who had fired the shot handed his rifle to the Sgt and went off by himself. By force of habit I rewound my camera. The screaming birds had settled down. I stood listening to the rain dripping off leaves.

He concludes the piece:

I shot hundreds of close-ups. But to this day I only remember one with clarity. His eyes still look up at me.

Writing about it was another way of trying to come to terms with it.

Des was promoted to director by Tony Richardson, the main man at Woodfall. Richardson had worked at the Royal Court, and directed movies of their hit plays – *Look Back in Anger* and *The Entertainer*. He was, incidentally, father of Natasha and Joely. One night, after shooting, he said to Des, 'You want to direct don't you, Desmond?' Des nodded, and Tony lobbed a book at him. 'Have a look at that, then.' It was Edna O'Brien's novel *The Girl with Green Eyes*, and it set Desmond on his way.

We met in a bistro near the BBC doughnut in Wood Lane. I had never been asked to meet a director over lunch, but Des was always immensely respectful of actors. He was working on *Wings*, a hit BBC series about the Royal Flying Corps. One episode centred around a court martial, and Des wanted me to play the wounded major in charge. He had seen Dr Watson, been reminded of me by my photo in *Spotlight*, and thought I looked heroic!

This was very different from my disastrous meeting with David Lean some years later. He was insulting about my stills, and criticised my agent's failure to provide video footage (England didn't really do video then). Lean was domineering and snooty. I hated him. If he had asked me (very unlikely!) to do the film he was setting up – about Fletcher Christian and the Pitcairn islanders – I like to think I would have turned him down. But the film was never made.

Des has great sweetness of nature, but he is made of steel, and can, if need be, push his team hard. On *Wings*, Des showed them how to shoot the flying sequences with model planes. He had worked quite a lot, with – and *in* – aeroplanes. He always researches his projects carefully so he was completely on top of court-martial protocol.

It was a long scene – over half an hour, as I recall, and we – Tim Woodward, Jeremy Child, Michael Cochrane, Anthony Andrews and me – were naughty boys. We got such terrible giggles over one line we could not get past it without breaking up. I am ashamed to tell you, but the line that finished us was, 'Gerry was two hundred feet below us, sir, so I ordered him to go down.' Pathetic. But group hysteria meant that every time we did the scene it got worse. I decided to take notes at that point, so I could keep my head down. On studio day, an accident to one of the cast delayed us, so when we finally got to camera rehearse we were way behind. The dreaded line came along, and once again we 'corpsed'. Des came down from the gallery and wiped the floor with us. It was white-hot anger. That was the only time I saw him lose his temper with actors.

My major made occasional interjections, but his main contribution was summing up, which necessarily came at the end. Last shot of the day. I knew that at 10 p.m. – on the dot – the electricians would simply pull the plug and plunge the studio into darkness. The summing up lasted two to three minutes, and we began shooting at ... well ... two or three minutes to ten! I had rehearsed myself strenuously, but the tension in the studio was palpable. It went fine. I finished and the studio went black.

Later, Des found me in the bar and thanked me for my professionalism. He said he was really glad we had worked together, and assured me that we would again. I was fairly used to directors saying this sort of thing, and you never heard from them again, but Des was as good as his word.

A year later, in 1977, he cast me in a lead role in a BBC adaptation of L. P. Hartley's trilogy, *Eustace and Hilda*: three films, one for each book. *Eustace and Hilda* traces the relationship of a brother and sister, starting with the devoted innocence of their childhood in Book One, *The Shrimp and the Anemone*. Hilda's first, and catastrophic, love affair leads to the confused alienation of poor Eustace, who says, when he is happy that he is in his '*sixth* heaven' – the title of Book Two – explaining feebly that he likes to keep one heaven in reserve. It's heartbreaking and comes to a sad end in Book Three.

The first film used child actors. In the other two I played Dick Staveley, Hilda's lover. Hilda was my old friend Sue Fleetwood. The cast was superb, with support from Dame Flora Robson, Billie Whitelaw, Robert Stephens and Desmond Llewelyn – Q in the Bond movies. Christopher Strauli (Eustace) and Richard Heffer (Anthony Lachish, a wicked impersonation of Lord David Cecil) were also there for the ride.

The story is as powerful as the author's more famous *The Go-Between*. Hilda is seduced by their childhood friend Dick, the cad, the bounder who takes the fragile childhood relationship and breaks it. It breaks him, too, and I had a great final scene, talking to Eustace, subtly revealing the damage the affair had done, set during a violent thunderstorm, in a bar in Venice.

We shot in Hunstanton, L. P. Hartley country, and then in the old Ealing Film Studios – used for the Venice scene! Des was on fantastic form, creating an excited family feeling on the unit. The best of the three films is the first, with the children: it is tender and sweet, and by the time you have Richard Rodney Bennett's lilting theme tune playing it is very touching. It won Des an award at the Venice Film Festival.

Des introduced me to real filming. There is one exterior scene in which Dick questions Eustace. We rehearsed it, but Des could not decide how to shoot it. Over supper that night he explained that he saw the camera as another character in a scene – this is basic cinematography, but it was new to me – and said he never knew how to shoot something until he had decided what that character was; was it an outside observer coolly relaying events, or did it take a subjective point of view?

Being more interested in word pictures, I had never thought deeply about cinematic imagery, but Des taught me to visualise more. Next time we rehearsed the scene with Dick and Eustace, he staged it in a field with Dick's family home in the background: this was the first visual statement – Eustace came from a humble background, Dick had money, status and family. Eustace was stationary and I walked slowly round him, asking questions. Des shot a couple of differing wides, then put the camera where Eustace stood and followed me round. He then laid circular tracks, so the camera could be me, circling Eustace. It captured the essence of the scene: Dick literally running rings round his victim.

I remember that shoot with particular affection. One evening, Pam arrived in Hunstanton with Tom, who was just over a year old. We took him to the sea. The coast of eastern England boasts sandy, flat beaches, ideal for children. Tom was a fearless child, who walked from ten months, and as soon as we set him down he raced across the sand and into the sea. It was wonderful to watch him surging into the shallow water. We were nervous, but he wasn't. He loved the sea immediately, and always has.

When Des did *The Girl with Green Eyes*, he had to cast about 20 of Rita Tushingham's Irish male relatives who angrily invade the house where she is living with an Englishman. As he was shooting in Ireland, Des opted for a bunch of actors from the Abbey Theatre, Dublin. It was a day of utter, glorious mayhem. At one point, Des was unable to make himself heard above the happy, raucous din. Peter Finch, playing the Englishman, materialised on Des's shoulder and said, ruefully, 'Like playing chess with mice, eh, Desmond?'

In 1978, the BBC began televising all Shakespeare's plays: we called it '*The Bardathon*'. This was a Reithian mission, masterminded by that great old TV producer Cedric Messina, whose name I had seen on countless productions as a teenager. Des fought Cedric to get me the role of Angelo in *Measure for Measure*. He succeeded, and once Cedric felt he could rely on me, he was just great fun, a sheep in wolf's clothing.

The TV studio is a thing of the past, and drama today is more commonly shot on location. The old electric cameras were cumbersome things, giant Daleks on castors. Over the years I got

Angelo in Measure for Measure, *BBC TV, 1979*

to know the cameramen at the Beeb, who were masters at using them with an artistic subtlety that belied their bulk. One of the doyens was Jim Anderson, who could be difficult, subversively expressing his views about the way something should be shot, sometimes even telling the director openly he had got it wrong. I gained early respect for him because I overheard him talking to a young cameraman who was shooting one of my scenes. Jim was speaking quietly, unaware that I could hear. 'You know when he [me] leans on the desk? That's an important moment for him. So as he comes forward, just push in and down a touch. I don't want to be aware of *your* move, and if you do it on *his* move, I won't be. All right?' Recording in a Beeb studio was a Rolls-Royce ride, a family working together.

When we did *Measure for Measure*, Des wanted to get Jim on side, so he set him a challenge, asking him to track Claudio leaving jail, in a long sequence that circled the studio three times, and those old studios were bi-ig. Electric cameras were juiced by cable, so enormous lengths had to be plugged together and pre-laid. The cable was gathered up as Jim backed his way three times round the studio! He pulled it off superbly. The tracking cleverly made Shakespeare seem modern and immediate, which is a challenge when you are putting large language on to the small screen, so Des killed several birds with one stone and Jim's achievement was applauded in the studio.

One of the best images Des created in my work with him was also in *Measure for Measure*. Angelo is a man of ice-cold heart who has a dark, introspective speech about his surprising, uncontrollable lust for the young novice Isabella: it is Isabella's purity that arouses him. I was wearing a trimmed black wig, and had grown a tight, manicured beard which was also blackened. Dark, shady, evil. The soliloquy was shot in a small, candle-lit, mirrored room. The overall impression was of disturbance, the images in the mirrors suggesting a fractured personality dodging its shadier impulses. At the end of the speech, Angelo is in a fever of anticipation, awaiting the arrival of the young nun. The last shot of Angelo was a close-up. I turned towards the sound of a door slamming loudly, with something like fear: Isabella was here, and how was Angelo, so full of despicable desires, going to cope? Over this was laid the slam of huge doors crashing shut, and there was a cut to the large hall outside Angelo's cell, and there, at the far end of it, in front of the huge doors which had just slammed to – and with their echo still sounding – there was Isabella, a small figure in white – white for good, purity – the novice – an innocent, doomed figure. Simple, but effective; you could have taken the words away and the pictures would have told you both the story and its inner meaning.

My Angelo gained some attention – especially from Clive James, reviewing in the *Observer* – and from now on, thanks to Des, quality television work came my way.

12 A

Upwards a Bit

No Chapter Thirteen. There is never a Dressing Room Thirteen. The theatre is a superstitious world.

Simon Cadell's mother passed the ghost at the Haymarket on the back stairs – a Victorian gentleman, hatted and caped, who smiled at her. I *think* I saw a ghost at the Theatre Royal, Bristol. When I asked our stage manager who the stranger watching rehearsals was, he said, 'Who do you mean?' When I indicated, the stalls were empty. I described the man, and was told, matter-of-factly, 'Oh. That's the ghost.' The shade of the great actress Sarah Siddons has been seen walking through walls at the Bristol Old Vic.

The most tenacious theatrical superstitions surround *Macbeth*. Its history is dotted with stories of people being hurt, ghosts appearing on set, terrifying screams coming from the ether, and – more infectiously – productions which have bombed. I have always loved stories about *Macbeth*, but I never believed there was any substance in them, until I appeared in it.

On the first night at the Bristol Old Vic, back in 1969, during the opening fight, an axe head flew into the auditorium. It landed in the one empty seat in the house. During the last performance, at the outset of the climactic Macbeth/Macduff duel, a sword blade broke off at the hilt and flew at eye level between me and another soldier. We eventually found it – buried to the hilt in one of the polystyrene blocks of the set. It could have gone straight through someone's head. The first and last night symmetry of these close shaves made them just that little bit spookier.

The sword blade that had come within a foot of killing me came from Macbeth's sword, and left Julian Glover, our fine Thane, standing, helpless, with a sword hilt in his hand. Someone remarked later, 'All Julian was holding, was the plot … in tatters.' Without thinking I slid my sword out from between my shield and my back, and skimmed it, 30 feet across the stage. With a whoosh, the hilt caught under Julian's foot, so he was able to grab it and finish the play. People were full of praise for my daring, but my view about superstitions is … don't mess with these things. No Chapter Thirteen.

The year after *Measure for Measure*, Des introduced me properly to the world of the big screen. Working on a follow-up to their movie *Jason and the Argonauts*, Ray Harryhausen, the iconic animator, and his long-term producer, Charles H. Schneer, came up with *Clash of the Titans*. They wanted innovations: the first was to have characters that were both models that Ray could manipulate, and fully acted characters: Calibos would require facial close-ups of an actor; Pegasus would be both a maquette and a real horse. Secondly, they wanted better actors. In Des they had a director with technical understanding of Ray's Dynamation who could also assemble a classy cast. We had a *very* classy director of photography, Ted Moore, BAFTA and Oscar winner for *A Man for All Seasons*.

Ted was an easy-going genius. He taught me – invaluably – how to keep my eyes open when shooting in bright sun! Our film is superbly shot, but I don't think Ted, who was not that old, ever worked again. It was heartbreaking to read of his death, in 1987, in poverty in a bedsit in Lambeth.

Ray Harryhausen did *not* die in poverty. He was lucky to have a partner like Charlie, because Charlie was good with money. Ray had worked on the original *King Kong* and he was a slightly eccentric man, who, on sunny days, wore a bizarre 'umbrella-cap' to shield his bald pate. He was like a child playing with big toys. His Super-Dynamation involved a painstaking process. His maquettes are exquisitely detailed creations, about 8 inches high, with moving parts. Working, as he did, in 16mm film, you have to shoot 16 frames for every position the model is in. If you want the model to move an arm up, you set it up, shoot 16 still frames, move the arm a fraction, shoot 16 more, and so on until you have raised the arm to where you want it – days of work for this simple movement. Then you put the sequence together, and if there are any jumps in the upward movement of the arm you have to start all over again. Ray's technique of 'dynamation' was a combination of fantastic imaginative powers and laborious craftsmanship.

If he had one limitation it was his assumption that actors could be manipulated like his models. He was never unpleasant, but he spent most of his time with models that did what he made them do, and he expected actors to be the same! He asked me, in my death scene – when I had been stabbed in the back, something I was miming so he could dynamate Calibos, the killer, in later – to 'lower yourself – backwards, Tim! Slowly to the ground. Slowly!' Not easy.

He is rightly revered in the world of animation, and although his once revolutionary technique was left behind by computer technology, it has a charm, and life, that eludes most digitised film. People mainly see *Clash* on television, but in 2014 there was a special screening at the BFI to which Des and I were invited for a Q and A. I had not seen it since the cast and crew screening in 1981, and I was surprised that in the cinema it really holds up. Dynamation looks antiquated on TV, but is less outmoded on the big screen where the story rises into enchanting mythical fantasy.

Before my deal could be clinched, I had to meet Charles H. Schneer. Des warned me that he had rough edges. He was wearing a red-check lumberjack's shirt, which was unusual, and he was very direct in his questions, 'Do you *like* doing Shakespeare?' he asked, as though Shakespeare was a creature from outer space. He had a reputation for being the tightest man in film, and he kept an eagle eye on the finances, but he was kind to me. Unlike everyone else in the film I was on a weekly wage, and, unlike all the other actors, my contract had an overtime clause. The first assistant, the great Tony Waye, whom I still see, told me that every single day I filmed, Charles asked him, 'Did Tim do any overtime today?' Is that being tight, or just doing a good job? My work on *Clash* meant that in 13 weeks I earned twice as much as previously in a year.

Des had assembled a stellar cast led by an ailing Laurence Olivier, playing Zeus. His cotton costume had to be lined with chamois leather, because if he were to bang his elbow and split the skin, it would not heal, apparently because of the cancer drugs he was taking, which also affected his memory. You would scarcely have known it. He would heave himself out of his chair, and potter to the set, but, once there, he transformed into a powerful god-figure, and that unmistakable voice cut through the studio. Scene over, a weak old man would be led back to his seat. On one occasion he clearly dried, and after a very long silence, Des called, 'Cut!' Olivier turned to him and snapped, 'Have you never heard of a dramatic pause?'

On the studio floor at Pinewood, in addition to Sir Laurence – who celebrated his seventieth birthday while we were filming – were Ursula Andress, Claire Bloom, Maggie Smith and, of course, Sue Fleetwood. Flora Robson and Siân Phillips joined us during the shoot. John Gielgud was offered the part of Ammon, and I was very excited about the prospect of spending time with him. Unbelievably, the studio bosses back in Hollywood had not heard of him – this was before his success with *Arthur* – and the part was given to the diminutive Burgess Meredith. Buzz, as he was known, apart from being a terrific screen actor, was quite eccentric. When we flew, his hand luggage was a small square tartan box on four wheels, which he dragged after him on a leash. He called it Fido.

When we were in Granada, Buzz was determined to see some genuine flamenco. He made endless enquiries, and one night he organised a couple of taxis to take seven or eight of us up into the hills above the city. We drove until, at the end of a dirt track, we were met by a couple of big, rough, Spanish-only-speaking guys and ushered into what was little more than a low barn with a scattering of tables and chairs, and a wide, low stage at one end, with side and back walls simply painted white and green to look like rural cottages. I had a feeling that John Gielgud, wonderful companion though he was reputed to be, would not have brought us to this place. Buzz was rubbing his hands gleefully. Ranged along the sides of the stage were a dozen or so chairs, and on the chairs, waiting for us, were the dancers and two guitarists, who acknowledged our arrival with polite nods. We sat at the tables, were given terracotta jugs of wine, and, without ceremony, the dancing started.

There were only two men, who played guitar. The women were mostly of middle age, dark, swarthy and utterly magnetic: *they* were in charge. Stamping, swirling, their earthy focus on their dancing was intense. There were moments that seemed improvised, but the order of the dances was clearly rehearsed, *pas de deux*, *trois*, *quatre*, starting slowly, and building to a colossal ensemble climax. This was no accident of a show, but something that had been worked on, refined. I have seen good flamenco at Sadler's Wells, but this was in another dimension. It was feral, blood-curdling, witty, sexy. This was the world of *Carmen* – don't mess with me ... or my woman! Occasionally, competitiveness flared up dangerously with the swell of the music, and some dances were accompanied, not by guitar, but by clapping – syncopated, harsh, violent clapping. It was raw: both alien, and instinctually, powerfully accessible.

Actors, if they are well entertained, make appreciative audiences, and at the end of an hour of spellbinding dancing we stood and simply roared our approval. The dancers joined us for a drink afterwards, and the youngest and prettiest sat on Buzz's knee – *she* knew who was footing the bill! Conversation was limited, but we learnt that this was how these people earned their living. It was the real thing, genuine, inherited, unsophisticated flamenco, handed down through generations – gutsy peasant passion.

I had another adventure with Buzz. Our last location, Malta was an important naval base for the British in the Second World War, and the atmosphere was still vaguely colonial – the interiors of the old buildings, the names of restaurants and their menus – spotted dick and custard was not something I had expected to find! People all spoke English. On a day off I was strolling round Valletta, looking for its renowned theatre.

It was a hot morning, and I was wandering lazily when I bumped into Buzz. When I told him I was looking for the old theatre in Valletta, he said, 'How about this, Tim? I will get us one of those horse-drawn rickshaw things – I believe they are called "sulkies". We will only hire a driver who knows where your theatre is, but first he will take us on a tour around the island. We shall stop for lunch, and end up at the stage door. Whaddaya say?' This was an offer too good to be refused. We had a great tour, a superb fish lunch at a beachside restaurant, and, late in the afternoon, ended up, as promised, at the stage door.

We went in: there was no one to be seen. We called. Nothing. I walked to the end of the corridor, pushed the pass door open and – wonder of wonders – there was the beautiful Manoel Theatre, built in 1731 – 35 years before the Bristol Old Vic! Buzz and I stood and gazed at its perfect dimensions: the curve of the theatre's proscenium, mirroring the curve of the auditorium, the painted ceiling and chandelier, the combined grandeur and intimacy of the space. It was in impeccable condition – the gold lacquer paint glowing in the half-light and the pelt of the deep crimson velvet seating, smooth and unpressed. The curtain was raised and the lit stage was empty. Buzz and I strolled our separate ways around the auditorium, taking in the ghosts of actors past, and then Buzz, recalling a conversation at lunch, called out, 'You like Shakespeare, Tim! Give me some!' The pass steps to the stage were in place, and I ran up and let rip with 'O for a muse of fire!' Then I said, 'OK Buzz, your turn.' I sat in the middle of the theatre. He nipped up and did a Robert Frost poem, strolling about, speaking very quietly. It was sheer magic. As we left the auditorium, there was still no sign of a stage doorman. We slipped out into the street without anyone ever knowing we had been there. Two more ghosts.

Big movies like *Clash* walk a tightrope between things happening smoothly, and sudden, complete disaster. This is when the director has to use all his skills to pull the picture through. There is a sequence in *Clash* in which Perseus is seen growing up: first we glimpse him as a babe in arms; then as a toddler, walking along the seashore, hand in hand with his mother. The next shot in this sequence was planned for sunrise one morning. We were in Palinuro, southern Italy, and the now teenage Perseus was to ride a white horse, bareback along the beach, jumping on and off the galloping horse. The final vignette would introduce us to the grown Perseus, as he throws himself down into the sand – a montage lasting less than a minute, taking our hero elegantly from baby to Harry Hamlin – the handsome LA actor playing our hero.

A stunning white horse was hired and a teenage horseman/ stuntman – a dead ringer for Harry – came down from Rome. The morning call was 2.30 for breakfast in the hotel, before bussing down to the beachside location. The aim was to catch the dawn, and play the riding sequence in silhouette against the sun rising over the sea, to camouflage any differences between the stunt boy and Harry.

So the film army of over 200 people assembled, and, as dawn approached, Des rehearsed the young boy and the horse. In the half-light it was ethereal. The camera was brought out and positioned on the beach, and it was then, just before sunrise, that someone pointed out the camera was pointing west over the sea, and the sun was about to rise *behind it* – in the east! Big films are planned down to the tiniest detail by squadrons of brilliantly accomplished and experienced people, but one crucial thing can be forgotten or overlooked. Des demanded that a boat be brought as quickly as possible. The camera was transferred swiftly from beach to boat, and thus, shooting into the sun, the silhouette effect was achieved.

Des and I share a love of Raymond Chandler. He will often quote something like:

Man meets girl in a bar.
Girl: Have another …
Man: No thanks. I'm the kinda guy who goes out for a quiet
        drink, and ends up in Singapore with a beard. How
        about you?
Girl: No thanks. One more of these and you couldn't prise
        me off the chandelier with a crowbar.

Together, we set about creating a British Sam Spade – Bogart's character in *The Big Sleep* and *Lady in the Lake*. We named him Duggan. Duggan, digging, dig … spade. Duggan is a Kentish Town schoolteacher whose wife and child are killed in a car accident. He finds the circumstances suspicious, visits a private eye, based in the high street and tells him his tale. Together they start unwinding a complex mystery involving pharmaceutical experiments – a dark, surreal yarn. Every new clue led to a surprise development. This Chinese box quality of the story was our tribute to Raymond Chandler.

The BBC commissioned the first two parts of four, and Brian Clark wrote them. They were well received, and the Beeb were on the point of commissioning the remaining two when Jonathan Powell, head of drama, defected to Carlton. Drama development at the Beeb went on hold for three months. Alan Yentob was then appointed and he swept 92 projects into the bin, including *Duggan*.

The fate of the elderly director is harsh. Jobs are given to the young, as indeed they should be, but it means that people like Des, with a lifetime of skills to offer, are twiddling their thumbs. Hitler's architect Albert Speer had a workplace rule that anyone over 40 should be paired with someone much younger. I think we should do a Groucho Marx on this and implement the contrary: any director under 40 should be paired with an older director. When John Cleese set up *A Fish Called Wanda* he persuaded Charles Crichton to come out of retirement. Crichton directed *The Lavender Hill Mob* and *The Titfield Thunderbolt*, so he knew a thing or two about film comedy. When John Birt started 'reforming' the BBC (introducing a 'counting paper-clips' regime), and older people were pushed out, someone created the T-shirt logo *Too Much Experience*. Our profession wastes valuable experience. Des sits in his sweet home in Kentish Town, and writes, and works: he keeps himself active. But his skills as a director and cameraman lie unused.

In *Wanda*, Pam plays the flat owner who interrupts Cleese when he is speaking in tongues, stripping, to seduce Jamie Lee

Curtis. Cleese grabs a photo and holds it over his private parts – a photo of Pam. She asks him, 'Are you Archie Leach?', Cary Grant's real name. In the background is a pale-faced little boy, trying hard not to laugh – our son Tom, aged 11.

14

THE TV CLUB

Thanks to Desmond Davis I felt that I had been allowed into the TV club. I was offered better roles, and, because of *Clash of the Titans*, it even looked as if I might have a film career, not something I had ever considered: my dreams were always of the theatre.

When Roland Joffe (*The Killing Fields* and *The Mission*) offered me one of my first villainous roles, I was making a film for television called *The Day Christ Died*, taken from the book of that title by Jim Bishop, author of *The Day Lincoln Was Shot* and *The Day Kennedy Was Shot* – I do not lie. This was a documentary approach to the crucifixion and it worked surprisingly well; I was playing Pontius Pilate's right-hand man.

When I first met Maggie Smith, she said, 'I was watching you on television last night.' She was referring to *No Mama No*, an improvised film I had made with Roland. 'Very brave', she added, nasally. That tells you all you need to know about *No Mama No*. The film was about a decaying marital relationship. The wife subsided into silence, and as I was playing the husband I improvised about 60 per cent of the script! In spite of the fact that the editor used my back for most of the film, I was delighted when Roland's offer to play Vasques in a BBC film of John Ford's Jacobean revenge play, *'Tis Pity She's a Whore*, reached me in Tunisia. Ironically, one of the reviews of *No Mama No* was headlined *'Tis Pity She's a Bore*.

The BBC originally asked Roland to make a film about the painter Stanley Spencer. He had a script; he had cast Kenneth

Cranham and Alison Fiske; he had a director of photography – the great Nat Crosby; he had a crew; and permission to shoot in Spencer's house. He was suddenly told he could not use the *inside* of the house. Roland said he could manage with the *outside* – shooting (for example), the Alpine sequence, on the roof! Permissions were again rescinded, and with 'the first day of principal photography' two weeks away, he had a budget, but no project – more often, it's the other way round. Roland and producer Richard Broke suggested to the Beeb that they could use the team already assembled, to film *'Tis Pity* in Chastleton House, an untidy Jacobean pile near Moreton-in-Marsh. Wonderfully, insanely, the BBC agreed. It could not possibly happen today. 'Tis pity.

I had filmed at Chastleton once before, on *Joseph Andrews*, in 1976. The house was owned by the Clutton-Brocks who tried to run their house as a home, renting it out unwillingly when times were hard. Lady C-B liked having film people about; her husband, decidedly, did not.

I had played a cavalry officer in *Joseph Andrews*, and one sunny morning I was strolling round the grounds in my – I have to say – rather dashing, knee-length scarlet tunic and thigh-length, black leather riding boots when I noticed Lord C-B hoeing in one of the flower beds. His hoe, like all the wood at Chastleton, was riddled with woodworm. I rather suspect *he* was, too. As I passed, I said 'Good morning, Lord Clutton-Brock.'

He grunted, without looking up from his hoeing.

'Nice to see you,' I said, endeavouring to suppress any irony.

As I walked on, he muttered angrily, 'Dis*gust*ing to see you!'

He never reconciled himself to this shameful way of raising money.

Chastleton (built in 1612) was a wondrous place, perfect for *'Tis Pity*. Boasting a superb Long Gallery, panelled state rooms, evocative kitchens and a secret priest's hidey-hole, it was the ideal location. Roland's decision to Victorianise the play was inspirational, making it look at home on television. My Vasques became a vile Mr Hudson – the butler from *Upstairs, Downstairs*. I had

Vasques in 'Tis Pity She's a Whore, *BBC TV, 1980*

real fun with it, rogering Hippolita in the secret room, before poisoning her, throwing boiling water in the face of the maid and manipulating everyone while remaining as cool as a Victorian cucumber. It was quite a useful lesson in 'baddy' acting: Vasques was rotten to the core, but he offered the world an acceptable face, in order not to arouse suspicion. This tension, between his perceived and his *actual* character, encouraged a response to the shocking interior. 'Who is that ... rogering that woman from behind? It's the butler. It can't be!' Baddies easily have more than one dimension; goodies can only be good.

From Angelo on it didn't seem to matter whether the piece I was in was successful or not; I was *in* the TV Club and further decent parts were entrusted to me. It was a great club to be part of, churning out exciting, quality drama. *School Play*, by Frederick Raphael, Oscar-winning writer of *Darling* and the TV series *The Glittering Prizes* (in which I had a very small part), offered me more baddy practice. Set in a boys' public school, the pupils were played by adults. Jeremy Kemp was our head boy, Denholm Elliott was the school cad and I was the school shit, Perkins. Freddie had written it years before, but when it came out it looked like an imitation of Denis Potter's lauded *Blue Remembered Hills*, which used the same child/adult trick. The director, Jimmy Cellan-Jones, head of drama at the BBC, had known Freddie Raphael since their days at Charterhouse, on which our fictional school was based. As a way of gaining influence, my character, Timothy Perkins, organised the exposure of the school cad, of whose morals he disapproved. My character was based, I believe, on William Rees-Mogg, and my victim on Simon Raven, who was expelled from Charterhouse.

When I was a kid I had a thing about my ears, which stuck out. One of my less happy nicknames – and there were many – was Pig-Ears. I didn't mind being teased, but Pig-Ears hurt. I used to press my ears hard against the pillow at night to persuade them to lie flat, but the hairdressing mores of the time were not on my side: every two weeks, Dad took me to have my hair cut.

Timothy Perkins, School Play, *BBC TV, 1981*

Mr Montgomery, who had an old-fashioned red, white and blue revolving pole outside his salon, placed the electric clippers by my ears and went straight up the side of my head, giving me what amounted to a head shave. When I had more hair, and with less barbarous barbering, my ears were not so protuberant. But I used this unhappy memory for Perkins, getting the make-up department to give me a severe short back and sides, and putting nose putty behind my ears to make them stick out. It was a great part. Jimmy said to me, 'It was your show, Tim, until the new boy snuck in at the end.' The 'new boy' was Michael Kitchen.

Then there was *Hannah*, an adaptation of the novel by E. H. Young. Helen Ryan played Hannah. I was a dried-out Mr Blenkinsop, whom she brought to life. Superb director – Peter Jefferies. Patsy Kensit, aged 12, played a little girl. It was written in four half-hour episodes that introduced a disastrous new format: Tuesday Thursday, Tuesday Thursday. Beautiful piece of work. Nobody watched.

I was fortunate to be an actor who nearly always worked, and I was now making a living in television, but my hope that it would give me more time at home was naive. Up to about this time, Pam, who was also doing really good TV work, and I managed a reasonable balance between looking after Tom and working. But from this point on I was obliged to spend more time away.

I was at least able to work from home when David Giles, whom I knew from the video of *Hamlet*, asked me to play Hotspur for the BBC's *Bardathon*. Our *Henry IV (i)* was thrilling in rehearsal, but on the screen it appeared workmanlike. Moving from rehearsal into the theatre or studio is a dangerous moment in the life of any play.

The best thing in it was Anthony Quayle. He had been a famous Falstaff, and he brought an impishness to the part, aided by a cheeky, turned-up false nose – you only had to look at him to smile. He moved from comedy to sadness with ease and skill, his onstage experience shining through. Sadly, the only interaction in the play between Hotspur and Falstaff is when he lugs off Hotspur's dead body. We wanted our one moment together to be telling.

Mr Blenkinsop in Hannah, *BBC TV, 1980*

Hotspur represents honour in the play, but ends up as dead meat. Tony managed to hook my legs over his shoulders and carry me off upside down – clanking in my armour, so we achieved a final image of Hotspur that was a complete inversion of the vaunting glamour of his early scenes. Tony and I talked a lot about one more fundamental issue ...

Hotspur is described as being 'thick of speech'. Actors have dealt with this in different ways. Michael Redgrave played it with a Northumbrian accent. Olivier, showman that he was, stuttered on the letter 'w'. As he dies Hotspur's last words are:

... and food for – *(he dies)*

– he is obviously going to say *worms,* and this dying word is whispered for Hotspur, by Hal –

For worms, brave Percy.

By stuttering on the 'w' Olivier could prolong his death:

... and food for w-w – *(he dies)*

Naughty but clever. I borrowed this idea to an extent, forming the letter 'w' with my lips, before plummeting forward to my death. But that was not enough for 'thickness of speech'. Hotspur is over-active, a doer not a thinker – the text offers amusing descriptions of his excessive energy. Driven by a misplaced sense of his own glorious destiny, he lacks emotional control; unable to monitor his thoughts, he just gives them voice. I decided that the best way of achieving these qualities was to have him rush through certain passages, language pouring out of him *thick* and fast. I hoped this would catch the essence of the man, moderate the florid language for the small screen *and* provide something that held true for 'thickness of speech'. Tony favoured Northumbrian, with a guttural 'r', based on his acquaintance with a Northumbrian who was 'an herreditarry mole-catcher'. I liked the idea but wasn't sure I could

Hotspur's death scene, Henry IV Part I, *BBC TV, 1979*

hold on to the accent, and also felt that Hotspur needed to sound upper-class. In England 'nobs' don't speak with regional accents, although they might well have done so at the time. I think my idea worked, although I was not happy with my performance overall: there was too much swash and buckle for the small screen. The Beeb seemed happy enough, though, and asked me to do a publicity tour of the States, where the *Bardathon* was to be screened on PBS.

While filming *Clash* in Rome, I had been invited to meet Rose Tobias Shaw, a major casting director who was working on a big film about football in a Second World War prisoner-of-war camp, to be directed by the legendary John Huston. Rose and I met in the bar of the Hôtel de Ville: it was all so grand I felt it was happening to someone else. She was interested in me for one of the English POWs – a member of the escape committee – a part which ran through the film. When could I meet the producer, Freddie Fields, who lived in LA? The BBC publicity tour took me from Boston, to New York, New Orleans, Cincinnati, Kentucky, Chicago, Dallas, ending up in LA, where I hired a car and drove up to Freddie's house. This was glamorous film country: the massive security gate, the entry phone answered by a servant, the curved, rising driveway, the manicured hedges, the low, white, long-windowed house, the fountain, the statuary, the pool. The view over the valley. It was like being in a movie.

I was ushered to the poolside by a charming, uniformed black maid who offered me a drink and assured me, 'Mr Fields will be with you momentarily.' Freddie, nudging 60 now, was a serious player who had made big money as a producer on the TV show *Dallas*. He was a charmer. Nut-brown with white baseball cap, white shirt – with rolled cuffs – royal-blue jumper over his shoulders, white socks, white trousers, sandals and gold-rimmed shades. Freddie had a script under his gold-braceleted arm. From the umbrella'd shade of a lounger he informed me languorously that the cast thus far was Sly – Sylvester Stallone – Michael Caine, Max von Sydow, Daniel Massey, the Brazilian footballing god Pelé, the English footballing god Bobby Moore, Ossie Ardiles, Mike Summerbee and the Ipswich Town football team. 'Has such a diversely talented group ever been assembled for a film before? Huh? Soccer is the coming thing in the States – a-a-and we have a great director.'

The shoot would be in Hungary where the POW camp was already being built. Although I had not been afforded the luxury of reading the script, it was accepted that I would be doing it – who would not want to be part of such a Hollywood tutti-frutti? It was unreal, not to say unbelievable.

Next spring I found myself with Dan Massey and my old mate Julian Curry, aboard a Malev flight to Budapest, where a very real ten-week sojourn in a POW camp awaited us. I love my job; *Escape to Victory* looked good on paper; I would be with mates; the family would be comfortably off that year; but leaving home for ten weeks was ghastly, the worst yet.

John Huston was a mighty impressive man: tall, rangy, thinly bearded, ruggedly handsome with massive craters beneath beady eyes, he had charisma in spades. He was, nevertheless, getting on, with a Vesuvian cough, a symptom of the emphysema that took him, seven years and four films later, aged 81. Because of his health, we were working five-day weeks and, apart from the huge centrepiece of the film – the 'Big Match' – we were shooting sequentially. We Brits could have done our stuff in half the time, but this Huston-friendly schedule meant a lot of waiting, and two days off a week, kicking our heels in Budapest at a time when food was not on the menu. In ten weeks I saw one banana. I queued for it, and the person in front of me bought it! We got to know the museums and art galleries, steamed ourselves in the famous baths, became masters of the public transport system, and Dan introduced me to opera. Dan was an opera nut and we went regularly to the National Opera which, benefiting from heavy subsidy, meant ludicrously cheap seats. Maybe it was the distance created by Hungarian, that most opaque of languages, that helped me towards an appreciation of opera; anyway, I began to enjoy it.

When the work *happened* it was quite fun, but we had to hang around for ever at the POW camp, some 20 kilometres outside Budapest to which we were coached every day at 7 a.m. We were also detained there until the end of each day's shooting. It doesn't matter how conscientious you are – you can play chess, backgammon, read, kick a football about with a legend, have some decent food in the middle of the day courtesy of good caterers, meet fascinating people, chat with stars – eventually you are worn down by such imposed, sustained inactivity. Exactly, I imagine, like being a POW.

One of the most interesting people available for a chat was Major Pat Reid, who had escaped from Colditz, the special German high-security castle for serial escapees. Pat was our POW-camp adviser, and he was always happy to talk about his extraordinary exploits: indeed, one got the impression that he had never again had such an exciting time as when pitting his wits against his German captors.

Max von Sydow was also great company. Here was a film actor I revered, star of Ingmar Bergman movies, notably *The Seventh Seal* in which he is the noble knight who plays chess with Death, and, of course, *The Exorcist*. One might have expected this statuesque Scandi blond to have been a rather grave man, but, in addition to being a stunning actor, the endearing surprise about Max was that he had a delicious sense of humour. We spent many hours compiling limericks about the cast and crew, and he bought me a book of dirty limericks, inscribed *In all decency. Max.* He was a gentleman. In the decade after the film, whenever he was in London he rang. He saw me in plays, he and Pam and I went to concerts, he came to dinner. I was sad when we lost contact but when his first marriage broke down he went to live in France. I tried writing to his agent, but he cut himself off. No one could reach him.

When Huston was fully engaged with a scene, he was a terrific director, but it often seemed the whole thing was a bit of a chore for him: one afternoon he actually dozed off during a take. I think he was less well than anyone realised. He had a short temper, and that kept people on their toes. The first shot we Brits were involved in required the camera to track, coming to rest looking through one of the hut windows at a car arriving at the main gate. Timing was of the essence. Huston set it up carefully, and then expected it to happen fast. It went wrong on the first take, *and* the second.

Huston slammed his fist down, saying, 'Goddam! We'll have to go again!' On the third take, the driver made an error, and Huston uttered the chilling words, 'If he gets it wrong again, he's fired.'

The plan for the centrepiece of the film – the Big Match – was to shoot all the specific incidents over three weeks – Pelé's overhead kick, a nasty foul, the penalty – and then to open the stadium to the public for the match. For 20 forints, a very small sum, they would provide us with a crowd, and in return, see two legends on the pitch *and* a football match. Dan, Max and I were part of the crowd, so Huston needed us in place all day, every day, for three weeks, in case the camera caught us in the background. This was tedium on a scale so intense that we longed to be back in prison.

There was *some* comedy. Sly was eager, but he had clearly not thought to ask – and nobody appeared to have informed him – of the difference between soccer and American football. You did not want to be tackled by Sly. He ended up in goal but did not know that when defending a penalty the keeper has to stand still until the ball is kicked. Sly's antics, before he was informed of this rule – leaping about, shouting as if he were a college cheerleader – were ... well ... worth seeing.

When Huston staged a foul giving rise to a penalty on the half-way line, it became evident that our august director shared Sly's ignorance of association football. When it was pointed out to him that the foul had to be committed in the penalty area, he was furious! 'Goddam!' he expleted. 'Stupid game!'

Huston's attitude was captured in an interview. Two hundred press who were flown in for a big PR bonanza. One question was 'Why do you make films, Mr Huston?'

'Either to make money,' he replied. 'Or because I like them.'

The smart-arse reporter persisted, 'Why are you making this one?', implying that anyone involved in our movie was several studs short of a football boot.

After a weighty pause, Huston swatted this cheek away with, 'For both reasons.'

Filming sport is immensely difficult, but piece by piece they worked through the essential set-ups. It was always a joy to watch

Pelé, and to see that Bobby Moore, although 14 years older than when winning the World Cup, was the same calm, strategic force on the field that he had been in his finest hour. After three weeks' painstaking shooting, the approaching Big Match brought extra cameramen to Budapest – the hottest sports photographers in the world. It was exciting, and, because the success of the film was entirely dependent on the game, the tension increased tangibly. In the event, they shot 17 hours of film for a thrilling 15-minute sequence. One story illustrates the heightened atmosphere.

The day before the match I found myself on the pitch having a rare conversation with Huston. Freddie Fields came over to speculate on the bi-ig day. It was a relaxed enough conversation not to exclude me, and we were joined by Tommy Shaw, the props guy. Tommy was a short, square man, with arms like tree trunks – he always made me think of Michelangelo. He enjoyed a drink, and on this day of relative relaxation he had clearly enjoyed more than one. He was warmly welcomed, despite a slight unsteadiness in his gait as he weaved his way across the pitch towards us. Talk of the Big Match resumed when Freddie suddenly gasped, 'Oh, my God!'

We gazed in surprise. 'What is it, Freddie?'

'Oh, my God!' he cried again,' Oh. My. God!!! What the fuck do we do if it rains?'

There was a complicated silence.

'Football is played in the rain, Freddie!' I said. I was ignored. Tommy couldn't have cared less, and if Huston had a view he did not share it with us.

Freddie was off, though. 'Oh no! Oh no! What the fuck do we do? Fuck! Fuck! Fuck!'

'Shtop panicking, Freggie,' said Tommy. 'It'sh rain. Like Tim shaysh, there'sh nod mush we can do!'

'We gotta do something!' howled Freddie in pain. 'I mean … heeeee-eelp!' Then suddenly he cried, '*I* know, I *know*!' We waited. Eventually our patience was rewarded. 'Umbrellas!' cried Freddie triumphantly. 'We need umbrellas.'

We stared at him. Huston observed cryptically, 'Oahh! Ye-es! Umbrellas.'

'Umbrellash?' repeated Tommy, seeing a props issue material-
ising like Omar Sharif in *Lawrence of Arabia*.

'That's right, Tommy. Umbrellas,' said Freddie with convic-
tion; although what he intended to do with them was still darkly
obscure. The angel of silence descended again, and I began to
wish I was elsewhere. 'Got it!' said Freddie dynamically, rubbing
his hands. 'Got it!' We awaited a verdict from the oracle ...

'Tommy ...'

'Yesh, Freggie?'

'Tommy ... I want you to go into Budapest ...'

'Yesh, Freggie?' Tommy repeated uncertainly.

'Go into Budapest ...' the suspense was agonising ... 'Go into
Budapest ... and buy ten thousand umbrellas.'

I swear to you Freddie said, 'Go into Budapest, and buy ten
thousand umbrellas.' Would I make this up?

'Ten thoushand umbrellash?' squealed Tommy as the mirage
became real.

'You heard me. Go into Budapest, and buy ten thousand
umbrellas.'

'It'sh Shaturday, Freggie.'

'So?'

'You can't buy a mack in Budapesht on a Wedneshday.'

Freddie was stymied, but he was not to be denied. 'Tommy!' he
insisted, 'go into Budapest, and buy ten thousand fucking umbrellas!'

'Aw,' said Tommy with a dismissive wave of the hand, 'shtick
ten thoushand umbrellash up yer arshe!' and he tottered away.
Freddie was completely unfazed. He looked at Huston for sympathy. Huston remained silent. He was no fool.

Freddie gave up, 'Pah!' and added, more in sorrow than in
anger, 'Tommy!'

Inscrutable as ever, Huston pushed his lips out in a characteristic gesture. 'Mmmmmn. Ye-es,' he said.

I found some excuse to slip away. They didn't notice, or care.

Tommy did nothing, of course. Shame. I would have loved to
see the bill for ten thousand Hungarian umbrellas which had
been purchased, but not needed. Big films.

15

ESCAPE

My last week of Hungarian exile was scheduled to finish on a Tuesday. I was thrilled because Pam had booked us into *Nicholas Nickleby*, the RSC's hit show. We had tickets for both parts, matinee and evening on the Saturday, and that was to be the last performance ever.

My final scene went OK, so I planned to watch rushes on the Wednesday evening, to be sure that I was clear, and just melt away. I collected my last per diems and asked the production office to book my flight home for Thursday morning. Julian Curry was livid because he was being made to stay on to shoot an unnecessary scene, which originally involved only Dan. In the film, the escape committee give Stallone's character permission to escape. Dan was always scheduled to *watch* him do it, at night, from the window of his hut. A dopey scene; and, to make it dopier, Dan was now to be joined by Julian! As if it wasn't idiotic enough, Freddie decided that he might put *me* in the shot, too; *three* people watching Stallone escape – secretly – at dead of night!

In this age of instant electric playback, viewing rushes is not the sacred rite it used to be. Back then, all heads of department would gather nightly to watch everything that had been shot the previous day. Actors were rarely invited, and with good reason – you tend to look at yourself, which is depressing. Watching rushes is an art: make-up people look at make-up, hair people look at hair, costume people look at costume. You would rarely reshoot for a bad performance, but if there was anything wrong technically that could not be covered in post-production – bad focus, mike in shot, dodgy continuity – you would shoot it again the next day.

For an actor, looking at take after take of uncut film is sheer hell. Imagine the rushes for one of my little scenes with Michael Caine. First we did the wide shot – say, two takes. Then we moved nearer for the establishing two-shot – three takes – and, finally, close-ups on each of us lasting half a minute for each take. Say we did two or three takes on Michael, and two or three on me, although the whole scene cut together would end up at 30 seconds, in rushes you would sit through six to seven minutes of uncut film.

That night my rushes were fine. I packed and booked my own cab so I could slip away without anybody noticing. Then, my master stroke, I shaved off my moustache and went to bed. In the middle of the night I woke to find the red light on my phone winking. A message from Freddie told me *not to go* because they *were* going to use me in the dreaded night scene. I didn't sleep much after that, but the die was cast – I could feel the cool night air on my top lip! When I left for the airport next morning, I sent Freddie a diplomatic message, apologising, but explaining that without my moustache there might be a continuity problem.

Being home with Pam and Tom was sheer heaven, and *Nicholas Nickleby* was unforgettable: I wasn't to know then that it would go on for years, when I *could* have seen it without breaking my contract. Because I had been naughty, for about three weeks I jumped every time the phone rang: was this a call from Freddie, threatening me with the legal might of the studio? I was still jumpy the night Julian called to tell me he was home, and ... right off me. 'Frankly, Piggers old stick, your behaviour was less than collegiate,' he railed, his tongue firmly in his cheek. His ire had been justifiably wound up by the fact that he and Dan had been called for this silly night shot at seven on Friday evening. By two o'clock on Saturday morning, they had still not been used – unimportant shots are always left till last. After ten weeks of hanging about, this was the last straw.

As dawn approached, Julian and Dan were in the catering hut, bemoaning their fate, when Freddie came in. He was annoyingly cheery and asked them how they were. They explained that they were just marginally pissed off, and why. Freddie beamed at them. 'Aah! You should have done what Tim did,' he said, 'he shaved his moustache off, and fucked off home.' On big American movies it's not until you behave badly that they treat you with respect. I am thoroughly ashamed of my behaviour, but, in my defence, I was on the edge of insanity. The conductor Georg Solti, a Hungarian himself, said that the Magyars are the only people in the world who can go into a revolving door behind you and come out in front. Ten weeks on this crazy movie had turned me into a Hungarian.

By the end of this experience I felt very strongly that this world was not for me. I sensed that such parts would do nothing for my career, absolutely nothing for my mental health and less than nothing for my relationships with Pam and Tom. The only *up*side was the money, and it simply wasn't worth it. As Hollywood seemed less than interested in me, I never really had to choose.

Michael Caine, whose performance is central to the film, was exemplary, as an actor and a man. He knew everyone on the unit within days, and he would still know them today. He was completely professional, even towards the end, when Sly started turning up late on set – he was busy writing *Rocky Seventeen*. Michael was friendly, amusing, and a lesson to watch. He was private: he did not join us in the evenings, and used to go to Paris at weekends, largely because he wanted a decent meal. I had no social time with him in Budapest at all, so I was surprised, when the movie broke up, that he invited me to get in touch if I was ever in LA. By chance, I *was* in LA the following year. I was staying with friends, and one evening when I got home from meetings they excitedly played me a message on their Answerphone. There were the unmistakeable London tones of Michael Caine. I had rung the number he gave me, and left a message, but never expected for a minute that he would return the call. Amazingly, this happened three times until we spoke, and he invited me up to his house.

Towards sunset, I drove up the steep, bendy roads to high above infamous Cielo Drive – where the Manson murders took place. Calling off a pair of vicious guard dogs, Michael greeted me with a glass of champagne and led me towards the stunning view over the ocean, flame-red in the light of the sinking sun. We gazed at this staggering panorama. 'Tim,' Michael said dryly, 'one day, this whole fucking thing will be yours!' I hated to tell him that by then I really didn't want it. But I was knocked out by his kindness, and surprised that he had been watching me on TV: Angelo, Hotspur, you name it, he had seen it. I have met him only once in the intervening years, but I always watch his movies: he can be a brilliant screen actor.

Acting with Caine, you are aware of effortless control, and – and this is what marks him out – he creates a sense of reality by not acting. You have a feeling that there is life beyond the confines of the scene you are playing. This, for me, is the benchmark of good *screen* acting; theatre is different. It is simply astounding to act with such people. You float off into the world of the film. It's magic. I tended then, to see the camera as a lens for which I worked. Great screen actors don't work for it; they treat it as an observer that just happens to be focused on them. From such experience I developed the maxim that a scene was working if *it smelled true*. For me, truth is the great aim. And on film you *can* smell it. Olivier remarked that if something was true you could make it as big or as little as you liked, and it would hold.

With Michael, I got the added sense of an inner eye, watching wittily, objectively – maybe this is how he reveals so easily what he is thinking. He told me a story about Marlon Brando who was asked to walk up a hill, in long shot, with some Mexican extras. Brando asked the director not to call 'Action', and told the extras he would let them know when to start acting. As they walked, the extras kept asking 'when to act', and Brando kept saying, 'Just keep walking.' When they reached the top of the hill, the director called 'Cut!' but Brando had not told the extras 'when to act'. You don't need to act walking!

Even when Michael is going for posh or American, you can always hear *him*, but he is completely at home within himself. He has a relaxed presence, a fantastic face and superb, owlish eyes – I think a German actor taught him how not to blink: Michael once said to me, 'If you want to play strong don't blink.' He also said that if the audience is thinking what a good actor you are, you have done it wrong: all they should be thinking is, 'What is going to happen to him?' It's a cliché that good acting is no acting. But what does this mean?

Gregory Peck used to mark his scripts *NAN* or *AH*. A young actor asked him what the letters stood for, and why there were pages of *NAN*, and only rare *AH*s. Peck explained that *NAN* meant *No Acting Necessary* and *AH* meant *Act Here*. I never even saw Michael's script. When he appeared on set he was in complete command of the material. What you saw was the character, not the actor looking at his lines. I was very impressed by him and his approach, but there is a myth that grows out of this minimalism, do less, do nothing, which needs unravelling.

The problem is, 'doing nothing' is an impossibility. So when you hear Caine and De Niro saying 'don't do anything, it will just happen', don't believe them. If you don't do anything, you will find yourself in front of the camera with a pair of the emperor's finest trousers wrapped visibly round your ankles. A director, in frustration, once said to me, 'Mr Pigott-Smith, is it *possible* for you to do less?' I replied that I was trying to find out what the scene was really about – something he had so far been unable to help me with. To be able to achieve this fabled *nothing*, you have to have total understanding of the story and your character's place in it, so you can just live it. It will *look* as though you are doing nothing – it *should* look like nothing – but nothing is not what you are doing: you are doing everything invisibly.

The best thing Hungary gave me was a lifelong friend. Dan had a contact number, and towards the end of the shoot, in desperation, we decided to follow it up. We had a lovely evening with an actor and some of his friends, in spite of the fact that our host's dog ate the very expensive food – and good food was really hard to come by in Budapest in 1980! Among those present was a sweet-natured young director, Tamás (pronounced Tam*ash*), an assistant at the Madách (*Mah*-datch) Theatre. Madách was the great Magyar poet, so in a way the Madách is the equivalent of the RSC, although its role is more populist. Tamás asked us if we would like to see his *Much Ado About Nothing*. Knowing the play, we felt we could cope, and had a really enjoyable evening. It was superbly directed.

Some ten years ago, Tamás was made artistic director of the Madách, and he loves his theatre like his life. I have seen several of his productions, and they are massively impressive. Massive and impressive! For his *Phantom of the Opera*, the most astonishing feat of design I have ever seen, he had to close his theatre for four weeks for technical rehearsals. 'Timmy, darling,' he said to me, 'it had to be a hit, or my theatre is bust!' Tamás and I always raise a glass in Dan Massey's memory – he was taken cruelly by Hodgkin's lymphoma. The film we made together, which is a turkey, often brings me the envy and admiration of younger actors who like football.

Budapest is now an altogether different city. Tamás once said that in the old days – before the Berlin Wall came down – they had communist shit. 'Now,' he grinned fatalistically, 'we are trying to have capitalist shit. We are between two shits!' Streets have been renamed, you can buy bananas, and Budapest is fantastic value for money. Filmmakers are brilliant at finding cheap places in which to work; Budapest is one of them. I did a film there once, just to see Tamás and his Julia.

Back home, more good television roles beckoned. Hugh Whitemore wrote four one-hour plays about Nelson: the first story was told by Fanny, Nelson's wife; the second by Sir William, Emma Hamilton's husband; I had the third story – as Captain Hardy – and the last was narrated by a sailor on the lower gun deck at the Battle of Trafalgar. The overall title was *Aspects of a Hero*, and the point was that different people see heroic figures in different ways. They were classy scripts, well and expensively filmed, but events scuppered their screening. England was at war with Argentina over

A young Captain Hardy in Aspects of a Hero, *filmed on the* HMS Victory, ATV, 1980, *with Kenneth Colley and Michael N. Harbour*

the Falklands and, after three episodes had been transmitted, HMS *Sheffield* was sunk. It was deemed, quite correctly, that to screen our fourth film – in which a common sailor ended up in a home because he got a splinter through his brain at Trafalgar – was not something people would want to see at a time when our seamen's lives were at risk. ITV should have had the gumption to rescreen all four episodes later, but they didn't, so a good piece of television was wasted. In an act of madness, the fourth episode was screened on its own to celebrate Trafalgar Day!

David Giles asked me to play a cracking leading role in a television series for the BBC. Hamer Shawcross is Howard Spring's flawed hero in *Fame Is the Spur* – a lad who rises from poverty to be Prime Minister, based on Ramsay MacDonald. By counterpointing the stories of three youths who start out with Labour hearts, the novel highlights Hamer's betrayal of first principles, as his ambition spurs him on to political compromise. Now where have I heard that before? The great challenge with Hamer was ageing from 14 to 70 over eight hours.

Latex, in its infancy, was all the rage, and, indeed, for the last shots of the 70-year-old Captain Hardy we had used prosthetics. However, my director on *Aspects of a Hero*, Simon Langton, and I were agreed that, as the audience had spent 55 minutes with me as the *young* Hardy, it would not be long before they realised that the *older* Hardy was heavily made up. We calculated that after three seconds looking at the eyes, viewers would realise there was something different about the face, and look to the mouth. Two seconds there, then they would look round the face for clues. We reckoned we had seven or eight seconds of close-up time before I was rumbled. We started with a bald cap, on top of which sat a wispy white wig. A large latex piece and white sideboards covered my cheeks and lower face. The latex went all the way down my neck into my upper chest, successfully jowling me. Superbly shot, it really worked; but with Hamer I had so much screen time that such sleight of hand was not possible. At this time, *I, Claudius* was wallowing in latex, and we were under pressure to use the latest technology, but we opted for wigs, moustaches ... and acting.

An older Captain Hardy, Aspects of a Hero, *1980*

A very young Hamer Shawcross in Fame is the Spur, *BBC TV, 1982*

For Hamer, I started with a 'young' wig that covered my creased brow and flopped forward. Not quite 14 but it wasn't bad for a 35-year-old. This wig was then trimmed, parted and swept back until Hamer was in his mid-thirties, at which point we added a moustache which took me to about 50; then we had a salt-and-pepper wig which mirrored my own receding hair, and another matching moustache that, with gradually added flecks of grey, got me into the sixties; for the very old man we had a white wig and moustache. It worked, inasmuch as it was not distracting.

The cast was strong: George Costigan was one of my mates who became a wealthy store-owner; David Hayman was the other – who went to Wales to work with the miners, staying true to his socialist roots; Julia Mackenzie played *his* wife, Joanna David played mine. It was very well adapted in ten episodes, but the producer who proudly reduced it to eight ruined it, because the first six episodes covered 40 years, and the last two episodes then had to zoom through *30* years. It just got silly.

I was in India when it was broadcast, and got the impression that it did not create many ripples. But by then all my energy was going into the new series on which I was working – *The Jewel in the Crown*.

16

FINDING MERRICK

The trail of coincidence that led to the job that changed my life began in the summer of 1975, when, with Pam pregnant, we moved to Greenwich. From financial necessity I had become quite a proficient DIY man. I could handle all things domestic – except electrics: I was a dangerous electrician. I was up a ladder trying not to blow us up when the phone rang – it was our old friend Richard Heffer. Heff had rung to wish us well in our new home, but in his usual, savvy way he had something to impart: 'Do you know *The Jewel in the Crown*?' he asked. I did not. 'Oh, my God,' he cried, 'first of *The Raj Quartet*. You must read it ... there's a part in it you *have* to play!'

I started reading Paul Scott's great work. It was pretty obvious which part Heff had me in mind for! I loved the books, and read steadily, always alert to the possibility of a production. When I eventually heard, five years later, that it was happening, I had a shock, because the proposed director, Christopher Morahan, was a friend of ours.

Anna Carteret is an old chum of Pam's, and Chris, having lost his first wife to cancer, was courting Anna in 1973 when they came to stay in our little house in Stratford. Chris, at that time head of plays at the BBC, was one of our foremost television directors. He had a frightening reputation. This was the man coming to stay in our house! We were terrified.

Chris turned out to be a charming, kind, funny man. Like many people with reputations, he has little time for people with lower standards. We became good friends: he and Anna married, and their first daughter, Rebecca, was born three months after our Tom. We saw a good deal of each other: we were in Greenwich; they lived in Dulwich. Indeed, it was Chris himself who, in answer to our question 'What are you working on?', told us he was exploring the possibilities of televising two sets of great books – Anthony Powell's *A Dance to the Music of Time*, and ... be still my beating heart ... Scott's *Raj Quartet*.

At Christmas 1981, on the way to their party, I said to Pam, 'What on earth am I to do about *The Raj Quartet*?' Pam made it clear that I should be very cautious in talking to Chris about work – as we always had been. I was desperate to be considered for Ronald Merrick, but this was a ticklish situation ...

Quite late on in the evening I saw Chris – bottle in hand as a good host – without anyone to serve. I said to Pam, 'I'm sorry but I have to do this.' She protested, 'Tim! Don't!' But I was gone! I approached Chris, slightly short of breath.

'Chris,' I gulped, 'I'm sorry to do this, but it's about *The Raj Quartet* ... I know the books, and—' before I could continue, Chris, looking down at me, his eyes hooding characteristically, said, 'I know what you want to play.' Before I could launch into a speech of wild adulation about Paul Scott, Chris began to outline the project. We knew he had been away, but did not know he had been in India on a reconnaissance trip, identifying locations, drafting itineraries and making shooting plans. Chris told me that the actor playing Merrick would be contracted for about 18 months, with a considerable spell in India. He was very sweet and very clear about the potential excitement of the project – and completely non-committal. He excused himself and moved off with his bottle to continue hosting. I was in shock. I had done it. When I talked to Pam we agreed that not only had I probably damaged a friendship, but I would never hear another word about Merrick, until we read in the paper one day that someone else was playing *my* part.

A couple of months later I had a call from my agent, Jeremy Conway. Jeremy had bumped into Chris in Delhi, where they happened to be staying in the same hotel. Chris was on another recce, and he met Jeremy, who was sitting by the hotel pool, actually reading *The Jewel in the Crown*! By another magical coincidence, when Chris started casting, my name was at the top of the adaptor Ken Taylor's list of Merricks. Jeremy reported that Sir Denis Forman, chairman of Granada – whose pet project *Jewel* was – wanted to see tapes of my work. After an agonising wait (nearly five years) I was offered the part! Hard to believe that it had happened at all, let alone so easily.

When I finished *Fame Is the Spur* in the middle of 1981 I went to Pinewood to play Dom Philippe, a part that I described as 'Derek Jacobi's left leg' – Derek was playing Dom Claude. We were doing 'priest acting' in a TV film of *The Hunchback of Notre Dame*, starring Anthony Hopkins, a superb Quasimodo. It was a Norman Rosemont production. Rosemont was a massive, taciturn, Uncle Sam producer, with simple taste and huge drive. Outside Norman's Pinewood office was a sign which read, 'To err is human. To forgive is not Rosemont policy'. He mounted European classics for the American market: they were simply adapted, lavishly designed and peppered with names – David Suchet and Lesley-Anne Down also graced our cast.

One incident from the shooting was ... well, unusual. The exterior of Notre Dame Cathedral, built at Pinewood, was fantastically impressive, but the night before we started filming there was a torrential downpour. In front of the cathedral façade, the square, which had been covered with earth, was a swamp. The first scene is on The Day of Fools – so there were many strangely made-up people, and a number of dwarfs. Hundreds of poor extras were issued with polythene bags to protect their footwear.

Derek and I were lucky, being driven through the quagmire in a carriage from which Dom Claude espies Esmeralda, performing the infamous Fandango, which in the Pinewood mud had become a Fandango de la Boue! He stops the carriage, and calls a soldier over, from whom he demands the identity of the beautiful, mud-splattered dancer.

During rehearsal, as the soldier moved towards us, he slipped in the mud. I swear that what follows is true ... one of the dwarfs helped him up, and in this slithery *pas de deux*, the dwarf somehow became affixed to the soldier's sword belt, where he hung disconsolately. The soldier's dilemma was – do I remove the dwarf and move? Or do I move forward, with the dwarf hanging from my sword belt, and just pretend he is not there? Brave soldier, he opted for the latter. By the time he reached our carriage, Derek and I were hiding, barely able to breathe, smothering our shameful, hysterical, laughter. The first assistant mercifully called 'Cut!'

I took with me to Pinewood, daily, two large carrier bags containing Ken's 13 scripts for *The Jewel in the Crown* – a real test of the viability of this massive project. The story-telling in Scott's books is not sequential: disparate strands of the tale come together, but not always chronologically. Ken had decided that the only way to adapt this twisted, kaleidoscopic marathon was to iron the narrative out. As I devoured the scripts – with annoying interruptions to film – I was thrilled to discover that the story still developed with great power, without losing the suspense and excitement of its original. It was a staggering achievement, to condense Scott's material for the small screen without losing the scale of the story. Ken's work was well-nigh flawless. The 'pivotal' figure, as Chris always described him, was Merrick. He was the link, the character that joined together the different elements of Scott's epic tale.

Jim O'Brien was appointed as the second director. Chris was overall producer and decided that he and Jim would direct alternate episodes. When I had the pleasure of meeting Jim and Ken, I was asked to comment on the script, and was able to say that from Merrick's point of view I thought there were two brief vignettes missing, not much from four huge novels. The first was the scene in which Merrick finds a cobra in his bath, lures the snake with his false arm and slices off its head with a kukri. This seemed to encapsulate both the scary and the admirable in this damaged man. In Ken's draft the snake scene was 'narrated'; he merely added that you also *saw* ... Merrick's calm, calculated courage. This was a very privileged way to work. You are always allowed input as an actor, but not often consulted in this way.

The other slight loss, I felt, was Merrick's relationship with Susan's baby son. I loved the notion that this resistible, manipulative man, with one arm and a face deeply scarred from burns, was good with a young child, a boy who adores him. A tiny scene was put back in, but this vignette did not survive: it emerged that Scott slightly confuses the child's age, something you don't notice when reading, but visualised it looked wrong and, sadly, had to be cut.

My task now was to get inside the character of Ronald Merrick. Scott writes all the other characters' minds and feelings. There is, for example, an insight into the retired missionary, Barbie's, fear of sex, when she fills her pen and finds the action of squeezing the ink sack, sucking the ink into the pen, somewhat troubling. With Merrick, you never get anything like that. Scott deliberately paints just the surface: this helps explain the power of the character – each reader is able to create Merrick in their own imagination. Whatever facts you learn about him, you *never* know what is going on in his head. At first, I thought that Scott saw himself as Guy Perron, Charles Dance's character, and our 'sort of' hero who represents the reader in the fourth book, but I came to believe that the fascination, the spell, the power of Merrick came directly from the author, who had, with searing honesty, poured his class complexes, his own racial and sexual confusions, his fears and darkness, into the soul of his twisted anti-hero. But because Scott never explains Merrick, merely recounting what he does, it was difficult to get inside this complex man.

When Merrick meets the Layton family, Aunt Fenny spots immediately – because of the way he speaks – that he is not 'top-drawer'. Like Merrick, I was a lower-middle-class grammar school boy. so I began to work on something in my speech that suggested someone *trying* to be upper crust, but falling short. Chris suggested my 'o' – as in 'open' – might be of use; so I worked on making that sound pure and manufactured, in contrast to other, less diamond sounds. The class issue was central to all our work, because the first time Merrick meets Hari Kumar, he speaks to him in Hindi, and is taken aback when this drunken Indian layabout – as he sees him – addresses him in clipped, public school, superior-sounding English. A trick of speech *can* open the door to a character. Not this time.

The best way to explore a part, if you don't find the answer immediately, is to play games: for example, you can do Shakespeare with an Italian accent, playing a scene in cod spaghetti – 'My 'orse-a, my 'orse-a! My keengdom-a for a 'orse-a!' And you can try swearing, interpolating Shakespeare's language with the worst possible abuse you can think of – it's not for the faint-hearted! 'My horse, my ******* horse! My ******** kingdom for a *******-******* horse!' It's just playing, but it can be very liberating. When I direct, I say to the cast that we have to become so confident in what we are doing that we can play – in the theatre what we are doing is even called 'a play'.

All acting aspires to the simplicity of playing. 'Hold that tin,' says a child offering you her empty hand. You take it. The child mimes pouring water into it. 'Don't drink it,' she says, 'it's from a dirty river!' You say, 'Well, we could boil it.' The child shakes her head, and says 'No. You can drink it. It's all right now.' Acting is fundamentally simple: it gets difficult when the imagination is not stimulated. My judgement on Merrick's character was hampering my imagination.

It is fatal to judge your own character because the absolute rule for me, with wicked characters, is that they don't think of themselves as wicked. The approach I had developed when play-ing 'baddies' can be reduced to two statements: bad people very rarely think that what they are doing is bad. Genuine racists think it's acceptable to despise black or Jewish people – *that* is the problem. The second notion is that even the most powerful people, the wealthiest people, the wickedest people, go home and cry because something in their lives is not right. Imagine a scene in which the villain in the movie has a beloved pet dog. The dog is killed. The villain mourns. As an actor, you have to play genuine grief. Leave reactions and moral judgements to the audience.

With Ronnie – as I increasingly liked to think of Merrick, because it took away the aura of wickedness – I hit on a way of speaking that was a pronounced, deliberate version of my own speech: it generated within me a slight sense of inferiority. It made him stiff, deliberate, calculated. I fancied that, like me practising to find Ronnie's voice, Merrick had worked hard to improve his speech. My own way of working on an accent is to master a short phrase – 'Stone the flaming crows!' would be a good start for Australian – and then count from one to ten. Do that with a Northern Irish, Northumbrian, French or a Bronx accent, and you get a clear idea of what sounds are working and what are not. I did this with Ronnie, but I still could not find the key – the switch.

It was partly that I was daunted by the scale of the responsibility I had been given. I talked to Chris and Jim who were insightful, but I still felt *outside* the man. I spoke to Greg Stewart, a specialist in criminal psychology, and he gave me one particularly useful thought: he talked about how hunters can, in time, *will* themselves to become the hunted – like the 'signature' of the serial killer who wants to be found out. Merrick is a policeman, hunting criminals, promotion and social position. He allows his needs to distort the truth, and has to conceal so much, some of it from himself, that eventually it devours him. The hunter becomes the hunted. But the way *into* the man still eluded me.

We began rehearsals in December 1981. Christopher and Jim had assembled a strong cast, some of whom had, like me, known the books and asked if they could be considered for their roles, and others who brought coincidence with them. An important character, early on, is Sister Ludmila – a Mother Teresa figure of Russian extraction. Christopher had an instinct that Matyelok Gibbs was the woman for the part: her mother, it turned out, was Russian.

We sat round a table in a wintry rehearsal room in Brixton, and with our hearts in our mouths we launched into the three-day read. You knew that Judy Parfitt was going to be superb as Mildred. You smelled the canny brilliance of Eric Porter's Count Bronowski. And there was a moment when the room was shocked by Wendy Morgan's explosive grief as Susan. Charles

Dance – whose character does not appear until late on in the series – didn't open his mouth for *two days*!

We then had the privilege of proper rehearsal, spending time on the history of the Raj, listening to tapes of the period, accent, as I have mentioned, being crucial. We discussed the piece, the characters and the challenge of the episodic structure. Ken's aim was to draw the audience into the love affair between Daphne and Hari, and create such a powerful sense of the agonising wrong done to them, that the viewer would be propelled into the story of the Layton family, the link being Merrick.

Hearing the entire story, and seeing how Merrick functioned within it, was useful, and Chris and Jim were both very clear on my character, but I was still frustrated by my lack of an instinctive reaction. I fed my inner computer with data – lower-middle-class, an orphan; a policeman working for the Raj, which gives him the family he never had; a longing to be in the army – better job than the police force; an absolute belief in what he is doing, never questioning his superiors or the validity of the Raj; upholding authority in a way others find reassuring. A repressed homosexual, Merrick doesn't like being attracted to men; he hates being attracted to Indians – because he regards them as inferiors. He is admirably brave. I chewed over all this information but I could not find the switch that set my imagination freewheeling. That meant that *I* would play the character, but the character was never going to play *me*. I prayed for that little internal click telling me that my character was in charge. But it would not come.

The day I finally found my way in to Merrick I was working with Elizabeth Pursey, a voice specialist who had been brought in to help us with 'class'. I knew Liz through Maggie Tyzack, who had been taught by her. Maggie once said to me, 'Liz is a witch!' At my first session, Liz asked me to demonstrate what I was after with the accent. Merrick gives a lecture to a group of soldiers – an unbroken chunk of text that I had been playing with – so I did it for Liz. She asked immediately if Merrick was gay. She *was* a witch! She had only read the first episode, but she was on to that secret. Scott conceals the revelation of Merrick's homosexuality until well into Book Two, and Ken had placed it near the end of Episode Six. Liz said that what I was doing confirmed her suspicions that he was gay. I decided then that, although I wanted to be true to the character, I did *not* want to give this secret away, and would further suppress his gayness.

Liz observed that people trying to get on in society often work too hard. She sat me in front of a mirror and asked me to push my lower jaw forward a little. When I did this, my mouth fell effortlessly into an expression of contempt. Click. This released in me something central to the writing...

Merrick is strongly motivated by his need to master the contempt he has always felt from his social superiors. He makes himself feel better by handing this contempt on to his social inferiors, subjecting Hari to his theory of 'fear and contempt'. By pushing my jaw forward, I was in touch with this 'contemptuousness', and it became the way I got into character over the next 18 months. To begin with, it took me maybe a minute – concentrating, in order to allow the internal sensation this prognathous position produced – to take over from its physical unfamiliarity. It got easier and quicker with time: after six months, it took seconds. It became the switch I could throw, that released my imagination and when the imagination works, it works fast, and, suddenly, you are playing. One minute I was me; the next, I felt like a different person.

I was Merrick.

As Ronald Merrick with Art Malik as Hari Kumar in
The Jewel in the Crown, *ITV, 1984*

17

Being Merrick

One purely practical problem facing us was that, for half the series, Merrick is without most of his left arm, and his face is burnt. An amputee showed me how to manipulate my false arm, strapping the leather harness on to the shoulder, forcing the stump down perpendicularly, to bring the false forearm up to a right angle, then pushing it forward, which simultaneously raises the thumb and locks the elbow. I was given a false arm for reference, which I kept in the wardrobe. Pam didn't like it at all and it *was* a bit weird. Props made me a tight-fitting, flesh-coloured plastic sleeve that I slipped over my forearm. This was held in place by my watch. A glove concealed my hand. So, for the arm, it was just a question of practice, but the facial scarring offered a different challenge.

Anna Jones, our make-up lady, organised a face mask, and a very skilled prosthetician produced a wafer-thin latex piece that Anna stuck on. It didn't work. We then tried smaller pieces in specific places on my face. That didn't work either. The problem became clearer with each disaster: when you have been burnt, you *lose* flesh, the skin contracts. These latex pieces looked exactly like what they were – additions, bits stuck on.

Merrick's left side is burnt when he tries to rescue Teddy from a blazing jeep. I suggested that the only features we could 'deform' were my eye and ear, so, using liquid latex, Anna stuck a small piece of gauze to the outer edge of my left eyelid, and, while she allowed it to dry, created a burn map on my face, with reddish purple colours. Then she pulled the gauze down, deforming the

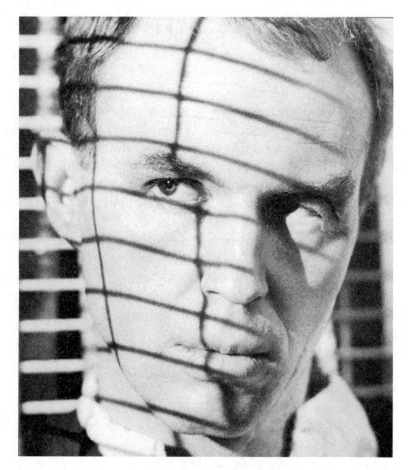

Ronald Merrick, The Jewel in the Crown

eyelid. She stuck the loose end to my cheekbone, and used the same technique with my ear, wrapping the gauze round and tightly under it. She then brushed liquid latex over the whole burnt area. If I held my head slightly to the left, the impression created, was – at last – of skin that had been lost – burnt away, and we felt we had something that we could shoot on from any angle.

We went to India in January 1982.

The first scene I filmed was the last but one (of 13 episodes), a sequence in which Merrick is thrown from his horse. He blames his fall on a stone being thrown. True to form, Scott does not tell you whether someone did actually throw a stone, so – is Merrick lying? In Episode Four a stone *is* thrown – breaking the window of Teddy Bingham's car as he and Merrick make their way to the wedding: this incident is immensely significant, informing Merrick he is being watched, pursued. For the scene with the horse I had to decide – is Merrick lying?

In the days prior to filming this scene I had time to consider the implications because I was working daily with my horse. As riders go, I was an actor: as actors go, I was a rider. But this beast was something else – a magnificent Indian thoroughbred. As I mounted him the first time, the Indian groom said sweetly, 'He is a prince. He will ride till you are off his back.' When I returned from my first outing I had learnt that if I held this fiery beast too firmly on the bit, he chafed and rankled. If I loosened my hold, he would be at full gallop within four paces – he did it once, and I just clung on! It was his way of testing me – 'is this an idiot on my back?!' If I got the tension on the bit right, he was good as gold, willing, obedient. I grew to admire and love this highly sensitive, intelligent, proud creature. I do not say this lightly because it was unprecedented for me to entertain feelings of this nature for an animal. As a child we lived in flats and I was never allowed pets. I have always found people's devotion to animals rather surprising – until I fell for this staggering creature. He was named Chetak, after a fabled Indian warrior horse which had sacrificed his life to save his master. The same groom who had filled me

Rehearsing for The Jewel in the Crown *on 'Chetak', India, 1982*

with dread as I mounted Chetak told me that a month before we arrived, they had lit a wall of fire and galloped all the horses in the stable straight at it. Chetak was the only one who went fearlessly though this blazing wall. This was why he was a prince.

Chetak and I rode past the location for the stone-throwing incident daily. I decided that in this scene, in this location, no stone could possibly have been thrown – the terrain was too flat; any attacker would have been seen. So ... was Merrick fantasising, unhinged or both? I decided that he knew, deep down, that he had done wrong – that he could not deny to himself that he had twisted justice to nail Hari Kumar, and that years of being followed, harried, reminded of his culpability, was getting to him: the stone was a hallucination brought about by suppressed guilt. Merrick was temporarily unhinged – 'Mad Merrick' was how we sometimes jokingly referred to him.

With the end point of Merrick's journey fixed, I used a technique I had learnt from Freddy Young, the great director of photography, with whom I had the privilege of working when he was in his eighties. He told me that Robert Donat used to create graphs for his character – a story graph, a character graph and an emotional graph – so that when he was obliged to shoot a scene out of order he would turn to his graphs and know at what level to pitch it. This had been useful with *Fame Is the Spur* and now, with Merrick, I could build my graphs, knowing that by the end, I needed to arrive at a state of mind in which he acknowledged his guilt and had been driven to the edge of madness. Maybe he wanted an end to it all – to be punished for his wrongdoing, the hunter, hunted. Just before we started shooting I had found my switch and my journey. I could relax a bit.

Years later, I met an old codger who told me how *Jewel* had been put to the board at Granada. He said, 'Well ... Denis [Sir Denis Forman, chairman] said to us one day, "I have these four books about India that I want to make into a series." He told us about them. He also told us that shooting in India might well be a nightmare. We asked how much it would cost. He said 5.6 million, and we said, "All right!"' This simply could not happen nowadays.

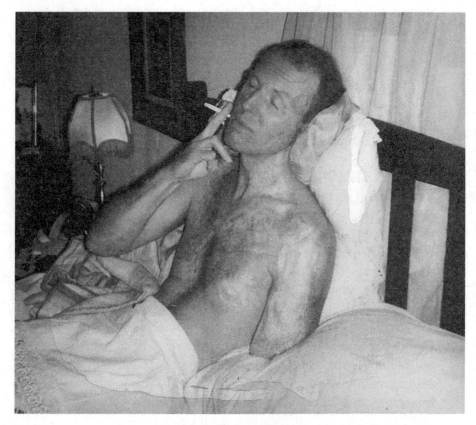

A one-armed Ronald Merrick awaiting his death

Projects go through committees, and although that makes sense in a harsher financial climate, it blunts the edge of passion, which is the only reason for ever making anything.

We began with nearly five months' shooting in India, and, as Denis had predicted, it had its moments. On one occasion our online producers, Bill and Ian, en route to the airport, popped in to a large, classy Delhi hotel to confirm the booking of 27 rooms, awaiting the arrival of Granada personnel. They met them off the plane. They took them straight back to the hotel, where all the rooms had been let. There were other issues – financial, culinary, health problems, cock-ups over transport – but we more than got by. We had two superb Indian producers, Tejbir and Valmik, and our local fixer was a fabulous, charming, wily guy, Bhaskar, who got us out of all sorts of scrapes.

I have known creative film directors mess up because they are not organised. I have known directors of medium talent make good films because they *are* organised. A really good film director – like Mick Jackson, Peter Kosminsky, or Paul Greengrass – will know pretty much what the whole picture is going to look like in his head, and maybe on his storyboards, before he starts shooting. Christopher combined immense creative talent with natural organisational skills, and he was responsible for planning *Jewel*. Jim was a perfect foil because while Chris was planning, he took a more relaxed, broader view of the material. Christopher also had the help of experienced associates led by Milly Preece, and the organisation of *Jewel* – which won many prizes – was an amazing feat, worthy in itself of an award.

We used our Indian locations to the utmost – not shooting interiors: why go all that way and film something you could do in a studio? This made perfect sense but it required immensely detailed planning. Chris and Jim tried to make every shot in India count. For example, Daphne Manners came out on to a balcony in Udaipur, an early shot in India, making the most of the view of the surrounding countryside. Months later, she ran across a set in our Manchester studio – to reach that balcony.

171

The most extraordinary bit of planning was probably Guy Perron, throwing a ball in Simla, to be caught, eight months later – in Manchester. But when Vic Symons, our experienced, brilliant designer, found a perfect old Raj club in Mysore, it was decided that on our last day there, we would use it to shoot one longish, unscheduled scene between Merrick and Teddy Bingham. We did not generally work on our last day in any location – there was no time for rushes to be sent home, checked and reshot if anything was amiss. But as this was an interior, if there was anything wrong Vic knew he could recreate the club in England. In the event it was fine, so we gained time and a perfect set. There was only one bit of material from my five months in India that we had to reshoot in England: Jim thought I had missed something in a scene in the car with Daphne. It had been shot at night, so it was relatively easy to restage.

The shoot in India was followed by a year in England, mainly in studio at Granada, with the brief, judicious, use of Wales, doubling for Simla. People are astounded by how much was done in and around Granada. The Bibighar Gardens, where Hari meets Daphne, were just outside Manchester, and the midges there rivalled Indian mosquitoes! Burma was Alderley Edge! We would have got nowhere without Vic, but I could say that of everyone – there was not a weak link in the team. The climactic train massacre, considered too inflammatory to be shot in India, was filmed at Quainton, near Aylesbury, where steam railway enthusiasts maintain suitable old trains, rolling stock and buildings.

I kept a diary while in India – not just accounts of heat and dust, and days of feeling queasy – talking to God on the big china telephone as we called it – or because I thought such memories might be useful acting reminders come December in Manchester (which they were), but because the country was so astonishing, and this trip, from the beauty of Rajasthan, to the heat of Mysore in central southern India, via Delhi, Bangalore and Bombay to Simla and Kashmir, was overwhelming. I have only been back to India once since then, to make some documentaries about Calcutta, when I was again knocked sideways by the country and its people: I met rich people who were kind and generous, but the same qualities of warmth and welcome were shown me at every level of society. Most moving of all were the people with nothing, who *gave* everything. Beyond humbling.

Chris was a director so detailed in his preparation it was almost intimidating, although he was always adaptable and enjoyed being stimulated by new thoughts on the day. Jim was less premeditated: you felt that his camera just happened to land on something, picking out a detail suggestive of a wider context. He brought, too, a heightened racial awareness: he would often start a scene off-piste – on the Indian bearer perhaps, sitting silently, able to hear the actual scene being played out between white people.

On my first day working on set with Chris, Merrick was to meet the Layton family arriving by train. Chris showed me the route he had planned out. 'You greet them coming off the train, lead them along the platform, and out through the station arch. You will see a turbaned policeman standing over there to your right. He will salute you. Just acknowledge him as you pass. Slacken your pace a little, and when Sarah Layton joins you, head for the cars – which will be waiting over there ... and ... just fall unconsciously into step with her.' He was fleshing out and making character points from what could have been a straightforward walk from train to car. Phenomenal stuff.

We spent six weeks in Udaipur, a ravishingly beautiful city, graced by man-made lakes and therefore known as 'the Venice of the East'. In 1982 it was quite primitive – you couldn't telephone England. It is now an electronically up-to-date city, with one café showing the Bond movie *Octopussy* non-stop, which was filmed there just after we left, when Udaipur had innocence as well as beauty.

Jim wanted to shoot Merrick's long scene with Sarah Layton – as per the text *and* Ken's adaptation – at sunset, at that Magritte moment when the earth is suddenly dark, but the sky is still light. We shot on Jagmandir, an island in one of the lakes. Beautiful does not even begin to describe this island temple – *mandir* is the word for a temple – with its row of carved elephants by the landing

stage. At sunset it was breathtaking. Merrick has a prosaic, defla-
tionary line, which takes all the mystery from the fading day, when
he says flatly, 'Water reflects the light.' The scene was close on
seven minutes long, but the sunset only lasted three! We rehearsed
with Jim, in a detailed, theatrical way, so that we were completely
on top of the text, and the brilliant schedule took us back on three
consecutive nights to make the most of this awe-inspiring location, and to give the scene an authentic feel of happening in real
time. We had three miraculously identical sunsets!

In Mysore it was baking hot, and I got ill – the Hindu Two-Step
as we sometimes called it. Chris had to rejig the schedule because
I was out of it for 24 hours with fever and hallucinations! I
came back from rehearsal one morning – we were preparing
for the shoot that night – feeling increasingly light-headed and
sweaty. I remember running faster and faster through the endless
marble corridors of our massive hotel and reaching the bathroom
just in time, before passing out.

The shoot in India was arranged so that, as the heat increased,
we went north, rather as the British had in the days of the Raj,
taking refuge in the Himalayan foothills of Simla, and then still
further north, in the houseboats of Kashmir. These boats were a
very English solution to not being allowed to own land in this
extremely beautiful diamond of territory. Moored in the most
spectacular scenery – mountain-fringed lakes, lily pads and
willow trees – were floating relics of the Empire, huge houseboats
converted now to holiday rentals, with gloriously inappropriate
names – *Ritz*, *Savoy*, *Prince of Wales*.

Kashmir was safer then. Under pressure from the English, the
Hindu Rajah, Hari Singh, agreed at a quarter to midnight, just before
Independence, that Kashmir would remain part of Hindustan. The
decision was delayed agonisingly because Kashmir has a largely
Muslim population, so there was also pressure to join *Paki*stan: *stan*
means place or land; *pak* means pure. Many Kashmiri Muslims
were intensely poor, and this, to simplify things, was the seed that
grew into the tragic violence which erupted not long after our
departure. We were blessed to see it at peace.

At midnight on 14 August 1947, Nehru made his famous 'tryst with destiny' speech which was used – Jim's idea, I believe – to bring our series to a close. As Guy Perron's plane left India, symbolic of the British departure, Nehru's words rang out and Hari Kumar heard them on his radio, a symbol of the damaged continent we left behind. It was one of the privileges of working over such a long period of time that changes and additions like this could be made. Some critics disliked the fact that *Jewel* was a British – therefore still an 'Empire' – view, but no one has come up with anything to rival it since, and it was pretty harsh on Britishness! I was personally attacked by people who said that a man like Merrick could not have existed, that no Englishman would ever have behaved in that way, referring to Merrick's mistreatment of Hari in prison. I used to reply that I was very much afraid that not dissimilar things were going on in prisons in Northern Ireland as we spoke. And that was before the dark days of extraordinary rendition.

There was a rather strange and disturbing coincidence: fire is a theme in the books – Edwina Crane, the missionary, incinerates herself; a young Indian boy puts a scorpion in a ring of fire; Susan Layton, in crazed imitation, puts her *baby* in a ring of fire; Merrick is badly burnt. One night I was in Manchester, on the point of going to bed at about midnight, when I had a call to say, 'Don't come in tomorrow, the studio is on fire.' I jumped in my car. By the time I got there, only the walls were standing. The roof had collapsed and the studio floor was a mangled heap of steaming, metal spaghetti. The fire had lasted 20 minutes, and it had taken with it five sets and quite a lot of Vic's designs. No one ever rightly explained the cause of it, but it was chilling, and seemed like a bad omen.

Chris took it as a personal affront, swatting it away like an annoying fly, rejigging the schedule and getting us shooting again within four days! It was staggering. The fire made it even more extraordinary that he brought the whole project in on time, *and* a quarter of a million under budget.

When you are working on a film you have no idea how it will come together, and none of us thought that *Jewel* would be massively popular. However, being led in this way, by Chris and Jim, and behind them Sir Denis, the feeling began to grow that our film stood at least a chance of being as classy as the books.

18

AFTER MERRICK

When *Jewel* was screened, old friends from school and university got back in touch. More than one of them told me that their partners hated Merrick so much they could not think of having me in the house. This kind of audience identification does not happen in any other medium. When you have seen *The Last of the Mohicans*, you do not expect Daniel Day-Lewis to be a Native American. When you have seen *King Lear*, you do not assume the actress playing Regan to be someone who habitually pulls people's eyes out! It only happens with television. And it happened to me with *Jewel*. It *still* happens. People recognise me, and think I am Ronald Merrick.

The impact of *Jewel* was international. In 1985, Pam, Tom and I were on holiday in Jávea in Spain. I was looking 'summery' – leather sandals, shorts, T-shirt, sunglasses, large, floppy sun hat – when some passing locals pointed at us – at me. They waved enthusiastically. 'Holà! Holà!' they cried. And when we waved back, they smiled. 'El Diablo!' they called happily. 'El Diablo!' We discovered that *Jewel* was being shown on Spanish television. Friends invited us to watch an episode. Dubbed in Spanish, it lost … something … and the deep Mexican bandito voice I had been given did indeed turn me into El Diablo!

I received mail from all over the world, which is not unusual with a successful TV show or film, but I received one letter from India addressed to Mr Pigot-Singh. As is common, Pigott was misspelt. My name often causes difficulty and I have been Tim Piggot-Smith, Tim Pitt-Rivers, Mr Dicket-Smith, Piggot-Browne,

Piget-Smythe, Robot-Smith – I swear – and Pigot-Mnith – every conceivable version you can imagine bar one with a silent 'q'. What was truly remarkable about the letter from India to Mr Pigot-Singh was that the only other word on the envelope was London, a great compliment to the combined efforts of the GPO, our then postman, Terry, and the Indian Postal Service, which is, ironically, one of the enduring legacies of Empire.

When I was in New York in 1985, two major screen offerings were vying with *Jewel* for popularity – *The Thorn Birds* and *Romancing the Stone*. I ran out of shirts one day and needed a decent one for yet another press conference. I went in to Bergdorf Goodman, where they used to have staff behind desks just inside the entrance, to guide customers to the relevant department. Bergdorf Goodman is a classy Fifth Avenue store, and the woman facing me from behind the desk was pure New York class: her cream blouse appeared to have been ironed five minutes before, specifically for my arrival, her coiffure was impeccable, her make-up restrained and her nails looked as if they had just been varnished; but when she caught sight of me, for all her class she had to suppress a scream. In shock, her cheeks blushing scarlet, she said, 'Oh, my God! It's him! It's the thorn in the stone!' In her confusion, which bordered on fear, this poor woman managed to get all her lines crossed, and she ended up with that mess – the thorn in the stone! I managed to calm her down, and with profuse compliments and grovelling apologies, she directed me to, *Shoits!* Whoops.

I used to say that *Jewel* was classy soap opera. Soap opera has extraordinary power: viewers become addicted to knowing what is going to happen – the great strength of story. Soap opera also explains why the television audience expects you to be like the character you play – week after week you visit people in their homes. Linda Thorson, who took over from Diana Rigg in the early days of *The Avengers*, showed me some of her fan letters. One viewer thanked Linda for coming to visit her every week. Another lady asked if Linda liked the new green curtains in her television room, thinking that Linda, being on her telly, could see them!

This surprise fame was welcome professionally, but personally I didn't like it. Recognition in the street can be disturbing, even if people are nice, but because of Merrick's nature people weren't always pleased to see me! I was stopped one day by a lady who was beside herself. She halted me physically and said venomously, 'Are you ... are you ... THING!?!' I was nonplussed, and a little concerned both for my own welfare and hers – she looked as though she was going to explode. In response to my bafflement, she said again, 'You're THING. Aren't you? THING!!' I sort of nodded, but she was not through. 'If you had a restaurant ...' she fumed and blustered, 'if you had a restaurant ... I would not EAT at it!' For some obscure reason that incomprehensible threat was the vilest insult she could muster.

There is one recognition of which I am actually very proud: I was filming *The Challenge* in Australia, a fun account of Australia winning the America's Cup. I had a three-week break in shooting between Perth and finishing off in Sydney, which coincided with the school holidays, so as Pam was free she brought Tom over and we travelled. We visited the Barrier Reef, one of the most unforgettable experiences of all our lives, and Ayers Rock, staying in nearby Alice Springs, where, sitting by the hotel pool one day – the only three people in the hotel stupid enough to brave the fierce heat – we witnessed a very dignified, extremely well-preserved, elderly lady in a one-piece bathing suit, sporting an extravagant floral bathing cap, go into the water, swim several lengths of the pool in an elegant crawl, get out at the far end and take up station in a lounger.

Sometime after this I felt like cooling off and swam a few lengths. Tiring, I got out of the water near this impressive-looking lady, and as I emerged – up the pool steps – I recognised Lauren Bacall. She had removed the floral bathing cap. She looked hard at me and sat up, shaking her hair loose –

'Oh, my God!' she said. 'It's that ba-ad, sa-ad ma-an!'

It was pure Raymond Chandler, delivered with the savvy drawl of a great film star. I had met her briefly once before, backstage at the Royal Variety Performance, but here, by the pool in Alice

Springs, we had a nice chat. She was in Australia touring with a Tennessee Williams play. Acting is fun, but that's not the whole truth. Here was a huge international star, touring Australia in her twilight years. Touring is hard. Like old age, it ain't for cissies. Her description of Merrick is one I have always treasured.

One very unfortunate aspect of being recognised was the extraordinary level of discourtesy shown to Pam. I would introduce her to someone as my wife. They would turn and look at her as though she was a piece of furniture, and literally turn their backs on her, to continue talking to me. I was very bad at handling this, but I didn't know how to deal with such rudeness.

The welcome professional reaction was also double-edged. In one week after *Jewel* I was offered three disabled parts – Nelson, some man with one arm, and yet another, whose feet had been tortured, leaving him with a terrible limp. It is easy, and sometimes very useful, to be catalogued as an actor – *You need X for this part* – but *this* level of branding was hard to believe. My rise in status also meant that when I turned up to see people for work their expectation was immense. I was completely incapable of responding positively. It froze me. I was briefly a star, but I couldn't cope with it. I was lousy at it. I had played a star part, but I don't have glamour, and you can't be an unglamorous star! Charlie Dance is a star. My old friend Jeremy Irons is a star. Helen Mirren is a star. They are glamorous. All I had ever really wanted was to play good parts, with good people in good plays. I enjoyed the razzmatazz immensely, but, looking back, it was a complete distraction from what I wanted to do.

One of the many wonderful people I met on *Jewel* was Judy Parfitt. She had great success at the Royal Court with D. H. Lawrence plays in the sixties, and she was nominated by BAFTA for her performance in our film – her confrontation with Barbie is one of its most powerful scenes. *Jewel* won just about everything at BAFTA in 1985. There were two notable omissions: Ken Taylor could not even be nominated – there was, absurdly, no category for Best Adaptation; and George Fenton's evocative music lost

With (from second left) Christopher Morahan, Dame Peggy Ashcroft and Jim O'Brien at the BAFTA awards, 1985

out to *Robin Hood*! For me, these injustices undermined the validity of the many awards we *did* win.

Judy knew from the start that Dame Peg was likely to win her category, but Judy had *always* been wryly cynical about 'the business'. In Simla, she found a tailor to make her a fantastic silver fox fur floor-length coat – attitudes to fur were more relaxed at that time. When asked why she was being so extravagant, she replied, with a smile, 'The better dressed you are at the first interview, darling, the bigger their first offer!' Judy always had an aura of glamour, and with the wind of *Jewel* in her sails she spent many happy years working in Los Angeles. She joked that there were five stages to her career, and this is what they were:

1 Who is Judy Parfitt?
2 Judy Parfitt is too young.
3 Get me Judy Parfitt!
4 Judy Parfitt is too old.
5 Who is Judy Parfitt?

Extending the self-defined limits of her own career, she has recently been giving some of the younger members of the cast acting lessons as Sister Monica Jean in the BBC's *Call the Midwife*.

The boat may not leave on time, but it does go more than once!

Before *Jewel* was screened I had a call from my agent, telling me that Michael Codron, the best producer in the West End, was mounting a new play by Michael Frayn – one of our classiest writers – to be directed by Michael Blakemore – one of our finest directors. Codron, Frayn and Blakemore formed the impressive trio which had created *Noises Off*, and this felt like my territory. They asked me to look at Michael's play, and, if I liked it, choose which of the two men I wanted to play. *Benefactors* is a four-hander, two men, two women. I opted for the less prominent of the two men's parts, because I did not quite understand the main character, who was excellently played by Oliver Cotton. Patricia Hodge was his wife, and Brenda Blethyn stole the show as mine. It's wonderful to play great parts from our classic tradition, but the thing an actor really wants – it's certainly what I look for – is a good new play, and here it very clearly was. This meant that just as *Jewel* finished screening I opened in an outstanding production of a new play in the West End. I was only adequate in the part, but the play did well, winning every Best Play Award that year.

It was a very happy time. Pam was at the National Theatre playing Clover in Peter Hall's production of *Animal Farm*, which was stunning, and it was easy for us to meet up after the play. The Vaudeville is a West End theatre which is very close to the NT and I remember this geography feelingly, because one day I stood outside our theatre talking to Michael Codron. He had moved the centre of his activities from Shaftesbury Avenue because it was becoming less glamorous, and the development of Covent Garden had brought crowds further East. Michael was happy in his new patch, but he pointed out that, within a mile of where we stood, there were now two state-subsidised buildings – the NT and the Barbican, then home to the RSC – offering *five* competing auditoria. Times were getting tougher for the commercial sector. Michael Frayn's *Copenhagen*, with the same team – Codron and Blakemore – many years later, opened at the Cottesloe (now the Dorfman), before transferring to the West End. This form of subsidised, pre-commercial try-out has become more and more common. Perhaps the most successful example of it has been *Les Misérables*. When the RSC was in financial difficulty in the early 2000s, the continuing royalties from *Les Miz* helped see them through.

It really did seem that everybody watched *Jewel*, which featured in Jak's *Evening Standard* cartoon three times. The first cartoon related to a catering dispute. The second caught a moment in time when the Yorkshire and England batsman Geoffrey Boycott had made insensitive, uncensored – undoubtedly true – noises about the difficulties of staying healthy and playing cricket in Pakistan. Jak drew a cricket ground, with billboards displaying ads for Collis Brown and the like. The pitch is peopled by heavily bearded – Pakistani – fielders staring at the new batsman, who just happens to be ... one-armed Ronald Merrick. The caption reads: 'The rest of the team flew home sick, but luckily Colonel

183

Merrick was making a sequel to *Jewel in the Crown*!' My agent, Jeremy, generously bought me the original of this cartoon for the first night of *Benefactors*. Interestingly, Jak was not the only one to spot a similarity between Merrick and Boycott. In its 'Lookalike' picture spot, *Private Eye* showed the great man, with *my* name captioned beneath. Next to ... a picture of *me* in a solar topee, with GB's name underneath. The target of both the picture and the cartoon was Boycott's apparent racism.

Jak's funniest cartoon appeared just after the screening of our last episode. He drew a suburban garden in which a large, temple-like pile of logs has been built. On top of the logs is lying an army woman, with a flaming torch in her hand. She is about to set fire to the logs beneath her: this is someone from Surbiton committing 'self-suttee', quite a shocking but amusing idea. Two neighbours are watching this ritual and one of them comments: 'Doris has taken the end of the *Jewel in the Crown* very badly'.

Jewel was the last really successful mini-series. Granada's next venture, *Lost Empires*, was about the vanished world of the music halls, but it did not achieve mass appeal and was jokingly known in the profession as 'Lost Tempers'. But times were changing and the fate of the mini-series in England is demonstrated by the following facts. In 1997, Chris Morahan finally got to make that other great project which he had been working on for many years: *A Dance to the Music of Time*, Anthony Powell's stunning magnum opus. *Jewel* was an adaptation of *four* large books over *14* episodes. Thirteen years later, the *12* books of *The Music of Time* were reduced to *six* episodes! Broadcasters had by then lost faith in the format. Mini-series were costly, and if they failed you lost big money. The Americans, with some of their great series like *The West Wing*, *Breaking Bad* and *House of Cards*, have gone back to the extended story – soap opera; it is a natural form for television drama.

Fashions changed, but Margaret Thatcher had it in for the media. Disgracefully, she put the BBC under pressure to play the statistics game, one which our present government has, ironically, reversed, in yet another right-wing attempt to undermine an institution which is the envy of the world. But Thatcher's cleverest move was to weaken the opposition by redistributing the independent television company franchises. Anyone who said this would result in a lowering of standards was dismissed as a prophet of doom, but it has become harder and harder to make decent television, and when drama is forced to play the numbers game, standards will not rise! If you want more people to watch, reopen the Colosseum tomorrow.

Back in 1962 when my mum and dad finally bought a telly, I was able to broaden my theatrical education by watching great drama on television – Shakespeare, of course, Chekhov, Ibsen, Shaw, Sophocles, Wilde, Pinter. In the early seventies, when Chris Morahan was head of plays at the BBC, on average 90 pieces of new drama were produced a year – nearly two new plays a week! Not possible today. I find our current fare depressingly parochial. And there is less *of* it. As a young man, Sir Denis Forman, *Jewel*'s mighty executive producer, embraced the medium of television because of its democratic power. Sir Denis lived into his nineties, and acknowledged in his later years that television was not as easy, productive or exciting as it had been when he and the medium were young. Ronald Merrick belonged to an earlier time.

Merrick was not only harried by people who threw stones at him. Another symbol of his corruption was a mangled bicycle – dumped, anonymously outside his quarters, to remind him of his perversion of justice. On the press night of *Benefactors*, in April 1984 – almost as our final episode was being screened – Charlie Dance, in a moment of crazed inspiration, deposited a mangled old bike at the stage door of the Vaudeville Theatre. The picture made the *Evening Standard*.

Jewel is the mangled bicycle of my career – it's always on my doorstep. It never goes away. I can tell when it is being screened, or the DVD has been reissued, because people stop me in the street and I get more fan mail. How lucky I was to have been part of such an extraordinary piece of television, something that audiences still remember 30 years after it was made. When I came through the stage door of the Music Box, where I played King Charles III in 2015, I was humbled by the huge

The first night of Benefactors *by Michael Frayn, Vaudeville
Theatre stage door, 1984*

distances old fans of *Jewel* had flown to see me. They came from all over – Boston, Miami, California.

One of the people I was most fortunate to get to know while filming *Jewel* was Dame Peggy Ashcroft, and the next chapter is devoted to her because she, and people like her, are being too fast forgotten.

19

DAME PEG

When I went back to Stratford in 2001 to play Cassius in *Julius Caesar* for Ed Hall, we rehearsed in the Ashcroft Room, the most beautiful rehearsal space in the country, above the Swan Theatre, on the site of the old theatre that was burnt down in 1926. With its high vaulted ceilings and long windows looking out across the Avon to the verdant Warwickshire countryside, it is a practical, holy space, a fitting memorial to a great actress.

After some weeks, one of the young actors said to me, 'Why is this called the Ashcroft Room?' He had not noticed that the staircase is lined with pictures of Dame Peg, cuttings about her, many of her awards certificates; there might even be a BAFTA mask there. Even more upsetting, when shown this display he still had no idea who Dame Peg was.

I was shocked that an actor in his late twenties did not know that Dame Peggy Ashcroft, who had been dead exactly ten years, was a founding member of the company for which he was now plying his trade. It is arguable that without her he would not have been there, because in 1964, when Dame Peg and I first met, Peter Hall – inspired by a visit to England from Brecht and his legendary Berliner Ensemble – had just formed the Royal Shakespeare Company. Wanting to build the first real acting troupe in this country, Peter needed the commitment of a major star, a magnet to attract other quality actors. His first call was to Dame Peg, and when she said yes without a moment's hesitation, other leading actors came on board – Donald Sinden, Eric Porter, William Squire, Roy Dotrice. This represented, from everyone, not just an *artistic* decision, but a political commitment to something new that reflected the social developments of a changing world.

Set this against theatre in Leicester at the time – run down and unsupported – where the old Haymarket closed – something my father reported unhappily in his paper. One evening Dad said he had to interview the theatre manager. 'Had I done my homework?' I had. 'Did I want to come with him to the theatre?' I did.

While Dad worked, I sat alone in the empty balcony and watched the last play staged at the soon-to-be-demolished Haymarket. It was a drawing-room comedy, and the poor actors were working overtime to get something out of the dribble of paying customers, scattered about the stalls. I remember a tall, curved proscenium arch, framing a fragile, spare set, and on it a lovely, lively woman in a yellow dress with a cigarette holder. She fluttered and sparkled – the only thing that seemed alive down there on the distant stage. I was entranced and saddened that a performer of such energy and beauty was stuck in this tangibly decaying world. Osborne's *The Entertainer* – which captures the atmosphere of the dying days of the music hall – always reminds me of this doomed yellow butterfly.

Before the RSC, the Memorial Theatre held an annual summer season of Shakespeare, mounted by Barry Jackson and Anthony Quayle, who were building it into a theatre of international repute by asking great actors and emerging directors to work there. The first play I saw there was *The Merchant of Venice*, with Emlyn Williams as Shylock. One of my most powerful memories was of Dame Peg as Katherine in *The Taming of the Shrew* in 1959.

Opposite the young and emerging Peter O'Toole, she was fiery and funny. At their first meeting, waiting for her to appear, O'Toole hid behind the door. My first sight of Peg was entering like a tigress, twirling her long auburn pigtail aggressively. The apparently empty room took the wind out of her sails; Petruchio slid up behind her, took her by surprise – *big* laugh – and the contest between them, one of witty equals who were immediately drawn to each other, was under way. O'Toole was charm incarnate and he got the better of their first contest, as Petruchio should, with a piece of delicious business. O'Toole was thin and very tall. He sat on a stool, stretched his legs out downstage left, crossed them, and leant back on his elbow on a sturdy inn table. Thus arranged, he looked about ten feet long! In his free hand he held a tankard. Dame Peg tiptoed up behind him – you knew she was going to push the stool away and dump him ignominiously on the floor. Petruchio pontificated. Kate crept up, and, with her foot, shoved the stool from under him. It went skidding downstage. But O'Toole did not move a muscle. He remained absolutely as he was – a long, thin, unmoved bridge. Then he took a swig from his beer mug. Fabulous. More furious pigtail-swirling and stamping of feet ensued.

Featuring the diminutive Jack MacGowran as Christopher Sly, running wildly up and down the stairs of a glorious revolving Lila de Nobili set – taking us inside and outside an Elizabethan inn – it was theatrical magic. When, in the final scene, Dame Peg placed her hand, as the text requires, *beneath her husband's foot*, it was not a gesture of submission, but one of public acknowledgement that she had met her match. There was also a twinkle in her eye that said – 'It won't be like this when we're on our own, you know.' I have never seen another *Shrew* with anything like the same humour, sexiness and genuine sense of love that Peg and O'Toole generated.

The Shrew has recently been bogged down in deadening sexual politics which kill the central motor of the play. You cannot allow modern moral judgements to subvert the ethics of a play. The racism of *The Merchant of Venice* might not be to our liking, but it *is* the play, and if you don't engage with it the play does not happen. Inevitably, you filter things through your own contemporary mindset, but you change the ethical motors within a play at your peril.

Before that performance of *The Shrew*, the audience stood for the National Anthem. It was around this time that the great Guy Wolfenden orchestrated the piece to create an uplifting Elizabethan atmosphere, but the real move away from the past was the fact that there was no curtain: the stage was open! This was still not the norm, but it signalled another conscious change: theatre was no longer an act which allowed an audience to peep in on a concealed, secret world: the audience was now acknowledged to be in the same space as the actors. This echoed Brecht's great phrase 'We are working, not cheating'. And here, at the forefront of change, was Dame Peg. I wanted to *be* O'Toole, but I was fascinated by Dame Peg.

As an enraptured teenager, I learnt from theatre magazines that not only was she a respected and established actress who had long been successful, but that she was also something of a political activist. And she evidently liked men. The moral climate was very different before the war, but Dame Peg had been married more than once, first to Rupert Hart-Davis, who graduated from acting to a distinguished publishing career, then, very briefly to the Russian director Theodore Komisarjevsky, and later (in 1940) to the distinguished liberal QC Jeremy Hutchinson.

Dame Peg had a career that was conspicuous almost from the start. She was lauded by the critic Harold Hobson for her appearance in *Jew Süss*, in 1929, and there is a very beautiful still of her as Naemi. She *always* seemed to get good notices. In 1930 she played Desdemona opposite the legendary Paul Robeson, with whom she had a brief affair. Again her gifts transcended what was regarded as an ordinary production: *she* came out of it well. As for the affair, her conscience was stirred – so the legend ran – by the fact that Robeson, playing Othello at the Savoy Theatre, was not allowed to reside at the adjacent Savoy Hotel because of his colour.

Gielgud invited Dame Peg to join his Old Vic Company in the early thirties, and it was here that she began to cut her teeth on decent parts – Mary Stuart, Lady Teazle, Kate Hardcastle. One of the features of Dame Peg's eightieth birthday celebrations at the Old Vic was her turn as Lilian Bayliss – with idiosyncratic glasses and a slightly off accent – one of Peg's specialities. The young actor who had not heard of Dame Peggy Ashcroft is, I am sure, equally ignorant of Lilian Bayliss. So ... forgive me:

Bayliss is part of theatre folklore. At the Old Vic, that unfashionable spot south of the river, she ran an adventurous repertoire on a shoestring, salvaging the theatre from its always precarious fate. She had a demanding relationship with God, to whom she used to pray for funding! And she would fry up in the prompt corner – outrageous behaviour which would not be tolerated nowadays. There are stories of her ghost at the Old Vic: Sheila Allen told me that on her first entrance on to the stage, a female whom she took to be LB materialised, slapped her face harshly and vanished. I have never *seen* a ghost back-stage at the Vic, but I *have* caught a strong whiff of bacon in the prompt corner!

Peter Shaffer told me an amusing anecdote about LB. One day she was knocked down by a large omnibus in the Waterloo road. She lay on the road as a small crowd of onlookers gathered round. Only her legs could be seen, protruding from under the bus, so someone asked who the victim was.

The reply came, 'It's Lilian Bayliss.'

'Lilian Bayliss?'

'She saved the Old Vic!'

Then, from underneath the omnibus, came LB's voice, loud and clear, '*And* Sadler's Wells!'

It was under this unconventional woman's aegis that, through-out the thirties, Peg developed her classical powers on Chekhov and Shakespeare.

She was not drawn then to the cinema, and if you watch Hitchcock's 1935 *The Thirty-Nine Steps* you can see why: she has dignity and beauty – emphasised by her pale, almost white skin – but she is ill at ease with the accent and seems uncomfort-able as a Scottish crofter's wife. She displays the theatre actor's tendency to be slightly too large for the camera, and, conse-quently, she appears a bit melodramatic. This unusual display of something untruthful in her work is horribly unrepresentative. It was not until much later in life that she came to enjoy acting for the lens. She did not have much fun doing *A Passage to India*, feeling bullied by the director, David Lean, but her performance as Mrs Moore won her a BAFTA and an Oscar, by which time she had also won a BAFTA for Barbie in *Jewel*. After the screening of *Jewel*, she said she was regularly recognised in the street for the first time in her life.

When I had time to talk to her – on long days filming in India – I learnt that she had done a play called *The Silver Cord*, with Fabia Drake, who was now playing Mabel Layton, her landlady. Fabia, then the leading lady, had advised the young ingénue to change her name, as she thought Peggy somewhat common. Fabia and Dame Peg, filming out in India, had not worked together in the intervening 56 years, and Fabia wryly admitted that Peg had had the last laugh.

My favourite scene in the entire series is a short one between these two veterans. Mabel (Fabia) is in bed and Peg, the lacklustre missionary and tenant, pops in to check that she is all right for the night. Mabel has fallen asleep, reading: Barbie removes her spectacles and retrieves her book with great tenderness. She makes to go, but Mabel stirs and asks Barbie to stay and talk. This is an intimate development in their relationship, surprising to Barbie, who thinks she is boring and unwanted. She stays, sitting on Mabel's bed, and talks. It's not a long scene, but it is spellbinding and the dialogue was entirely the invention of our adapter, Ken Taylor.

What Dame Peg always found in the theatre were the joint strands of established classics – Viola, Nina, Mistress Page, Cordelia, Electra, Madame Ranevskaya – and the chance to cut her teeth on new work. These two elements guided her career to the end. She had a great hit with Marguerite Duras' *Days of the Trees* in 1966. In the 1970s I saw her at the Aldwych in Pinter and Albee, still taking risks. She performed more Pinter, and Beckett's *Happy Days,* at the National in the seventies. You might label the eighties her camera decade – *Caught on a Train, Jewel, A Passage to India, She's Been Away*. Her last appearance onstage was as the Countess in *All's Well* for the RSC: she had a gift for autumnal sadness which this play and Trevor Nunn's superb, delicate production exploited, and through it shone Peg's very own love of youth. She also loved cricket, and relished developments like the radio Walkman that allowed her to keep abreast of the action.

Only people who care about the wrong things need you to know they are important, so acting with her seemed quite normal. You just felt you were working with another actress, not a great, long-established star. She was unashamed to display insecurity. Barbie is a garrulous character, and Peg loved to sit and run the lines, because Barbie always had lots to say. I went through the lines, not just of my big scene with her, but several other scenes. She would sometimes ask a question, 'Do you think I should throw that line away, or is it important?' or even, 'Do you think that's all right, that bit?' She never threw her weight around, treated everyone as an equal, never admitted to being fatigued by the stress of living and working in Simla at 8,000 feet, and joined in with company fun. One day, when the weather did not cooperate, a large group of actors had to wait indoors for a long time, as potential rain cover. We played charades. Dame Peg joined in.

Having got to know Peg on *Jewel*, she kept in touch, came to see our work in the theatre and involved us in her life. On one occasion she asked me to read some political poems with her on behalf of Amnesty, at the behest of the Dean of Westminster. We read in Star Chamber – an astoundingly beautiful room so named because of the stars painted on its blue ceiling – whose court records go back to 1485. Henry IV died in this room. It was a great privilege.

Peg rang one day and said that she had been asked to help an Indian charity. She knew that I had an anthology in my repertoire – *Passages to India*. Pam and I used to perform it with Zia Mohyeddin (Mohammad Ali 'Mak' Kasim in *Jewel*) and Viram Jasani, a sitar player, and it was later published in a different form as *Out of India*. Dame Peg wondered if she might prevail upon Pam and me to perform our anthology with her. We were happy to do this, but Peg only needed 40 minutes, so I popped round to her house to do some cutting. She poured us both stiff whiskies, took up a horizontal position on the sofa and asked me to read to her. I explained that it was in two parts, roughly an hour and three-quarters in length. She was not perturbed.

With Dame Peggy Ashcroft at a reception for The Jewel in the Crown, *1985*

So I read. Within a few lines of each piece, she said 'Yes' or 'No'. Sometimes she might say, 'Read that one again', but in a couple of hours we had worked our way through the whole anthology and she had cut it to a coherent 40 minutes. It was a much better programme. Her instincts were astounding.

On another occasion I drove her down to the South Bank at five one morning. The remains of the Rose Theatre had been unearthed – then the only Elizabethan theatre ever to have been discovered. The acting profession was attempting to stop developers from building an office block over the revealing footprint of this old theatre. Dame Peg was in the forefront of this movement, appearing on a rickety platform at one end of the site while an enormous pile driver approached ominously from behind. She was undaunted. A grisly compromise was reached, but even that would not have been achieved without Dame Peg, whose presence got them to stop the drills and hold talks.

It felt to me that she died quite suddenly. One minute she was there, then, before her time, she was gone. I was angry with myself that I had somehow taken my friendship with her for granted, and never asked her enough about herself, but she had a tendency to deflect such questions. She was not young when she died, 84, but she was always full of youthful energy. She went to Canada to visit family, came back feeling unwell and suddenly she was dead. She had had a stroke. It was 1991, and I was touring with my company, Compass, playing Salieri in *Amadeus*. Peg's memorial service was held, fittingly, at Westminster Abbey. I was asked to read at the ceremony, a fantastic honour, but unfortunately that week we were playing Aberdeen.

I discovered that no one under 30 had a clue who this woman was – this revered star and political activist. Acting is smoke, but to be so soon forgotten is a sign of the changed world we are in. Or maybe it was ever thus.

> O heavens! Die two months ago and not forgotten yet?
> Then there's hope a great man's memory will outlive his life
> half a year.
>
> *Hamlet*

20

THE BITTER SMELL OF SUCCESS

When I was handed success I had no idea what it entailed, although there are enough plays and Hollywood movies about wanting it, fighting for it, getting it and coping with it from which I could have learnt. Modern 'celebrity' started just before *Jewel*, at a time when the eighties were moving us away from a drab decade. Success, for me, was a heady, flattering mix of suddenly being asked to do all manner of things that I had never wanted – big but not necessarily suitable roles, opening fêtes, appearing in charity events, playing cricket for the Lord's Taverners, being asked to put my name to things I knew nothing about – even modelling! This came with the invasive sensation that *everybody* suddenly knew who I was, and all about Pam and Tom. It was grotesque.

Adulation gives you a phoney sense of your importance. People defer to you. They call you a star, although that always made me uneasy. There is a sequence in George Cukor's film *A Star Is Born* when James Mason, quoting the great British actress Ellen Terry, defines being a star is 'having that little bit extra'. I felt I had played a *part* that had *that little bit extra*; if people expected me to bring something special to the table I simply was not able to do it. The more pressure I felt, the less able I felt to provide the stardust people were waiting for. But success is alluring, and, like a fool, I lost sight of what it was I wanted. If it hadn't been for Pam I might have got completely lost. In acting, the least bit of self-importance is destructive. I now believe that it isn't until you see yourself as completely insignificant that you can really serve a play. This is tricky, because without self-confidence and self-belief an actor can't get out of bed in the morning. So you learn a complicated balancing act.

Take this scenario: you are on your way to your first morning's rehearsal of a new play – an apprehensive time – you are vulnerable, nervous. Will you be any good in the part? Will the play hold up? Will the cast be nice? Will the director be a schmuck? You see a large poster outside the theatre – a poster featuring your name and your face – which advertises the play you are about to begin work on. As you approach the theatre a couple of people thank you generously for your work. You arrive at the stage door feeling quite good about the world. The stage door person looks at you as though you are a dangerous intruder, and says, 'Yeah?'

Do you point out that if the stage doorkeeper were to turn round, he/she would see your name and face on a poster? Do you mention that two complete strangers in the street outside just asked for your autograph, but that you, the stage doorkeeper, the one person I have met today who *should* know who I am, does not appear to know what is going on in the theatre that employs you? Well, only an idiot, or someone so insecure that they needed help, would be so foolish. But it *is* bewildering. And the added difficulty for the actor is that your product – what you are selling – is you, *your* face, *your* character. It is deeply personal, and it can be embarrassing and painful not to be recognised.

I heard of a very well-known actor who, thus provoked, asked the dangerous question, 'Do you know who I am?' The withering reply was 'Why? Aren't you sure?' And the truthful answer to *that* question is 'At this moment I really am not at *all* sure who I am.' A good stage door will welcome you warmly: 'Ah, Mr. Pigott-Smith, how nice to have you here. Here is your mail. Tea and coffee in Rehearsal Room One ...' That's all it takes and you will feel slightly less like going to the job exchange!

When I was talking regularly to students I developed a theory for them, that – assuming they all wanted to be actors in 30 years' time – it was useful for them to have in mind what *kind* of an actor that would be – a great classical actor, a light comedian, a soap star, a farceur, a film star, a musical star? It helps to *define* yourself by thinking I would like to be ... Laurence Olivier, or Ruby Wax, or David Jason, or Meryl Streep, or Danny La Rue. This gives you a constant sense of direction (which I lost, briefly). It helps with large decisions such as should I do this play? And it guides smaller issues such as do I like this play enough to take my clothes off? You might *have* to show your arse just to pay the rent, and there is nothing wrong with earning a living, but this helps you decide where to draw the line.

I always wanted to be a leading actor in the theatre. I started off clearly enough, and it was undeniably a thrill, in the wake of *Jewel*, to see my name in lights above the awning of the Vaudeville Theatre, because I was proud to be appearing in a fine new play that had something to say. But I didn't stay focused. Frustrated by the work I was being offered, I looked for ways of doing things on my own. I have always resented the random lack of responsibility of being an actor: standing in line to be chosen or rejected. I am impatient, and it would have made more sense for me to have waited, but I commissioned a one-man play. They were fashionable at the time.

Over the nearly two years I worked on *Jewel*, I read 'Indian' literature – anything I could lay my hands on about India: history, novels, poetry and biographies – like *Bengal Lancer* by Francis Yeats-Brown. This remarkable book was very different from the dopey Hollywood movie into which it had been turned, featuring Gary Cooper. Two things in it really appealed to me: I had an instinct that Y-B, as I came to call him, was a performer, and I was intrigued by his interest in yoga, because at the time I practised regularly. When we were filming in Mysore, I found a guru: indeed, I went to what he called his Yoga Workshop every day for nearly four weeks. My guru was a monster who taught Ashtanga yoga mercilessly, but he really put me through some stuff in the small hours of the morning, and it was an unforgettable experience. No pain, no gain was his mantra. A young American girl he was teaching said he took liberties with her while he was 'helping' her. Dirty old guru.

As a lancer, Y-B became a member of the most romantic of all regiments in 1907. When he developed an interest in Indian spiritualism – unusual for any Englishman at that time, let alone a soldier – he didn't go back home when he had leave, he went to Benares, found a guru and studied yoga. The First World War converted cavalry regiments into the Royal Flying Corps. That is why, in photographs – and the BBC's *Wings* – airmen wear jodhpurs. Some Lancer regiments were deployed, and Y-B found himself flying reconnaissance planes over Turkey. When his aircraft was damaged on a forced landing during a reconnaissance mission, he was taken prisoner. In a violent Turkish prison what saved him was his yoga. After the war he returned to Benares, hoping to study full time, but his guru told him he had spent too long on the path of violence to be able to devote himself unequivocally to the spiritual demands that yoga would make of him. That is where the book *Bengal Lancer* ends. Y-B returned home, became a writer. Like a surprising number of people, he placed his faith in Hitler and Nazism as a bulwark against communism. When he realised he had backed the wrong horse, he dwindled away, a broken man.

When I discovered (in one of his other books, *Lancer at Large*) that Y-B had dressed up more than once to escape from prison, it added to my suspicion that here was a man who was playing roles in life – romantic soldier, spiritual disciple, escapee – because he was in search of himself. This quest for self made it ideal in my mind for a play.

I met William Ayot, who had a knowledge of India, and wanted desperately to be a full-time writer, although he was obliged to pay for his writing vice at that time by being a croupier. Willy wrote a sample 15/20 pages. He was clearly gifted, inventive, liked rich language, had a sense of humour and emotional awareness, so I commissioned him to write the play. I gave him some guidelines, and the main one was that I wanted to play, not just Y-B, the central figure, but – following the notion that Y-B was a performer – other roles in the play, other people that he spoke

With Mark Buffery in Sexual Perversity in Chicago *by David Mamet,*
Bristol Old Vic, 1978

about. The driving idea was that, through becoming other people, Y-B was trying on different personalities in search of his own.

Willy wrote a massive draft offering me 23 parts! It was crazy, but the core was true. Michael Joyce, with whom I had done the British première of David Mamet's *Sexual Perversity* at Bristol Old Vic, was keen to direct, and David Aukin, then the general manager of the Haymarket, Leicester, offered us a budget and the studio. Bob Crowley agreed to design, George Fenton came on board for the music, and we set about the massive task of caging the mad beast Willy had unleashed. Our overriding aim was to create a play, not a 'one-man show'. *Krapp's Last Tape* is not a one-man show, it is a play for one actor. During the run of *Benefactors*, and while filming a disastrous movie called *Chain Reaction,* with Martin Sheen in Paris, I learnt the monster, and taught myself unhorsed lance drill from an old Lancer training manual.

The movie could have been good, but in the event it was a stinker. I was playing a priest in a fascinating story about a nuclear scientist who develops conscientious objections to his work. The intelligent script offered good reasons to be wary of nuclear proliferation, and was funded, I discovered, by the Blue Army: the blue of the army being the blue of the Virgin's robes. One central image in the movie was the appearance of the Virgin to the children in Fatima – a famous twentieth-century miracle.

God is bad box office, but this script led you brilliantly to those spiritual areas which were both at the film's core and its greatest commercial danger. When I discovered that Martin and the director were born-again Christians, I suspected we might be in trouble. On the day I met 'the money', I knew we were scuppered.

When 'the money' appears on a film set, people behave differently. Everything has to appear shipshape, a worthy investment of insane amounts of money. I was aware that the atmosphere in the studio was heightened when suddenly ... I saw 'the money' – a tall woman with a lot of blonde hair and noticeably red lips, dressed in ... well ... blue. She was a nice woman, but the *Virgin Mary* blue was unnerving.

We were chatting – necessarily about the brilliance of the script – when she said, 'Do you know how you got this job?' I suggested that my agent had put me up for it. 'No,' she said sweetly but firmly. I offered that it might have been through David Graham, the LA casting director. 'No,' she said, firmly and not so sweetly. I admitted that she was going to have to tell me how I got the film. 'Your birthday,' she said, smiling, 'is the same day as the first appearance of the Virgin to the girls in Fatima.' I knew the film was sunk. I know only one person who has seen this film, and he said it was so badly lit it was hard to see anything at all. Or, indeed, *hear* anything, because the dialogue was drowned out by religious music. 'Tim,' he said, 'it really is the worst movie ever made.'

My one-man play *Bengal Lancer* was uncharted waters, but at least I had some small element of control. We all knew that what we started with was not what we would end up with, because Willy had provided us with some potent stuff, pushing the boundaries as requested, but in the process creating some high fences to be cleared. In the first half, I had to 'shower', and then redress myself in full Lancer gear, which is quite impressive. It is nevertheless easier to write *Y-B dresses in full Lancer uniform* than to achieve it ... swiftly ... on your own.

In the end I emerged from my shower – a tantalising gauze drape – putting my jodhpurs on; then boots with boot hooks; then the tunic – easy; then – help! – a 4-yard cummerbund – this was why British officers needed personal staff. Bob provided me with a fixed upright bamboo pole, downstage right, to which I knotted the cummerbund. I was then able to stretch it to its full length across the stage. Wrapping it once round my waist, I spun my way across, twisting into the cummerbund, freeing the tied end and tucking it in. I then slung the sword belt and popped a ready-made turban on my head. When really slick, it earned a round, but it took a lot of figuring out.

My reading had unearthed a book called *Two Monsoons* by Theon Wilkinson, so-named because if an English child survived two monsoons in India he stood a good chance of reaching

Bengal Lancer, *Leicester Haymarket and Lyric Hammersmith, 1985*

adulthood. Many, of course, didn't, and Willy wove one epitaph into this haunting sequence which opened the second half. Y-B was by now in kurta and pyjama, mirroring his spiritual move away from being a Lancer towards India.

> Further along the road, beyond the jheel lake, stood an
> ancient banyan tree. Huge tree. Its branches had rooted
> long ago, forming a vault like the bones of a ruined
> church. Inside, in its quiet shade, stood a group of crosses,
> Victorian graves. All children. 'Lucy – from the cholera'.
> 'Georgie from a snake'. 'Amelia Jane. Departed this life
> the tenth of April 1857. Aged seven months, seven days
> and one hour'. With the inscription – 'In the morning it
> was green and growing up. In the evening it was cut and
> withered like a flower'.

Willy's language was rich and muscular, good to speak, but the constant textual changes in rehearsal were demanding in the extreme, and as I was the only actor I never had a break. Every day we cut and honed and gradually found a way for me to become all the different (16) characters, and revert seamlessly to being Y-B.

The sands of time and memory were my environment: the relic of a Nandi – a sacred Indian bull – which emerged from the sandpit Bob had created – and a small, gauze-covered table were the only bits of set. All the props I required were half buried in the sand. I picked them out when needed, as though they were ancient memories. Situation is a fundamental challenge in a one-person piece, but as the play developed, we created a style which gave us freedom to take real risks, so that my morphing in and out of the different characters was clear, and part of the pleasure for the audience: I jumped on to the Nandi, with polo stick in hand and solar topee on head, changed accent to sporty gung-ho, and then described and 'participated in' a polo match; to the hummed – pre-recorded – Death March from Handel's *Saul*, Y-B supported and slow-marched a mimed coffin, as he described the death of its inmate; the guru sat cross-legged beneath an old umbrella. It was simple, fluent and fun. There was, of course, a snake sequence. Removing my belt in preparation for going to bed, I placed it carefully, curled on the small table. With clever lighting, this belt 'became' the snake.

The Turkish prison was interesting: Y-B, although not tortured himself, could hear other prisoners being abused – hung upside down so the soles of their feet could be beaten. Y-B described this vividly, adding that his yoga helped him cope. I was barefoot in the second half, so for this prison sequence I did a headstand – which I had always found easy – and spoke the whole 'bastinado' section standing on my head, which, as well as being quite unusual, gave the audience images both of yoga and foot beating.

Acting on your own is hard and unrewarding, but as the characters and situations became more extreme, we increased the risk, so towards the end I stood atop a mound of the sandpit, wearing a sort of sadhu's jockstrap; I filled a brass pot with water, from a mighty brass urn buried in the sand, and poured it over myself; this was Y-B bathing in the Ganges. Draped in a long piece of pink silk, I even managed to assume the character of a young Indian girl. It was dangerous, but her only line was magic: 'One does not fall in love, one rises into it'. After good reviews in Leicester, the show sold out instantly.

We came to town, to the Lyric Hammersmith. The poster there read Tim Pigott-Smith as Francis Yeats-Brown, produced by Robert Cogo-Fawcett ... well it made *me* laugh. We did respectable business. In those days, I used to look at reviews when the show was over. The press was very kind, apart from the aptly named Martin Cropper (or was it Cutter?), who wrote that I was a reasonable actor, to a certain level, with a small talent for narration. The story goes that this man was so disliked by other critics they had him removed. The *Observer* liked it very much and gave perhaps the truest description of it as a 'labour of love'. It *was* – I was in love with India.

The play brought the great reward of getting to know Y-B's delightful family. One of the themes of Willy's play was time. Partly to illustrate this, before I even spoke I took out a half-hunter, looked closely at it, tapped it and slipped it into my waistcoat pocket. When Y-B's daughter saw this, she told me her heart stopped. Every morning, her father would descend the stairs; every morning he would stop in front of the grandfather clock, take out his chained pocket watch, and tap it – the exact gesture I had employed. Engage the imagination and you are using a powerful and sometimes spooky tool. She was so affected, she gave me Y-B's Lancer insignia, an overwhelmingly generous and treasured gift. If your work touches one person as deeply as that, critics can say what they like.

21

BACK TO THE THEATRE

The best piece of work I did before I got back on track was a film for the BBC, playing the scientist Francis Crick, alongside Jeff Goldblum as James Watson. When the director Mick Jackson, whom I had known since university, took me out to lunch to interest me in the movie he was making about the secret of DNA, I nearly fell asleep over the soup. More fool me. When I read William Nicholson's script, *Life Story* – based on Watson's book *The Double Helix* – I devoured an exciting discovery movie which offered a magical glimpse of understanding of something infinitely complex, and provided a challenging moral commentary on the world of scientific fame and fortune.

At Cambridge University in the early fifties Crick and Watson made questionable use of Rosalind Franklin's research. She was working with Maurice Wilkins at King's College London, and although she and Wilkins were not participating in a race to find DNA, they were outflanked by the more ambitious combination of Crick and Watson, who smelled a Nobel prize for first past the post.

When we met for rehearsal, Mick spoke briefly, then asked Jeff if he needed a script for the read-through. Jeff said, 'Do you want to start?' Mick nodded, and Jeff set off. He knew the entire script. He changed one word, and explained why. I have never seen anything like it before or since, although, recently, the director Stephen Frears told me that at their read-through of *Florence Foster Jenkins* Meryl Streep performed the whole thing, songs and all. The downside was that at the end of a week's rehearsal

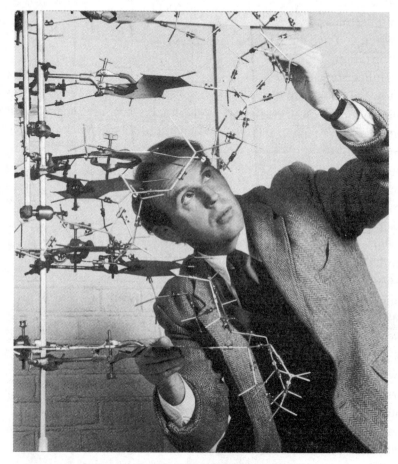

Francis Crick in Life Story, *BBC TV, 1985*

Jeff was bored, so when we started shooting he would pump up his energy by reading P. G. Wodehouse, aloud, in a sort of cod Noël Coward accent. The first assistant would call 'Action!', but if Jeff was mid-paragraph he would finish the section he was on, throw the book over his shoulder, cry, 'Come on, Timmo!', and off we would trot! There were days when this was infectious and useful, and other days when I would say to the first assistant, 'When you need me, I shall be behind that tree.' Jeff's cabaret was entertaining but it was dangerous to be sucked into the lunacy!

Juliet Stevenson was stunning as Rosalind Franklin, and Alan Howard consummate as Wilkins. After dinner one night during the shoot in Cambridge, Alan and I were walking back to our hotel and we passed the Cavendish. By chance, Mick had shown me – and I was able to point out to Alan – a sole light, burning in a basement window. Max Perutz worked with Crick and Watson on DNA, and he was still beavering away, late at night, in the same lab, over 30 years later. Alan gazed in wonder at this glimmer of light, and said, flatly, 'Mmmn. Not like acting, then.'

Life Story is an extraordinary film, winning a BAFTA in 1987 and helping Mick progress from filmmaking under the aegis of the BBC's *Horizon*, to Hollywood. When I was in LA, I visited him and remarked on the beauty of his house, which overlooks the Pacific. Mick nodded and said, with a wry smile, '*The Bodyguard.*'

Life Story was the sort of gem that could only have been made by the BBC at that time, but I did not feel I was really back on track until Peter Hall asked me to go to the National to do a new Stephen Poliakoff, *Coming in to Land,* starring Maggie Smith, and play Octavius Caesar in *Antony and Cleopatra* with Anthony Hopkins and Judi Dench.

When we placed *Coming in to Land* on the stage in rehearsal, you could see a fault line running right through it. It still offered a good evening's entertainment, and I had great fun as a customs official toying with Maggie's Smith's Polish would-be immigrant, but almost everyone who saw it commented on the incredibility of a wealthy yuppie bothering to assist an older, down-and-out

Polish woman to enter the country illegally, by marrying her. This was disappointing because on paper it had looked like a work of genius; at least I could look forward to *Antony and Cleopatra*, and I had experienced working with a great actress. Maggie Smith seemed slightly down through rehearsals, sensing maybe that the play was not quite what we had hoped. Through technicals and previews, her tension increased. She was demanding, living on a knife edge of danger, and, more than anyone I have ever worked with, she has the ability to keep things alive. We did 50 sell-out performances of the play, and the last one felt as fresh as the first. Maggie did not seem to be acting. I felt as though she was making it up; and I was learning again.

I had already had the privilege of working on Shakespeare with John Barton, and I was keen to learn more from Peter Hall. Peter *did* advocate a fairly rigid approach, but his aim was to create a kind of jazz – freedom within form. As a purist, I agree with him that you cannot enjoy the freedom until you honour the form. With an unprecedented 12 weeks' rehearsal on *Antony and Cleopatra* I decided that for six weeks I would do nothing more than implement Peter's theories about the verse. Something interesting happened ...

People started saying, 'Really surprising character you've got coming.' I was a bit miffed – I hadn't started acting. But this was a lesson. *Antony and Cleopatra* is a late play, and, by this stage of his career, Shakespeare, if you follow the verse, creates your character for you. Octavius is traditionally played as a cold, calculating fish, but by observing the text and the verse I was discovering a man of profound emotion. When Shakespeare wants tears, he puts it in the language, and there are clear references in the play to Octavius's emotions. On one occasion Enobarbus comments, 'Will Caesar weep?' To which Agrippa replies, saltily, 'He has a cloud in's face.' When he hears of Antony's death Octavius says, 'It is tidings to wash the eyes of kings.'

I loved the way Peter worked, so I just went with it. He has a great ear and, being musical, a natural sense of rhythm – one scene short and sharp, the next languorous, flowing, the next loud and harsh. He would ask us to repeat a scene – just the lines. Listening intently, he might point out that there was one word that ran through it that he needed to hear more clearly – would we nurse that word, whenever we spoke it – as though he was threading pearls on a string.

The English language was evolving at fantastic speed in the years when Shakespeare was writing, and one feature I relished was the juiciness of French-derived words – *dotage, reneges, emperor* – juxtaposed with Anglo-Saxon words – blunt monosyllables – *lust, stone, man*. Hamlet's 'To be or not to be ...' goes on to ... 'that is the question' – with *question,* a different sounding, different feeling word is placed alongside the monosyllables, and this nourishes their meaning, as it does again with Hamlet's ... 'quintessence of dust'. In the very first speech of *Antony and Cleopatra* we hear that Antony is dangerously obsessed by Cleopatra, his eyes turn ... 'the office and devotion of their view/ Upon a tawny front.' The words *office, devotion* and *view* have a courtly, French ring, even *tawny* has spin. But they slam into *front*. Bam. Point made.

On his best days Peter's elucidation of the text was so profound that you almost felt you were sitting with Shakespeare! I think he became more dogmatic as he got older, because he felt that too few people were teaching verse properly, and it became a mission of his to pass on his immense experience and knowledge, so that a verse-speaking approach *he* claimed went back via Dame Edith Evans and William Poel to Garrick would survive for future generations of actors. This sometimes made him very didactic, which was not characteristic.

He advocated that you should always read the line first with its iambic beat. Any shift of stress needed then becomes evident, and it helps clarify Shakespeare's intention. Saying O _for_ a _Muse_ of _Fire_ ... really confirms that he wants to kick off with a clarion-call, _OOO for a Muse_ of _Fire_ ...

Because blank verse is close to human speech patterns, it is the structure, as much as the language, that poeticises and heightens. I think verse just poured out of Shakespeare, and I suspect he did not have to work hard at its structure, but if you observe and *use* that structure, over the course of an evening, it releases the poet's subconscious energy and has an accumulative effect on the audience. They will not realise what is being done to them, but they are being affected in a way that is not possible if you do *not* observe the structure. *Un*structured Shakespeare is like music without bar lines.

Peter came in to rehearsal one day looking very smug. He explained that he had just instructed his secretary that he was not to be called out of rehearsal for *anything*! He had not been able to give priority to working on a play, over the burden of the building and the company, in the 13 years that he had run the National. The result was a sensational production. Peter used the scope of the Olivier Theatre to its uttermost – with messengers and trumpeters calling and fanfaring from the sides and the back of the auditorium, with exciting entrances and exits through the house. The staging of the monument was dangerous – literally – for both Tony, suspended in a net, and Judi, being helped and lifted down from high above the stage. The opening, after long weeks of rehearsal, was assured and bullish – one of Peter's favourite words. We played a hundred sell-out performances and closed to a standing ovation – not a common thing in English theatre then. My muscles were flexing again.

During the run, Judi was made a dame. The dressing rooms at the National give every impression of having been stuck on at the last minute when the budget was running out. They are arranged over four floors around a square open space, so that from your dressing room you can always see other people, and they can see you. On the night when Judi was made a dame, everyone in the theatre opened their dressing-room windows, leant out and let rip with a joyous chorus of 'There Is Nothin' Like A Dame'!

Another of my maxims is 'It doesn't matter who was offered the part, it matters who ends up playing it'. Peter was unable to cast a star for the role of Henry Moule in *Entertaining Strangers*, and it eventually came my way. This play was an adaptation of a community project that David Edgar had created with Ann

Dame Judi Dench as Sarah Eldridge in Entertaining Strangers *by David Edgar, National Theatre, Cottesloe, 1987*

Jellicoe down in Dorset – where it had benefited from a local cast of 120. It was the true story of a fundamentalist vicar who was hated for his rigorous views when he arrived, but who served his parishioners with such profound faith and courage – being particularly selfless when his flock was struck by cholera – that he eventually won them over. Judi was playing my main antagonist – Sarah Eldridge, owner of the local brewery.

Bill Dudley transformed the Cottesloe (now the Dorfman), creating a green slope that ran its entire length. A steam train arrived, there was a heavenly vision, and this was all done as we rubbed shoulders with our audience. The promenade element of the play was valuable, but we had to learn how to manipulate the audience physically. At one performance I turned around and found myself moving Stephen Sondheim up the grassy slope. At another, I was standing at the bottom of the slope, watching Judi at the top, waiting for my next scene, when I heard that awful *ssh-ticka-ssh-ticka-ssh*, leaking from a Walkman. A teenage boy was watching the play with headphones on. I tapped him on the shoulder, led him to the side and quietly suggested that the noise of his Walkman was troubling. He shrugged. I said, 'It's rude to the audience ... and *us*. Besides,' I added, 'you can't watch a play and listen to music at the same time.' He left.

Failure with teenagers aside, Moule was a wonderful part for me, ageing from 17 to 70. In the final scene Moule was praying by his son's tombstone, snow was falling and the atmosphere was rich as Judi played David Edgar's moving lines to perfection. When Jenny Galloway sang the final number, accompanied by our brilliant folk band, there was rarely a dry eye in the house.

My work at the National concluded with Peter's last project. His time as artistic director was drawing to a close, and the late plays of Shakespeare struck a farewell chord. He was always clear about doing *The Winter's Tale* and *The Tempest*, and eventually decided on *Cymbeline*, in which he asked me to play Iachimo. My other parts were Leontes in *The Winter's Tale*, and Trinculo in *The Tempest*. This was a huge project with an ensemble at its heart: one company – led by Michael Bryant playing Prospero,

Henry Moule in Entertaining Strangers

Iachimo in Cymbeline *with Peter Woodward as Posthumus,*
National Theatre, 1986-88

A villain, a king and a clown – Iachimo, Leontes and Trinculo, publicity image
for Cymbeline, A Winter's Tale *and* The Tempest, *National Theatre,1986-1988*

and the Old Shepherd in *WT* – three plays in three months. It was too much. I discovered that rehearsing three parts simultaneously is impossible. In rep I got used to *playing* one part and *rehearsing* another, but rehearsing three different parts (and, early on in rehearsals, playing two others) created system overload. On my way into the theatre one day, I thought, 'Why don't I just turn the car round and go the other way?' We were overworked and under-rehearsed, not properly ready when we opened. Touring Moscow, Tbilisi, Tokyo and Epidaurus, although quite thrilling, got to us all.

My big role was Leontes, whose jealousy spirals him into fury and madness. He says, in a fevered early soliloquy, 'I have *tremor cordis* on me' – shaking of the heart. This interested me, so I did some research into heart disease and discovered myocarditis, a condition of the heart that affects the brain for about three months. It goes on and off like a tap – just what happens to Leontes. Peter and I discussed the first scene when Leontes, watching his best friend talking to his pregnant wife, turns to the audience and says, 'Too hot, too hot!' – the moment when the tap is turned on ...

One of the fundamentals when using the structure of the verse is that when one line is divided between two – or, as is rarely the case, three – people, you work *together* to retain the linear structure. This is very pleasurable – tossing the ball about, maintaining shape. Leontes' explosion looks like this on the page: Hermione is talking to Polixenes about their relationship, and the verse runs ...

HERMIONE   ... Th'other
                    for <u>some while</u> a <u>friend</u>.
LEONTES   Too <u>hot</u>, too <u>hot</u>!

Two speakers, five stresses, one line: it is what we call a half-line pick-up. Shakespeare is clear that he does not want any air around this, he wants shock, an explosion. The play is set in Sicily, and the effect of this line on the play should be like Mount Etna erupting. This chimed with my discovery of myocarditis, so Peter and I went for it. It was great in theory, but it took me about six weeks' playing to find out how to take the audience by surprise without alienating them.

The later scenes are among the most magical I have ever acted. The primal power of *The Winter's Tale* is so immense that it seemed to rise up through the stage floor, and unless I held it at bay it simply engulfed me, and I could barely speak.

The 'resurrection' of Hermione usually places her – the statue – upstage centre, in the Elizabethan inner stage as it were, so the audience cannot *see* the faces of the speakers. Peter staged it quite brilliantly, bringing Hermione centre stage on a moving plinth, so that we could walk round her. Eileen Atkins was superb as Paulina, leading us through this final 'holy' scene with great delicacy. Encouraged by Peter, we felt that a cosy conclusion was unsuitable, but we learnt that if we did not hint strongly enough at a positive future, audiences simply did not like it. Resurrection is in the DNA of drama. It was a question of balance and it took time to achieve.

Peter was keen to illustrate the themes of madness, anger and revenge that the three plays share, and, although *Cymbeline* was majestic in the Cottesloe, it did not transfer well to the Olivier, and *The Tempest* was confused. So Peter's send-off was only good in parts and brought to an end my first, very happy and productive experience of working at the National.

When the RSC and the National were new, there was an energy about the concept of major subsidised companies which drove them. Times were changing. Immense cultural factories had been erected and now the job was not *just* to relish their existence, but to find sufficient quality material to keep the idea alive.

Our great institutions have to reinvent themselves constantly, not only by redefining the greatness of the past, and nurturing the writers of the future, but in reflecting the ethnic and social diversity of a rapidly changing world. It is harder for the RSC because they have to repeat ad infinitum the same plays. The fuel that should drive any play is passion – the need, the desire, to put it on. Directors queue up to do *Hamlet*, but fewer of them are burning to do *King Henry VI Part One*. It is beyond challenging, and the truth is you cannot please all of the people all of the time. That is one reason why subsidy is essential.

At an Equity meeting in 2008, I think (challenging yet another round of arts cuts), Miriam Karlin spoke. Great actress, old as the hills, she recalled a time when the Arts Council had been an ally, working hand in hand with our profession. By using sponsorship, Thatcher drove a wedge between us and our funding body, and, because cash is short, the relationship has never been repaired.

22

The Black Glove

During my time at the National, Dame Peggy Ashcroft reached 80. Celebrations were planned for a Gala at the Old Vic and the *Jewel in the Crown* company was asked to contribute. Charlie Dance cleverly came up with an old sketch based on the doggerel verse 'There's a one-eyed yellow idol to the north of Kathmandu!'. It provided lots of parts, and was aptly suggestive of the subcontinent. The sketch needed a fall guy, and, because Ronald Merrick was unpopular, I was given the role of the 'reciter'.

It was decided that everyone should wear one detail of costume that was reminiscent of their character in the series. The solution for Merrick was obvious – he lost an arm and wore a prosthetic with a leather glove on it. So I wore a black glove, and did a fair bit of silly, amputated arm acting. The sketch was part of a star-studded Gala, full of affection for Dame Peg.

I was asked recently what the generic term for actors was, and I suggested 'a babel' – put a bunch of actors together and they will talk and talk. And if there's any food around, they will eat it! During the melee backstage, Judi wandered into our dressing room and caught me rehearsing. She became almost immediately hysterical. For some reason my black-glove antics made her laugh. Judi has the most infectious – not even *bordering* on dirty – *filthy* laugh. Whenever she saw me in the course of the evening, she pointed at the black glove, put her hand over her mouth and suppressed helpless giggles.

The night *after* the Gala we were performing *Antony and Cleopatra*. In the great final scene of the play, Cleopatra waits to meet the young upstart Caesar who has driven Antony to his death. Judi was enthroned plumb centre, facing the main gangway of the Olivier, down which I clanked, in full armour to meet her. One of the joys of my final two entrances in the play was that between them I could stand at the back and watch Judi.

I dreamed there was an Emperor – Antony.
Oh such another sleep that I might see
But such another man.

The night after the Gala, just before I made my entrance down the gangway to Judi, I realised that I was wearing black leather gauntlets. The temptation was too much for me. I shoved one glove behind my breastplate, rattled my way down the gangway, and did as much one-armed, black-glove acting as I dared, without causing the audience to suspect that Octavius had suddenly become an amputee. Judi's eyesight has never been that great, so I practically stuck the glove under her nose. Nevertheless, she swore blind – as it were – that she had not seen anything. Other people had noticed, and asked me what was going on, but Judi pretended nothing had happened. It was like a challenge.

I plotted. The obvious place to put a glove was in the basket of asps that is delivered to Cleopatra. So I schemed with Greavesy, our props man, to place the black glove *on* the fig leaves in the basket, positioning the slow worm – the asp – on top of that, thus providing maximum visibility for Judi, but nothing that would be apparent to the house. That night I was watching like a hawk to see if Judi noticed. She took the lid off the basket, leant forward, and then, I swear, she gasped, covering her mouth with her hand. Not a bad reaction really – easily interpreted by the audience as horror at the sight of the venomous asp. I knew better. After the show, Judi said, 'You just wait, Pigott-Smith.' And so The Game began.

I framed a black glove and sent it to Judi for the first night of her Madame Ranevskaya in *The Cherry Orchard* at the Aldwych. Pam and I wanted to surprise her, and did not tell her when we were going to see it. At the interval, the company manager greeted us in the lobby of that gorgeous theatre – another gem designed by Frank Matcham. He said, 'Dame Judi sends her regards', and handed me a black glove. The witch!

From these simple beginnings in 1987, The Game has evolved into getting *any* black glove to the other person, in *any* shape or form, at *any* time. One of its most recent incarnations, sent by Judi for my birthday, was a box of marshmallows with pictures – photographs – on, of a black glove: we have been playing The Game so long, we are obliged to be inventive. My retaliation was to give Judi a mug with a black glove on it, for the first night of her Paulina in *The Winter's Tale*. A potter friend of mine made a tile with a black glove on for Judi's last birthday. My most recent gift from Judi was a cushion with a glove appliquéd on to it – a response to a tapestry 'black glove' cushion made for me by Joyce Nettles, our leading theatrical casting director.

As 'gloving' plans became more complex – and more competitive – other people became involved. No plot was more intricate than the one involving Kevin Spacey. I played Larry Slade in Howard Davies's production of *The Iceman Cometh* in 1998–99, so I was with Kevin on and off for about two years. Knowing him to be a great prankster, I felt comfortable asking him if he would 'glove' Judi when they were filming *The Shipping News*.

'How do I do that?' he asked.

'Well, you could tape it to her trailer mirror so that when she takes a look at herself, she sees it there. You're filming in Alaska, so for the glove to turn up at all will be a major coup for me. The possibilities are endless.'

'Like?' Kevin enquired.

'I once made a frame from a wire coat hanger, and planted it, with the glove on, in her dressing-room window box.'

'How did that work?'

'Well, Judi and I were doing different plays at the National. I was playing Leicester in *Mary Stuart*, and Judi was doing *A Little Night Music*. I knew there would be something for me on my first night …' (although even I had not expected a heavy box, delivered by Emma B, one of the National's stage management treasures). As Emma gave it to me, she said, 'I hope you like it. It nearly killed me!' Judi had given her the task of setting a black glove in Perspex. And during one of her experiments, it had literally blown up. The Perspex glove is in my study.

I explained to Kevin that on matinee days gloves went back and forth, each of us trying to outdo the other, enlisting anyone and everyone in our plots: the guy who pulled my boots off, onstage, slipped the glove into my hand. One matinee, when Judi opened her parasol, *there* was the glove, hanging in front of her nose. She organised someone to give it to me at the curtain call. I managed to get it into her serviette so that when she unfolded it, there was the glove. When *Mary Stuart* completed its run, *A Little Night Music* had not. This meant that I was leaving the theatre, but Judi was staying on. I knew she would want the last word.

After our final performance of *Mary Stuart*, we had a cast party with a cabaret, during which Dench, the wicked Machiavel, had arranged for me to be 'gloved'. Most people knew The Game by then, and this public gloving appeared to be a great victory for Judi. However, I had arranged for the security boys to let me into her dressing room. I slipped the glove that had been presented to me in the cabaret, on to the wire coat-hanger frame I had prepared, and stuck it in her window box. According to Judi's dresser, it was not until three days later that she finally noticed it. Pointing at it in fury she screamed, 'The bastard!!'

Kevin is a great company man, devising japes during the Broadway run of *Iceman* to keep us all happy. On one occasion he acquired a large rubber camel's head and, with the aid of two of the understudies and a large white sheet, he rode through the wings on the back of a camel, waving a sword, saying, 'We've taken Aqaba!' Hours of planning for a few seconds' glorious insanity.

In *The Shipping News* there is a scene in which Judi goes to an outside toilet shack, pours the ashes of her late brother down the latrine, sits on the loo and pees on them. Kevin ascertained from the director that he was going to shoot it so the camera closed in on Judi's face, with the *sound* of her peeing telling the story.

Kevin crawled into the space underneath the shack, waited for the ashes to fall, and then for Judi to sit down: she was sitting on her dress, so it was all quite decorous. Then he took the glove, placed it on a long-handled broom, and – in Judi's own words – 'He stuck it up my arse! No, he did! Can you believe it? He stuck it up my arse!'

When Kevin and Judi were promoting *The Shipping News* on *The Michael Parkinson Show*, they recounted the story of the glove. It was the then equivalent of going viral. Since then, whenever Judi does an evening in conversation with her biographer and friend John Miller, someone always asks, 'Where is the glove?' On one such occasion, I equipped John with a glove, so that when the question came up he was able to take it out and 'glove' Judi publicly.

I was asked to play the Foreign Secretary in *Quantum of Solace* – a day on a Bond film, very exciting. In the scene, I had to get quite strong with M, and I was really looking forward to putting Judi in her place.

The car arrived at 6.30 a.m., and, as I slid into the back seat, the driver turned to shake my hand. He was wearing a black glove. I said, 'Does this have anything to do with Dame Judi?'

He replied, 'What?'

'The glove,' I said.

'The glove?' he asked in amazement.

'Yes ... the black glove.'

'Oh no, sir,' he said, somewhat embarrassed, 'I have an unfortunate skin condition.'

I was mortified.

On set, most of the crew were wearing one black glove. I was so thrown by my earlier faux pas that I imagined some dreadful impetigo was going round, so I said nothing. Eventually, in despair at my apparent blindness, the director, Mark Forster, came close to me to give me a note. He too was wearing a black glove, and when he wagged his finger right under my nose I had to acknowledge what was going on. That fiendish woman had set the whole thing up – skin condition and all!

There is a coda to the Bond saga …

When she is passing time on a film, Judi sometimes embroiders. When *Quantum* was over, she sent me the fruits of her off-screen endeavours. In a small picture frame were 24 squares of green, red and blue. On top of them, in the shape of a gun with 007 on, is a piece of black silk. But it is not just a gun, it is also, amazingly, a black glove. Of all the gloves in my collection, this is my favourite. It tells you a lot about Judi – her boundless energy, her ceaseless creativity, her sense of humour, her naughtiness and her generosity.

The Bond glove. Handmade by M, alias Dame Judi Dench, on the set of
Quantum of Solace

23

COMPASS

By the end of the eighties I had reached a point at which I felt that I would be able to make a living as an actor and that decent work would come my way, although it might not always be what I wanted, and then fate intervened in the figure of Sir Anthony Quayle.

We had worked happily on *Henry IV (i)* and had kept tentatively in touch. But I suspect Tony thought of me at this point in his life because of an evening we had together when I was filming *Clash of the Titans*. We were in Malta. I had finished early and was in the hotel pool. I became aware that someone was trying to attract my attention. It was Tony. He had a house in Malta, and heard I was nearby. We arranged dinner at his house and talked all night about theatre.

If Peter Hall was the father of post-war theatre in England – and as a founder member of the RSC and the first artistic director of the National Theatre in its permanent home, he can lay claim to that title – then Tony is its grandfather, but history has a way of writing out those people who do not control the narrative, and this has been Tony's fate. Like Tyrone Guthrie, he did not hold the pen at the right time.

Tony's acting career began in 1935 at the age of 22, and was interrupted by the war, in which he was something of a hero. I heard it said that 'he had a good war'. I think it went further than that. He served in Special Ops in Albania, and turned his experiences, about which he did not like to speak, into two novels. It is not surprising that in films he seems completely at home in

233

uniform. After the war, he was asked to go to Stratford to help improve its standing.

Sir Barry Jackson, founder of the influential Birmingham Rep, had taken over Stratford in 1945, and when Tony joined him three years later, they started inviting the finest actors and directors to work there. Tony's departure coincided with my first visits to Stratford. After he relinquished the reins, he worked there as an actor, most notably as Aaron the Moor in Peter Brook's ground-breaking *Titus Andronicus* with Olivier. He told me that Olivier came up to him in the wings the first time he appeared in make-up – blacking up was the norm then – and with Tony looking stunning in his *ebony* black, which was *not* the norm, scrutinised him almost enviously. 'Bloody good idea, that,' he said. Tony was convinced that was the moment Olivier's Othello was born.

A story from his Stratford days gives a picture both of Tony, who was playing Benedick, and Gielgud, who was directing him in *Much Ado*. One day Tony came storming into rehearsals – he was a beef of a man, strong, commanding. 'Listen, Johnny,' he said to Gielgud, 'I have been doing some research and the genuflection, which we use in the church scene, did not come into common practice until at least a decade after the period in which we have set the play. Now are we going to do something which has some genuine integrity and historical authenticity, or just a bit of theatrical frippery-frappery?!' Without drawing breath, Gielgud replied, 'Oh, definitely frippery-frappery.' Gielgud, I am afraid, was right. *Much Ado* contains too much silliness to withstand close historical scrutiny; it needs flair and bucketloads of charm.

The Jackson/Quayle combination drew the eyes of the world to Stratford, and until Olivier sowed the seed of our National Theatre at Chichester in 1962 and established its London base at the Old Vic, by which time the RSC had been formed, the Memorial Theatre was, to all intents and purposes, our National Theatre. I understood from Tony that it was Lady Quayle – Dot – who identified Peter Hall as the coming man. No matter who, Peter came to Stratford, and when he and John Barton got together the future was set.

Tony enjoyed an important career in films – *Ice Cold in Alex* is probably his most famous movie, although I have a soft spot for Hitchcock's *The Wrong Man*. In the West End he originated the role of Eddie Carbone in Arthur Miller's *A View from the Bridge* in the fifties, and Andrew Wyke in *Sleuth* two decades later. Then, in his seventieth year, his conscience got the better of him. Recognising that there was a widening gap in the touring landscape, he bravely took it on himself to fill it. Theatre is hard, and touring is bruising. For a man of his age to pin his colours to the creation of a touring company – Compass – was noble indeed.

However, the day of the actor-manager was past – Donald Wolfit was the last relic of a bygone age, and Prospect, the only major company addressing the needs of the provincial touring circuit, was gone. By the eighties they had run into trouble with internal rivalries, and died with an infamously bad O'Toole *Macbeth* at the Old Vic. The national companies, the RSC and the NT, did some touring, but they are what I call 'landlocked' companies: their prime duty is to fill their own big theatres, a massive task in itself. When, in later years, they were placed under pressure to tour by a panicky Arts Council, the result was patchy: touring is specific, and both the RSC and the NT had disasters trying to fit complicated sets from their landlocked theatres into differently sized regional theatres. I blame the Arts Council, not the companies. The RSC subsequently did, and still does, amazing work, taking a complete auditorium round the country to sports centres and civic halls.

There are always commercial tours, sending round a film or television star with a popular play, but the world of touring, as even I had known it 20 years earlier, was looking very thin. The Actors' Company, led by Ian McKellen, Edward Petherbridge, Robin Ellis and my old friend Simon Cadell, tried to give the actor back his prominence and power, but although their democratic aims were noble, and the work of a high standard, they didn't last. They couldn't. You can't have the cast selecting the director – theatre needs individual leadership. You cannot put stars in small parts – it skews the play. The English Shakespeare

Company, although never quite to my taste, did a good job of touring large classics to the regions and indeed the world, but they had had their moment. Kenneth Branagh founded Renaissance, and the light of celebrity shone briefly in medium-scale touring. But Branagh was always destined for greater things, and, as I warned Arts Council England (ACE), they would not be able to rely on him in the long term. Good luck to him.

Tony wanted Compass to be a touring company, which he would lead himself, taking well-cast, major classics to the regions. He used his profile, his impressive credentials and gargantuan charm to persuade ACE to give him money. And when Tony turned on the charm it was quite something. A wide smile would cross his huge face, which would crumple, almost closing his sharp eyes: he would beam at you and light you like the sun. His rays had likewise been directed on to the wonderful Mr Blackett, sponsorship man at Prudential, and, with support from ACE and the Pru, Tony opened up offices in Covent Garden and set about casting *The Clandestine Marriage* by Colman and Garrick.

Tony's dream was one that even the halfwits at ACE could not refuse – the gap Tony had identified was all too real; but the awful truth was the halfwits were not completely wrong: the world had changed beneath Tony's feet. From day one, the work of Compass looked to the profession, and maybe to the punters, old-fashioned. The productions I saw were good, worthy, solid work, but they smelled of the past.

In addition to this unfashionable odour, the deeper problem Tony had was the nature of his ACE subsidy, which was project funding. As its name suggests, this was play-by-play funding, and what Compass needed desperately, in order to establish itself securely, was three-year funding. That carrot was endlessly dangled before Tony, although he once said to me, 'I wish we had enough money to kiss their ACE goodbye.' Gallows humour. Thanks to Mrs Thatcher we were now in the age of sponsorship. When introduced it was claimed to be vital and proper for the private sector to support the arts. Nonsense. Supporters of sponsorship swore blind it was not an alternative to subsidy. Pull the other one. Arts funding yo-yo'd up and down, depending on how tenacious the current Minister of Arts happened to be – David Mellor was a very good Arts Minister, but he only lasted three months.

Theatre companies learnt to perform an unpleasant juggling act, keeping the balls of subsidy, private support and sponsorship in the air. It wasn't easy for anyone, and for an outmoded septuagenarian it was impossible. Tony did valiantly for five years. He nearly killed himself, but he knew in his heart he was trying to hold back the tide. He knew he needed younger blood. He rang me and said he was coming to the National to see my Leontes, and asked if we could have tea afterwards. I should have seen it coming.

He told me he was going to leave Compass, and asked me to consider taking over. I had such regard for him I was flattered, but his proposition appealed to me because I had been brought up in the age of ensemble thinking – the ethos of the company. This meant that although I had been working for 20 years I did not know how to put a play on. This embarrassed me. I was part of a generation that had been steered away from influencing the direction our profession was taking. Actors are not generally interested in power, and we had relinquished control of our destiny to ambitious directors and designers, who were not about to let go the reins. This troubled me. Most audiences go to a play because there is someone in it they want to see, but, as actors, we had no say!

If there is one part and both Maggie Smith and Judi Dench want to play it, one of them will end up unhappy. In this scenario, the two Great Dames are unable to do anything to influence their fate. They are inactive. I hated that. I have never minded taking on responsibility, and here was an offer that could potentially enrich my artistic life, as well as addressing the areas of my discontent. When governments talk about subsidy they never take into account that actors subsidise the theatre all their lives with inadequate wages. I was playing good roles at the National, and able to balance the books with voiceover work. I didn't need to do Compass, but I liked the idea of influencing the profession in some small way, and perhaps acquiring a touch more control over my own working life. Tony's appeal to me was brilliantly aimed at the right person.

There didn't seem to be any particular time scheme attached to Tony's offer. He was at home writing, and I would call him to ask questions: who deals with the money? How on earth do I behave at board meetings? Who's *on* the board? One of his answers tells you something of the man. My question had been 'How do I deal with the Arts Council?' 'Well, my dear Tim,' he said archly, 'imagine you are adrift at sea in a small rowing boat. You are on one oar and the Arts Council is on the other.' Tony liked boats.

He had said there would be a salary for the artistic director, and, ignoring Pam's warnings, I instructed my agent to open negotiations. So the moment arrived when I felt it was both safe and necessary for me to go into the impressive Covent Garden offices and see what was going on. There I found the very charming general manager, Julian Forrester, and an office boy, Edward Kemp, later head of RADA.

'What is happening?' I asked.

'Not much,' they replied.

'Where is Tony?'

'Tony doesn't come in a lot these days.'

'Are there any plans?'

'Well, we have the rights to *Royal Hunt of the Sun*. And ACE backing for a tour.'

Royal Hunt is a massive *modern* classic, a really important piece that galvanised the theatre world in 1964 with its tale of the Spanish conquest of Peru. A dazzling production by John Dexter with a stunning star turn from Robert Stephens, as the fated Inca chief Atahualpa, made pure theatre. The play was famous for its stage direction – *The men cross the Andes!* – which Peter Shaffer wrote as a direct challenge to the cramped vision of the many kitchen-sink plays that had occupied centre stage since *Look Back in Anger*.

This choice of play was a departure for Compass, a clear move to shift the company's image, and quite a coup, as it was the play's twenty-fifth anniversary. Julian said the wonderful Denis Quilley had been approached and was reported to be 'not uninterested' in playing Pizarro.

'So when will this happen?' I enquired.

'Autumn next year.'

'And who will direct it?'

'Well ... we haven't given it much thought.'

I was getting a strong feeling that Tony had departed rather sooner than expected, and there was no one here taking decisions. Time was not exactly running out, but if things were not acted upon immediately I sensed there would be no company for me to be the artistic director of!

'Tricky piece *Royal Hunt*,' I said. They nodded. 'Do you have anyone in *mind* to direct?'

A piece of paper was taken from a drawer with a few names on. Perusing it closely, Julian said, 'Well, Trevor Nunn is top of the list.' Kemp nodded. They seemed pleased with this idea.

'You're joking,' I said.

They were not.

'Who is Trevor's agent?' I asked.

They told me.

'May I use the phone, please?'

Trevor was not available for the next two years. I knew this would be the case. 'Who's next?' I said.

'Adrian Noble.'

We repeated the same dance. Same result.

'Next?' I said.

'Andrei Şerban,' they replied. My jaw dropped.

Serban is a wild Romanian with great flair and a crazy reputation: the thought of him being interested in, or remotely capable of, tailoring his wildness to meet the demands of this huge play, in four weeks' rehearsal, for a UK tour was stark insanity.

'Does Peter [Shaffer] know about this idea?' I asked.

'No,' they said.

I rang Peter. I had met him in New York some years before, a delightful, entertaining man and a wonderful writer. At least he knew who I was, although he might well have asked himself why I suddenly seemed to be in charge of his play. I asked him how much contact he had had with the company about the production so far. He said there had been none. I made it clear that I had just popped into the office, and that there were, as yet, no real plans.

'Er, Peter ... do you know Andrei Şerban?'

'Yee-eees,' he responded with nervous caution.

'What do you think of Şerban for *Royal Hunt?*'

'Oh, for God's sake,' he cried. 'Noooo! We'd have Incas on motorbikes!'

'Don't worry,' I said. 'It won't happen. I just needed to cross him off the list. Peter, I will be in touch.'

So here I was. There was a company, just. There was a general manager. There were splendid offices. There was an impressive play. The rights were secure. There was money allocated. There were other names on the directorial list, although none of them were anywhere near being acceptable, and there was the ghost of a thought about a leading man. I didn't feel deceived by Tony, but this was not what I had been led to expect. And ... the clock was ticking.

In the next two weeks I waited for my agent to conclude salary negotiations and made discreet enquiries from home among director friends of mine and sympathetic agents about who the right person might be to direct. The play needed not only someone with textual skills and an eye for movement, you had to have – crucially – the right designer; get it right and it is a glittering pageant, get it wrong – if the costumes and setting are too gaudy, and the production does not have a gravitas which the play itself makes difficult to achieve – you have a Peruvian panto. In addition, our production had to be fit to tour. This was a massive challenge.

It emerged, embarrassingly, that there was not enough money in the company to pay the artistic director. My enquiries about directors for *Royal Hunt* got precisely nowhere. I should have listened to Pam who told me to get out now, before the die was cast, but I was hooked. I wanted to do this and make it work. My liking for a challenge, my ambition, my arrogance, or some combination of the three got the better of me and I went into the office to tell Julian I was very much afraid that unless I picked the production up, directed it myself and got things moving, the whole pack of cards would collapse. I could not see any other option. If Compass was going to work, just it as had been with Tony, the whole thing was on one man's shoulders.

I had done a fair bit of directing, at university, drama school and in my spare time at the RSC. Through the eighties I had done Beckett. My old friend Julian Curry and I did *Krapp's Last Tape* (which I had already done with my chum Paddy Godfrey), and Julian came to me with *Company*, a Beckett novella. With help from the remarkable Professor Katherine Worth, a Beckett scholar who had got permission to adapt from Beckett himself, we worked on this in our spare time, took it to the Edinburgh Festival in 1987, where the adaptation won a Fringe First, and on the coat-tails of that award we transferred to the Donmar. So I was not afraid of directing. *Krapp* and *Company*, however, are one-man plays; *Royal Hunt* is huge, and our budget allowed a cast of 28! This would be new territory for me, although I had once handled a large cast back in university days. But having seen the original production, and played a non-speaking Inca while I was a student – in a superb John David production with Julian Glover a fine Atahualpa at BOV – I felt I knew what the play needed.

Julian Forrester agreed to my proposal, on condition that I persuaded Peter Shaffer to let me direct, and Denis Quilley to come on board: if I managed that, he felt he would be able to hold the ACE money in place. And that is what happened. I was astonished and grateful that both Peter and Denis had faith in me. They did, and we moved forward.

My biggest challenge was to find the right designer. None of my friends, or any of the designers I admired, were available, so after a massive amount of research I chose Paul Hernon, who had several big shows to his credit. He knew and loved the play, and had designed Iain Hamilton's opera based on it at English National Opera in 1977. He was staggeringly inventive and at the same time realistic. 'It's easy having ideas,' he once said to me (lucky him), 'making them work is not so easy.'

When you tour, you play in a variety of theatres, big, medium, small, wide, narrow, some with wing space, some with very little, some with high proscenium arches, some with restrictive height. The first design decision we took was that for this play, which is very physical, we needed a basic module on which the play could easily be repeated by the actors – spatial relationships needed to be consistent. Working with the ground plans of our 12 theatres, Paul created a module that fitted into Bath, the smallest of our theatres, with half an inch to spare in each corner. It was metal-framed with screw height adjusters on all four legs to deal with differently raked stages. It would be placed centre stage in larger theatres, and, with our own solid side pieces, the wings would meld into black drapes, and could thus be adapted to fit all sizes.

The floor of the module looked like Inca stonework. It was dark grey, with large stones downstage, getting smaller as they moved upstage. From above, it looked like an Inca wall. The texture was firm but spongy, comfortable for the Incas' bare feet. It was raked, and it had three moving sections – two large flaps at the sides upstage – which could be hauled upright. Between the flaps, a long central column about 15 feet long and 4 feet wide could be raised to any angle.

With the side pieces almost vertical, Pizarro could walk up the partly raised central column, between the raised flaps and plant the Spanish flag. With strong back light and smoke, we had our Andes.

This central column would also be used for Atahualpa's death; ropes would be looped around his shoulders and threaded through big iron rings near the top of the column. Then, with Atahualpa lying on the column, sloping up to about 4 feet, he would be garrotted; one soldier stage left, and one stage right, would twist the garrotte, with Atahualpa isolated, struggling, and dying in the

Atahualpa's death scene in The Royal Hunt of the Sun *by Peter Shaffer,*
Compass tour, 1989

middle of the stage. The column would then be raised to vertical, with Atahualpa suspended by his shoulder ropes from the top, conjuring images of crucifixion. Pizarro hopes that Atahualpa will fulfil his promise and resurrect as the rising sun hits his body. As dawn broke, the dead Atahualpa would be lowered slowly to the stage floor, where he could be held upright, appearing to stand. As Pizarro moved towards him, full of hope, Atahualpa would fall forwards.

Paul's module offered strength and consistency; it would be easier to light than a space which altered and shifted. My colleague from the NT, Steve Wentworth, who had brilliantly lit several plays I had done there, would light. We would have the module for the last two weeks of rehearsal.

One of the problems with touring is that you set off without anyone to help you to – literally – keep the show on the road artistically. I was pretty sure this vast play would need that help, so I brought Rob Clare in to play the small part of de Candia, and be associate director. Rob held caretaker responsibility on tour. This was new: I had never encountered artistic directorial safeguards in a touring company. Responsibility for the quality of the performance generally devolves to the leading actors, and this, of course, can lead either to neglect or interference from the top!

It seemed to me wrong and dated to take our play to a city, perform it to the middle classes in their middle-class theatre for a week, and move on to the next place. It was important to me that we became, however briefly, properly involved in the life of the towns we visited. I thought it vital for a touring company to do 'outreach' work – both for our consciences and hopefully to build audiences. We raised money from the Baring Foundation to create an educational programme and to mount Trevor Griffiths' great play *Comedians*. Rob would direct this; it would rehearse on the road and play in prisons, an area in which Rob had considerable experience – in drama – not as an inmate! This was another first.

We were also able to do work with the deaf, which came about through the actor Michael Dray, who had his own company for working with the hard of hearing, Show of Hands.

He, too, would play a small part, and use actors from the company to visit schools for the deaf as we went round the country. These areas of work were a departure from all touring companies I knew, and it was the direction in which I felt Compass, in addition to performing a modern, as opposed to an ancient, classic, needed to go. It would provide evidence that we were up to date. This outreach work would have the added advantage of giving actors who did not have that much to do in the play – and *Royal Hunt* is basically a two-hander with (for us) 26 supporting players! – some extra room to express their creativity. We cast the extraordinary Jack Klaff as Atahualpa, and got in someone I knew, Simon Forman, to write new music, although the original score by Mark Wilkinson would take some beating.

We raised some extra money from my old colleague Robert Cogo-Fawcett, which gave him the rights to transfer the play, if he so wished, to the West End. And that, quite simply, was my aim – to get the play into the West End, to display Compass in a new and successful light. If we managed that, the future might not be assured, but it would be relatively plain sailing. I knew this would be hard, but if we could make it into London it would be difficult for ACE to ignore us.

24

THE CHIEF

As my artistic directorship of Compass theatre loomed, Ruth Boswell, doyenne producer, approached me with an idea for a television series. Six episodes, written by Jeffrey Caine, featured a tough, liberal-minded Chief Constable who found himself in constant opposition to the Home Office. It really appealed to me because the stories encouraged a questioning of the relationship between the police and government. Since Mrs Thatcher so shamefully used the police to suppress the miners, stopping peaceful demonstrations outside collieries and chasing protestors down Whitehall on horseback, there had not been a proper debate about the role of the police. This series was one contribution to it.

My character, John Stafford, was broadly based on a real Chief of Police, John Alderson, who provided a lot of ideas for the series as well as the fundamental stuff of my character. In addition to a dogged Yorkshire streak, John had a flair for drama, coining the name Europol for our series before it actually existed. Head of the Cornish force, he had clashed with the government over secondary picketing. Far from refusing to stop it, he told Queen Anne's Gate he would defend the miners' right to do it. If there was violence or threatening behaviour, he would deal with it, but he would not toe the government line and suppress freedom of expression. Great man, John. 'You have to be tough to be liberal' was one of his maxims. Didn't last long as a Chief; they didn't like his style.

One of our best episodes was about a middle-aged man (delicately played by Roger Lloyd-Pack) released from a mental

As John Stafford in The Chief, *Anglia TV, 1989-91*

institution because of a shortage of space. He forgets to take his medication, kidnaps a young boy and takes him to the one place where he was happy – a hospital. The hospital is now empty, closed, due to cutbacks. In this forsaken building, he keeps the boy in a deserted ward. He is not unkind or abusive, but he has a gun. The decision which confronted my Chief, when traditional rescue methods failed, was whether or not to shoot him. The story was exciting, but, importantly, it touched on cutbacks in public services and opened up another issue – police use of guns.

The Chief was intelligent, popular television. It would occupy six months of my time, and it was well paid. It came at the perfect moment: I could spend half my year subsidising the unpaid work I was beginning to relish with Compass, and if the series was successful it would improve the company's profile. Pam was always against Compass. She said it was past its moment, that I was wasting my time. She was right, but by now I was in too deep.

We went into rehearsals for Peter Shaffer's *The Royal Hunt of the Sun* with a terrific cast – a bunch of great bruisers as Spaniards, quite a few of them old mates, and some more refined actors as the Inca lords. We were allowed to give one Equity card to a young actor: Judi Dench had just directed *Macbeth* at the Central School of Speech and Drama. Judi said the most gifted actor in the cast was the Porter – in spite of his spectacularly bad performance. I like actors who can be fabulously bad; it carries the potential for being fabulously good. So we asked this young man in for a meeting, with a view to his playing the young priest in *Royal Hunt* and Gethin Price in Trevor Griffiths' *The Comedians*, our prison project. Within 24 hours, of his own volition he had learnt a chunk of *The Comedians* and asked if he could do it for us. It was electrifying, so we welcomed Rufus Sewell to the acting profession.

When our company of 28 gathered in St Gabriel's Church Hall in Pimlico, I went round the room introducing everybody, wardrobe people, designers, stage staff, actors, our movement director, Stuart Hopps, and our fantastic company manager, Colin Small. We had a read-through, Paul took the company through the set with the model box, I spoke briefly about the play and the way I wanted us to work, and that afternoon we started blocking – setting the moves.

I had blocked in detail all the scenes involving more than three people, and in the first half that means a lot of prep, but it saved hours of rehearsal time. Three intelligent actors can move a scene themselves, but the more people there are the more important it is to place them on the stage. Get the scene on its feet, get through it, and, as the meaning of the scene emerges, and people sense their characters more strongly, they will make their own adjustments.

On the second day of rehearsal I invited Frankie Armstrong to work with us. Frankie is a voice specialist with a great knowledge of folk chanting and primitive tribal calls – she could get a table leg to sing. By Tuesday lunchtime, with her liberating exercises, she had turned us into a company and the work proceeded happily and creatively. There were two train strikes during our four weeks, but not one person was late.

It was week three when our general manager, Julian, appeared and told me, with tears in his eyes, that Tony Quayle had cancer of the liver and had been given 11 weeks to live. I was shocked, but remembered Tony's unusually thin nose when we had met almost a year before. I spoke on the phone to Tony in the evenings, and he talked movingly about the fact that the company was in good hands – and we felt very close. Compass was a child to him: he had devoted his final years and the last vestiges of his monumental energy and creativity to it. I discovered that, in a way, I was like a child to him, too. I asked his daughter Jenny once why he had chosen me; she replied simply, 'He saw himself in you.'

I *should* have gone to see him, I am ashamed now that I didn't, but it was a frantic time and he discouraged me – he knew I was busy, and he was desperate to finish his autobiography, *A Time to Speak*. He was a bull of a man, and I don't think either of us quite believed he would be gone so soon. But he was. He hoped to make it to Bath to see the play, but he was too weak. His death left a mental rather than an actual vacuum. I had not known him that well, but when lost I had turned to him for advice. Our last conversations bequeathed me the added weight of needing the company to succeed more than ever. I didn't want to fail him. But now I really was on my own, although, mercifully, Julian was likewise determined to make things work in Tony's memory.

At this point, things looked good. Rehearsals went well, and there was a buzz about the place. Denis Quilley was hugely popular, and a complete pro, leading by example from the front. Jack was delivering, too, and the company was committed, contented and creative.

When you start putting work together, it can be dangerous. The knock-on effect of one scene on the next can be throwing. The words first run-through can strike terror to the heart of the strongest. So I developed a system of working in which the actors play scene one and you give them notes. They then replay scene one and go straight into scene two. Then notes. Then scenes two to three, and so on. At the interval you run the first half. And so on, to the end of the play. In two days you have worked through the play. It cleans troubling little things up, it gives a sense of continuity and it takes the pressure off.

The schedule was so tight, we managed only one full run, and it was clear there was *only one* real issue. Pizarro has to be a cold, hard man and Denis was too nice. I went to his Hampstead house after rehearsal on the Friday night to talk to him, and told him what was required. 'Denis,' I said, 'you have to turn yourself into the man who empties the pub. People come in, see you sitting in the corner and go somewhere else to drink.' He already knew this in his heart, but he was being required to leave his comfort zone of radiating charm which had made him such a stunning Hildy Johnson in Michael Blakemore's *The Front Page* at the Old Vic.

We were booked into our first theatre – Clwyd – for two weeks. We had four days in which to tech, with a first preview on the Friday. It could not have gone better. The cast were strong and adaptable, Paul's set and costumes worked and Denis began to turn the 'cold' corner. One night during the tech, Colin Small (company manager) came to me to say we had to stop. We were in the middle of a scene which Denis had always found particularly moving. I went down to the front of the stage and gently called his name. He carried on. I got on to the stage and said his name *again*, a bit louder. It was not that he had not heard me, he was ... in another world.

He was facing away from me. I walked towards him and put my hand on his back, repeating his name quietly. He stopped, and turned to me. He looked at me in wonder. He did not know me. He was so deep in character, it took him a few moments to leave the sixteenth century and come to terms with reality. He emerged from the power of his imagined world, grinned and shrugged. I apologised. I thought for a moment he might have hit me, but he hugged me. I adored him.

Denis once said to me that he was a simple man, but I knew how to get through to him, so he trusted me and once he recognised that charm was out of place – and that if he played it ruthlessly, the audience would go with him, sympathising with this barren man, feeling his pain – he never looked back. He simply got better and better. Every time I saw the play over the coming weeks he had improved. I admired him. The company loved him. Even during a full exhausting, eight-show week on the road, he would join them in the pub for a glass or four of Rioja, his favourite tipple. If there was a piano, he would play and sing. Singing was completely natural to him. He moved from speech to song without any vocal change. 'I love to vocalise,' he said to me, 'it's the first thing I do every day!' On press night, he gave me a card in which he said I was right at the top of his list of favourite directors, along with Michael Blakemore. I don't keep stuff like that, but I remember those words with as much pride as anything in my professional life.

One performance at Clwyd sticks in my mind, and it is representative of the audience response. My old friend Trevor Martin began the play as Old Martin. Trevor had a voice of gravel and thunder. One night as he began the play, a couple of Welsh kids barracked him. He turned them to stone with a basilisk glare. With the power of his voice he subdued them. They shrank back in their seats, and I shall never forget that at the curtain call those kids *stood* on their seats, yelling their approval.

The local press was terrific, for the play, the production, Denis, Jack, everything. It was bordering on sensational everywhere we went. But one review affected our fate, and thereby hangs a tale.

The first review I received from John Peter of the *Sunday Times* had been a poor one. He said it was a shame to have cast me and Ollie Cotton in Michael Frayn's *Benefactors*, because we were television personalities. I was inclined to agree with him that I was below par in *Benefactors*, but that was not because I was, at that moment, a name on telly – I just wasn't very good. During my time at the National Theatre, Peter changed his tune and a string of decent reviews followed. I don't look at reviews at all now.

When I took over Compass, John Peter rang the office and told Julian he was pleased I was doing this and if there was anything he could do to help, I had only to ask. This was very decent of him, so I took the bull by the horns and called him. We had a pleasant chat. I pointed out that Arts Council England read reviews, and the one thing he *could* do to help was bear that in mind when writing about our work. In the week before we opened, he rang and said that he would be coming to the first night in Bath.

Bath was the first move of the tour – the first time our set was to be dismantled and rebuilt. It was therefore by far the most stressful performance of the whole engagement. I rang and pleaded with Peter not to come on *that* night. He said he understood these things but if he did not see it that night, he might not see it at all.

In the event, the play began, annoyingly, ten minutes late, and it was a challenging evening. The theatre was unfamiliar, a cramped space, very different from Clwyd. New stage staff were doing things, unrehearsed, for the first time, and inevitably the show was a bit slow. We got through: a compliment to the whole team with such a massive play, and there was a very responsive curtain call from the packed house. It was error-free but it was dry. On the Wednesday, a *Sunday Times* photographer came to Bath to take a picture of Denis and Jack, so we were reasonably optimistic that the review would be positive.

On the Sunday, we turned eagerly to our papers. The opening sentence of John Peter's review read something like: 'I did not like this play when it opened 25 years ago, and neither of us have aged well.'

This man was trying to be helpful and had been warned of the implications of his views. Julian could not believe his eyes, I was in shock and Peter Shaffer was so upset he took to his bed for three days. He once said to me that he hardly ever put pen to page without sensing a critic on his shoulder.

In spite of this blow, the tour went well – a tribute to Denis and the company – and it was considered a success by Arts Council England, although they did not even notice the educational work, the prison play or our work with the deaf. The only place where the play really failed was Hull, where the Friends of the Theatre were at war with the theatre manager and were actively trying to *prevent* people going to see plays. Not without success. We performed our Saturday matinee to 25 people, who, incidentally, gave the cast a standing ovation. By then Rufus's line 'When I first came here, I thought it was paradise, but now I know it is Hell' offered our young zealot priest serious temptations.

Our West End ambitions were not just mine. Denis wanted it to come in, and Peter Shaffer was happy for that to happen, but because of John Peter's review our backer got cold feet. I tried desperately to persuade him that *Royal Hunt* in the West End, alongside the latest Shaffer offering – *Lettice and Loveage*, featuring the two Maggies (Smith and Tyzack in wonderful comic form) – would have worked commercially, but in vain. Sadly, and ironically, the play he decided to back instead failed and broke him. That one sentence of John Peter's scuppered us both.

25

ENDGAME

The Chief was mounted by Anglia TV – known in the profession as Nineteenth-Century Fox. David Puttnam, who was on their board, bumped into me one day, saying, 'Tim! *The Chief* has saved Anglia!' It had been well received so we were going to series two, which was good news. The bad news was that our main writer, Jeffrey Caine, had been spotted by Hollywood.

At Compass, Julian and I faced the issue of our next tour. I made a list of some 20 plays and we went to Arts Council England to ask for money. The meeting was a farce. They turned down every single idea – *all* of them. Dispirited, we rose to go. At the door, I said in a half-hearted way, 'I suppose I could offer de Flores in *The Changeling*.' 'That's the one!' Jack Phipps cried, jubilantly. 'It's a perfect part for you, and the venues will like it.' Venues? Diminishing, industrialised parlance. But agreement was reached: in the spring of 1990 we would tour *The Changeling*, a Jacobean revenge play, offering me a starry villain role.

Julian and I crept out of the room and looked at each other in amazement and horror: amazement that they had finally agreed to *something*, horror that it was this play!

'I shall never be able to sell that to the theatre managers,' said Julian.

'And nobody would come to see it if you did,' I replied.

Julian called those theatre managers he trusted, and they all concurred: *The Changeling* was a disastrous idea. There was a consensus, that with me as Brutus, *Julius Caesar* (which ACE had rejected) was sellable. I don't know how Julian achieved it, but he persuaded ACE to move the money sideways. I have always loved *Julius Caesar*, but this wasn't policy, it was survivalism.

I asked my old colleague Michael Joyce to direct. Things went well through casting, design and all other aspects of set-up. Annie Robinson – who had cast for Olivier at the Old Vic – helped us, out of good will. Terence Longdon, Drusus in *Ben-Hur*, would employ his magnificent Roman profile in the title role; Peter Blythe came on board for Cassius – perfect casting – and John Duttine, bringing his relaxed skills to Mark Antony, would also help the box office. Mike asked Pam to play Portia, Brutus's wife, which made good sense. The design, in spite of – maybe *because* of – budgetary restrictions was simple and clever. Stephen Warbeck would compose – timpani set in the wings, played by the actors. Perfect.

The first days went well: the company of 22 got on; we enjoyed working on the verse and exploring the world of the play. On day five, we started blocking, too late in my view, and as Mike wanted a precision that was hard to achieve at this stage we fell further and further behind. Since I had last worked with Mike on *Bengal Lancer*, he had been teaching – founding a drama course at Trinity College Dublin – and he was no longer a director; he had become an instructor. The company bridled at his didacticism. By the end of the third week (we only had four) we had still not blocked the play. Drumming rehearsals were going on apace, fight rehearsals were progressing, but there was no tree for these branches to hang from!

Things were not helped by the collapse of one of our sponsor's business affairs. He had promised us £20,000 but had gone bust. ACE, when approached, were tight-lipped, as well they might have been, so Julian arranged for me to dine with Mr Blackett of the Pru, who had, until recently, been our sponsor. If this meeting didn't work, I would have to tell the company that the tour was off. Blackett was a really nice man who had, like me, fallen under Tony Quayle's spell. We talked a lot about our mutual hero and I produced a postcard that I had treasured for 30 years, a picture of Tony as ebony-black Aaron, back in 1959.

Anthony Quayle as Aaron the Moor in Titus Andronicus, *Shakespeare Memorial Theatre, 1959*

Blackett had never seen this picture. He gazed at it, speechless. The next day Julian told me he had been moved by it, and was going to help. Divine man. So, by the skin of our teeth, we continued our uncomfortable rehearsals.

Mike scuppered all my plans for the prison play, and work with the deaf, and we were left with a minimal education programme. These things were important to me, and, as I had hardly chosen our play, they represented what little there was left that I might call 'policy'.

The cast just got on with it despite being stressed by the lack of proper rehearsal. I had a couple of spats with Mike about the way he was working, but he was grimly determined to do it his way, and after one dry, nervy run, we set off for Frank Matcham's beautiful Opera House at Buxton, where we began four days of ill-tempered technical rehearsals. Somehow we got the show on. There was not much wrong with it, but there was not enough right with it.

The severity of Mike's vision meant we were not living people. He saw Portia as representative of the great Roman past, which she is; but the other half of the story – that she is there to show real love and warmth, and humanise Brutus for the audience – Mike would not embrace. We had to introduce changes gradually, applying another of my maxims: 'if it's worth grumbling about, complain; if it's not worth complaining about, don't grumble'.

Slowly, we massaged the play into life. I would inform Mike of these changes over the phone, and he would shout at me that I had no right to tamper with his work. I would reply that I could not allow my company to go on a ten-week tour without addressing issues causing them discomfort, issues that had not been resolved in rehearsal.

The production was always, as board member Sir Ernest Hall described it, impecunious, but *Julius Caesar* is such a clear-cut play that lack of money per se didn't matter; once we had blood in the veins of Mike's concept, it got better and better. Using every performance as a rehearsal, this took about four weeks.

Mike turned up in Brighton, determined to change things back, but by then, tragically, he had been diagnosed with AIDS and was too weak to have his way. Although there was good cause for animosity between us, once we knew Mike was ill our long friendship took over. Disagreements over a play were nothing compared to the all too real drama of his life. He died in the Royal Middlesex four years later. Pam and I saw him the day before his passing. He drifted into a peaceful sleep; from which he never emerged. He was a good friend for over 20 years, and we were bereft.

I went off to do series two of *The Chief*, directed by my old friend Desmond Davis. I had to deal with Compass problems every day from my trailer and the hotel. My frustration turned to rage one day when I received a letter from ACE congratulating me on my three-year funding. For some time I had been complaining that a smaller company, registered under *another* name, was using *our registered* name – Compass – illegally. There were increasing instances of mistaken identity, culminating in this ludicrous error, made by ACE themselves. They didn't even have the decency to be embarrassed.

Things would have gone to the wall had not Peter Shaffer, who had been thrilled with our *Royal Hunt*, offered us the touring rights for *Amadeus* in 1991, the Mozart Bicentenary year. Even ACE could see this was an offer they could not refuse.

Rob Clare directed; Johann Engels provided fabulous designs; I was Salieri; Toyah Willcox was Constanze and Richard McCabe was a dazzling Mozart, composing and playing live his own piano variations. Martin Bax, deeply committed to what we were doing, clocked up his third tour. Michael Stroud was a fabulous Emperor. Terence Longdon was with us again, playing, as he termed it dryly, 'Some old count.' Michael Dray was in the cast, too, so our work with the deaf was resumed.

We commissioned a play for Toyah about Janis Joplin that went into prisons, funded again by the Baring Foundation. And the Hamlyn Foundation worked with us to create a schools' project called The Rock-me-Amadeus Roadshow that went into targeted schools in every city we visited. If the kids liked the Roadshow, for a pound they could come to see *Amadeus*: Hamlyn money paid the ticket price differential, and in this way we took 500 children to the theatre for the first time in their lives. We were able to give another Equity card, so, understudying Toyah, and appearing in the Roadshow, was Helen Baxendale. I am very proud of the unprecedented outreach work we did, and of Rufus Sewell and Helen, actors who began their fine careers under my wing.

The tour was a massive success. Theatres were busy to packed everywhere we went. The company was rock-solid. The Janis Joplin prison play was superb: Toyah, ably supported by Patrick Turner, played in seven prisons. And Michael Dray went into five schools for the deaf. In the Aberdeen school I went to see his work.

Michael had difficulty with one unhappy, isolated girl of about 11. He worked caringly on her, and eventually turned her into one of the most active members of the group. To see the smile she gave Michael when he left was a thing of great beauty. He gave her a glimpse of freedom. He might even have changed her life. I often wonder if that seed of creativity she found within herself that afternoon has blossomed.

The only weakness in all our wonderful work on this tour was the first ten minutes of *Amadeus*. I worked unceasingly at it, but it never came fully to life. We were on the edge of the West End after playing to packed houses on the road, but Peter Shaffer, remembering John Peter's disdain, and afraid *his play* would carry the can for *my inadequacy* (although he was too kind ever to put it that way), withdrew the West End rights.

In spite of my second failure to get us into the West End, we had an uncharacteristically happy board meeting, when it was revealed that *Amadeus* had been *so* successful that, for the first time ever, there was a positive balance in the bank. There was even heady talk of remunerating me for my services as artistic director. But things were changing at the Arts Council. Jack Phipps might not have been easy, but he did keep the company going. The new guard looked unsympathetic.

Salieri in Amadeus *by Peter Shaffer, Compass, 1991*

We put together a cast for a hypothetical *The Country Wife*, headed by Michael Rudman, hoping that an established director would help our cause, and to keep us alive I mounted a new play – an area I felt we needed to work in. The play was about August Strindberg and written by Ronald Hayman, with whom I had worked on the radio in a funny series called *Such Rotten Luck*, directed by the remarkable Piers Plowright. It featured Stephen Rea and Zoë Wanamaker.

Zoë was involved in another of my Compass adventures. While at the National Theatre, we were invited, with Barbara Leigh-Hunt, to do some readings from Saki for a Platform performance featuring Dirk Bogarde. The massive turnout, to see Dirk onstage for the first time in 40-odd years, was a reminder of what a star he was. Together, the four of us read four or five Saki short stories to a crammed Olivier. I felt that with very little effort this could be made into a really interesting, and lucrative, evening. Dear Robert Cogo-Fawcett offered us the Theatre Royal, Bath, and we raised money from Powergen to fund the evening. Jeremy Raison, the young director who had been assigned to us by the NT, and I put together an evening in which you learnt something about Saki himself, whose real name was H. H. Munro: he worked as a journalist in the Balkans; he died in the trenches; his last words, before a sniper got him, were, 'Put that bloody light out!' I commissioned music from George Fenton.

There was uncontainable excitement in the South West about Dirk's appearance. He read deliciously, with acid wit and great charm. The evening was a monster success. I shared a dressing room with Dirk that night in Bath, and he was quite apprehensive, but thrilled to see he could still command an audience. 'Come here,' he said to me just before we went onstage, 'your hair's a mess.' As he sorted out my hair, he said, 'Thank you for this, dear boy.'

David Puttnam crashed the post-show party. Powergen was very happy, and it created goodwill and pleasure all round. We performed it subsequently – and *did* raise money – with Alan Bates and Robert Hardy, an old, loyal friend of Tony's, deputising for Dirk.

Dirk adored Pam, who loved his acting and writing – which I am sure helped – and we remained friends, although, sadly, we did not see him again after he had his stroke. He did not want us to.

The *new* play was a brilliant four-hander called *Playing the Wife*. Its clever premise was that Strindberg was directing a play he had written about his first marriage. Playing his *first* wife was Harriet Bösse, who became his *third* wife.

A lovely actor, Paul Spence, playing the young Strindberg, brought with him some money from the Belfast Arts Festival. I needed another two thousand pounds to make a go of it, and ACE agreed to a meeting. I explained the situation to an officer, and expressed the hope that, as the amount was so small, they might contribute. She refused.

'Can you give me any help at all?' I said.

The woman shook her head.

ACE advertised its support then by a paper-clip logo saying, 'This production was mounted with support from ACE', so I asked, 'If I display your paper clip on our programmes, might you pay my actors' air fares to Belfast?'

'No. Sorry. I can't.'

I remarked tersely to this charmless woman that unless she was able to offer me some help I might be tempted to attach my own paper clip, saying, 'This play was mounted without any support *whatsoever* from the Arts Council.' She did not see the funny side of this comment. I said, '£500?' She shook her head. I said, '£200?' She just looked at me, dumbly. '£100?' I whined. I knew this was pointless, I was just rubbing it in. 'If I was Peter Brook,' I asked, 'would you say the same thing?'

'I am afraid I would have to,' she replied.

'That is probably why he has worked in Paris for the last thirty years,' I said, more in sorrow than in anger, and left the room.

I got the script of *Playing the Wife* to Barry Foster, an actor I had long admired, who was well known as the television detective Van der Valk. He liked the play and was happy to take on this limited small-scale engagement. I cast the young Julia Ormond as Harriet Bösse. I managed to raise the money needed, I called in favours from wardrobe, wigs, set and lighting people, and we rehearsed happily for four weeks, in a cold, empty room at the top of a school in Wandsworth, loaned to us by a sympathetic headmistress. We played a week at the Watermans Arts Centre to warm the play up, and flew to Belfast with ... no assistance whatsoever from ACE.

Barry and Julia were thrilling and Jonathan Goldstein wrote some spine-tingling music. It was a great success. One review described it as an 'electrifying four-hander'. We came to the Ustinov Studio in Bath for a week, in the hope that people whom we invited from London might see it, and perhaps move it to somewhere like the Hampstead Theatre Club. One local notice was a paean of praise for the play, the cast, the production and Compass, but only *one* person came down from town and she missed the first half, without which the play did not make sense. I felt like giving up.

Word came through that because we had made money from the *Amadeus* tour, ACE had decided they wanted as much as possible of their original investment *back*. The man who had taken over responsibility for touring took me to Chez Nico, a posh restaurant, to tell me they did not have enough money to fund *The Country Wife*. Tactless. Disgraceful.

'Could they not use the money we were giving *back*, to help them fund *Country Wife*?' I enquired pointedly over the lobster.

I told the ACE man that I had offered to create a partnership – the Bristol Old Vic were prepared to house us for a month at the beginning of a tour – to help reduce the overheads of *launching* a tour. ACE, I was informed over the petits fours, did not favour co-production.

'Keep going like this,' I said, 'and pretty soon you won't have anything else!' And, boy, was I right about *that*.

Every positive move I made was blocked. The last thing I said to the Arts Council was that they were the only body in the country whose defined purpose was to help people like myself, and that it was painful and incomprehensible to me that they were the *only* group of people who made my life difficult. Sponsors were queuing up to support us, but they would not commit unless they knew ACE money was in place. I could not believe that ACE were prepared to let such hard, decent work as ours, such good will and such good value, go to the wall, but even I could see the writing on it.

We called a board meeting and I informed our loyal members, ably chaired by Sir Richard Luce, ex-Arts Minister, that there was no will at ACE to keep us going, and that we should quit while we were ahead. We weren't ahead. Since ACE had deprived us of our small bank balance we had accrued debts of £14,000. Sir Ernest Hall and Sir Eddie Kulukundis nobly picked them up and we closed with a clean slate. Representations were made at the highest level to try and stop the axe falling, but ACE wanted rid of us, although they had nothing to put in our place. I was angry, I was bitter and I was disillusioned; but my adventure was over. Pam kindly refrained from saying, 'I told you so.'

I had failed because I was stubborn, idealistic, overconfident, and imagined that I could achieve, if not the impossible, the pretty bloody unlikely. It was a huge blow to my self-esteem. In *Educating Rita*, Willy Russell defines tragedy as 'something that is pre-ordained, inevitable. Macbeth ... is warned in the play, but ... he goes blindly on and on, and with every step, he's spinning one more piece of thread which will eventually make up the network of his own tragedy.' I am not suggesting Compass was a tragedy, let alone a tragedy of Shakespearean proportions, but when I spoke those lines in the Trafalgar Studios in 2010 they had a ghastly ring of truth for me: we are what we are. With Compass I had come face to face with the limitations of my character. And it hurt.

I tend not to have regrets, but I still chew over that period of my life.

26

STEPPING STONES

I have always been an actor who likes actors to have their say. For some time after Compass folded I felt I had no voice at all. I felt defeated. In the wake of running my own company the profession seemed confused about me, too, harbouring a slight concern that, having had control, I would still want it. Control. Ha! I had to reinvent myself. At least we weren't short of money and I no longer had to deal with the ignorant bureaucrats at Arts Council England.

Twenty-five years later, my career reached something of a high when Rupert Goold asked me to play the title role in *King Charles III*, Mike Bartlett's extraordinary play. Looking back, it feels as though there was a series of stepping stones that got me from the dark post-Compass days to my brief reign as Charles on Broadway.

In 1994, I went to see Mike Joyce when he was dying. I had just directed *Hamlet*. Mike hated me directing. 'You're a sensitive rugger-bugger,' he said to me, 'stick to acting.' But when Ian Talbot, who was dragging the Open Air Theatre in Regent's Park – known as 'the Park' – into the twentieth century, generously asked me to direct *Hamlet*, I was still feeling lost so I grabbed the opportunity.

Hamlet, a political and psychologically complex play, is not ideally suited to the Park. How could I stage it to blot out the pastoral setting? I asked our friend Tanya McCallin to take on the challenge of design, while I set to work with my old colleague Roger Warren cutting the text. Roger used to prepare Peter Hall's

Shakespeare texts, and we had worked together closely at the National. In the Park you are contracted to run two and a half hours, because if you overrun the Park gates are locked and the audience can't get out. Uncut, *Hamlet* runs four hours, so we needed to remove an hour and a half.

For my first cut I decided I would read the play, crossing out every single line I did not understand immediately. A lot of people see their first Shakespeare in the Park, so if I had to reread any line I cut it. I know *Hamlet* really well, but this exercise, to my surprise and embarrassment, took out almost an hour! Over the remaining 30 minutes, I had some choice.

The actor's job is to be his character. The director has responsibility for the whole thing, so when I am directing I read and reread the whole play, to see what ideas and themes emerge. Gielgud was once asked, 'What is style?' To which he replied, 'Being in the right play.' Looking for 'the right' *Hamlet* I felt the Park would favour the romantic side of the play, so the politics went – which hurt. I wanted to include Young Fortinbras – who gathers up the pieces at the end of the play – and I really wanted the great soliloquy 'How all occasions do inform against me', although it is not in the First Folio; so Roger and I winnowed and chipped away, making use of the Bad Folio in moving the placing of 'To be or not to be'. The result was so short and moved so fast, it inevitably reduced the sense of a man taking far too long to do nothing, but it was really true to the play! One review said, 'This Hamlet is having a ball!' This was the fault of our version, not of the *Hamlet*, but it was in the contract!

Casting went well, but I was without a Hamlet until Damian Lewis walked in: here was a star in the making. I offered Gertrude to Pam – I wanted a strong sense of mother/son. She shared Damian's colouring and our Tom was almost Damian's age. Paul Freeman played Claudius, David Collings Polonius and Rebecca Egan, Peter's daughter, made a stunning debut as Ophelia.

I asked Tanya to make the space more intimate. I asked her for a strong upstage entrance, entrances on *both sides*, and a small upper level. Tanya created a 30-foot-high, curving steel wall with

The set for Hamlet, *Open Air Theatre, Regent's Park, 1994*

a concealed staircase descending from a high platform, a hidden door at stage level, and hand grips so Hamlet could scale the face of the wall when desperately following the Ghost. There was a tall, wide steel pillar upstage left, concealing a curtain that ran out to the main wall, as an arras for the closet scene. The main stage in the Park is a solid mound, so Tanya brought the stage floor out into the auditorium – creating enough space to conceal Ophelia's grave, as well as providing some intimacy and visual balance. Simultaneously massive and minimal.

I wanted to keep the play mobile, to avoid actors sitting or lying on the stage floor, in case the weather turned nasty; so Tanya and I came up with two portable steel boxes which gave us thrones and, placed side by side with a wrap thrown over them, a bed for the closet. The Players brought all their stuff on in a cart, and the play scene was done with a white cloth on the deck. The only other time I let anyone lie down was when they were dead!

I tried to clarify a couple of things in the play. In Shakespeare, function is really important – you often need to ask what a scene is for. So ... what are the Players really *for*? They embody the themes of reality and illusion: their play – a lie – illuminates the truth. I wanted to try and make this theme more apparent.

When the actors arrive, Hamlet asks the leading man for an 'audition' speech: he recalls a speech in which the crucial words (to me) are 'blood of fathers' – surely Hamlet has chosen this extract subconsciously because of his obsession with his father. I had never seen this speech have any real point before, so I came up with something to illuminate it. It began with casting: I asked Ken Gibson (de Soto for me in *Royal Hunt*) to double as the Ghost (Hamlet's father) and the First Player, creating a clear connection between the two characters.

When the Players pulled their cart on, it was covered in a white sheet. When the cart was still, the sheet began, very slowly, to rise. Hamlet was transfixed by this strange, ghostly vision. When the sheet stopped rising, Hamlet moved forward and nervously pulled it towards him, in order to see what was underneath. What he revealed was the First Player, looking exactly like the Ghost.

Damian Lewis as Hamlet and Pamela Miles as Gertrude in Hamlet,
Open Air Theatre, Regent's Park, 1994

Hamlet recoiled. 'The Ghost' jumped down to greet him. On the line 'Com'st thou to beard us here in Denmark?' Hamlet put his hand out towards the First Player and touched his beard. The Player took a step backwards, leaving Hamlet holding a false beard in his hand. The Player is now clearly himself – not the Ghost – Hamlet's father. Hamlet, still holding the false beard, could then relate 'blood of fathers' directly to it, which helped his speech. It also illustrated the theme of illusion and reality central to the play: 'for there is nothing either good or bad, but thinking, makes it so.' I introduced other ideas of this nature to try and clarify subconscious elements in the play.

The first half of any play in the Park is challenging because of the broad daylight. When the theatre is cloaked in night and the stage is lit, it is easier to focus the audience, and atmosphere builds. I managed to bring the interval forward – to Claudius bellowing 'Give me some light! Away!' after the play-scene. This allowed our interval to use up 20 minutes of daylight, and the second half – which began with Claudius storming on, the Court still in attendance, confronting Hamlet and repeating, 'Give me some light! Away!' – happened in near-darkness. When the stage cleared, Hamlet was alone, holding a flaming torch, for the speech ''Tis now the very witching time of night/ When churchyards yawn and hell itself breathes out/ Contagion to this world'. It was thrilling, and the bonus – the real aim of this ploy – was that we could play the closet scene after nightfall. Ophelia's funeral was staged as if it was raining – with the company holding umbrellas, and a soundtrack of distant thunder. It looked stunning. Quite often audience members were fooled and got their umbrellas out. We were blessed with a blazing summer. The show was popular and we broke the box-office record for walk-up trade, and Damian, who was superb, was on his way to a stellar career.

One night I popped into the theatre on my way home and watched the second half. About ten minutes from the end, a young boy started walking along his row, but he wasn't leaving: he got to the aisle, then walked down towards the stage. He sat on the bottom step and watched, rapt. The ushers let him be. A couple of moments later, a young girl got up from another row and joined him. They sat together till the end, then stood and cheered and clapped.

You learn how to act, rehearsing a good play, with good actors and a good director. I grew a lot working with Howard Davies. The first show we did together was Schiller's *Mary Stuart*, in which I played a flamboyant Leicester alongside a steely Anna Massey as Elizabeth, and Isabelle Huppert as Mary. Isabelle was remarkable: she had a natural sensuality that I do not think an English actress could have achieved. The contrast with Anna was intense, and the great scene of the rival queens meeting – an invention of Schiller's – was electric. It was a starry National Theatre production, as was another collaboration, the Eugene O'Neill trilogy, *Mourning Becomes Electra*. Howard asked me to join workshops with Eve Best and Helen Mirren to test this unwieldy old monster. We spent a few days at the NT Studio where, one day, Howard received a note addressed to the director of *Maureen Becomes a Lecturer*! The work was reassuring; the plays held up and Howard asked me to play the Agamemnon figure – Civil War general Ezra Mannon. It hurt, but I had to tell him I did not feel comfortable in the part, and he cast someone else. And then, Fate intervened.

A year earlier, Howard was doing Christopher Hampton's *The Talking Cure*, with our friend James Hazeldine. Just as they began previews, Jimmy was taken to hospital with heart problems, and astonishingly, terrifyingly, within three days this handsome, vital man and superb actor was dead. All of us who knew him – Pam had done a play with him at the Court in the sixties – were shocked. It didn't seem possible. But there he was – gone. He was 53.

During rehearsals for *Electra*, almost exactly a year later, the actor Howard had asked to play Ezra experienced the same symptoms that had done for poor Jimmy, and was advised to leave the play. Howard called me. I was actually on a plane on the runway in Casablanca, on the way home from my first spell on *Alexander*, Oliver Stone's almighty turkey. The dates fitted, so I was able to help out. I was serviceable in the part, gradually feeling more at home, and my ordinariness did not mar a stunning evening. It was again useful to work unfamiliar muscles, and a privilege to act with Helen Mirren. She has a fierce natural intelligence, which, allied to her natural beauty, makes her a dynamic force on stage. She also had a light ease and freshness which helped me settle in the role.

Only the NT has the resources to stage such a huge work, and Howard's ambition paid dividends. It was a shame we did not have a longer run, but Helen and I were asked to repeat Ezra's death scene some ten years later as part of the NT's fiftieth Birthday Gala. Helen flew in from some glamorous location. We met up with Howard for an hour one Thursday afternoon, and staggered through it – it's a ten-minute scene. That evening we had a dress run, and the next night – with no more rehearsal – we were doing it to a full house of NT stars past and present, and the added pressure of online streaming. I must be one of the few people ever to have seen Helen nervous. She is a very cool, centred person, but at one stage during rehearsal she looked like I felt – white with terror.

My most successful collaboration with Howard was *The Iceman Cometh*. He had directed it once before, in a production famous for Ian Holm's breakdown. I happened to see the very performance at which Ian so tragically cracked up. He played a blinding first act, but did not appear for the second. Patrick Stewart told me that Ian was lying, rigid, on his dressing-room floor, in a state of catatonic shock. I don't think he went onstage for ten or 11 years after that.

When Howard returned to the play in 1998, he knew exactly what he wanted to do with it. He asked me to play Larry Slade – the old 'phoolosopher' as Hickey calls him. This is Hickey's main antagonist in the play, and, although he is 70 (I was then 53), I hoped I could create a rich character. And this was key to Howard's vision – bii-iig characters.

The play is set in a down-and-out bar in downtown Manhattan in 1911. The bar is peopled by an extraordinary array of alcoholic bums, and Howard wanted each character to be powerfully drawn, not only to help the audience distinguish them one from another, but to provide the energy of the play. Clarke Peters played the bar-room dogsbody with explosive passion; the leprechaun John Rogan, playing an Irishman, was paired with lean, tall, rubber-necked Roger Sloman; full of heart – how awful that his heart was in reality so weak – Jimmy Hazeldine played the Irish-American owner of the bar, Harry Hope; the magician Mark Strong played the Bronx bartender, Rocky; Paddy Godfrey was effortlessly eccentric as the Englishman; Duncan Bell was beautiful and damaged as Prince Willy; Nick Day was the Dutch Boer — outrageously incomprehensible and gloriously funny. Through this array of strongly etched 'men-on-the-edge', Howard released a crazy energy which drove the play forward with relentless speed. It didn't feel like four and a half hours, was the most common response. And sitting like a cherry right on top of the cake was Kevin Spacey, in the star role of Hickey, who tries to reform his drinking mates before revealing the tragedy at the heart of his own ruined life. Kevin's film *The Usual Suspects* was well known, *LA Confidential* was in the can, and here he was, this rising American star, giving his time to a small London theatre, the Almeida. Jonathan Kent and Ian McDiarmid had steered it to this pre-eminent position, and it was a tribute to them and Howard that they had persuaded Kevin to entrust them with his blossoming career.

Kevin always maintained that he was thrilled to be among a group of British actors, but the read-through was such an interminable shambles it must have crossed his mind to leave before it was too late! Of course we had not found our characters, or our accents, but it was downright embarrassing, bordering occasionally on farcical. Before he opted for stark, guttural Boer incomprehensibility, Nick Day was making such a hash of his Afrikaans that he started laughing *as* he was reading, commenting on how lamentable his accent was, and apologising. We were in stitches, but poor Howard – and Kevin – must have thought they were going mad. Read-throughs are nearly always sheer misery. In the days of weekly rep, managements insisted on a read-through, because it was not unknown for actors to study nothing but their own lines, and a read-through ensured that everyone heard the whole play!

We struggled through. Howard *might* have mentioned that we had left ourselves room for improvement and we set off up the mountain.

My character evolved gradually – arthritic hands arrived one day, and this led to my pointing things out with my thumbs, which led to bluntness of speech. I grew an unkempt beard and shaved off what little hair I have on top, chewed tobacco with damaged teeth, and hung old half-moon spectacles on a piece of string round my neck. Having built this character, I had the luxury of time on stage in *performance*, for which there is no substitute. I began to learn how to live on stage.

We might have developed a sense during rehearsal that *Iceman* had the potential to be good, but it was not until we had friends in for the dress rehearsal that we knew it was special. At the end, our chums just stood and roared! We were amazed. We had a hit run at the Almeida, went to the Old Vic, where Kevin fell in love with that beautiful old theatre, and a year later we were on Broadway.

Only five of the original cast were able to cross the pond. Kevin and Clarke had green cards, Jimmy was doing *Irish*-American, Paddy was playing the Brit, and Kevin went to American Equity in person to fight for me – I was playing American. He and Howard argued that without their Larry Slade the production would simply not be ours! I did indeed anchor the play, but I owe Kevin a debt of gratitude for convincing Equity that if we had a hit – and keeping the central ingredients made that more likely – we were making work for American actors – 20, plus understudies. Our transfer to Broadway welcomed on board classy Michael Emerson, charming Robert Sean Leonard and the then little-known Paul Giamatti – a fine cast. We were slotted for an 11-week run, but it was such a hit we extended to 17. First hundred-dollar ticket for a play on Broadway. Never an empty seat.

As Larry Slade in The Iceman Cometh *by Eugene O'Neill, Almeida, Old Vic and Broadway, 1998-9*

With Kevin Spacey in The Iceman Cometh

And in New York we learnt something new about O'Neill's masterpiece. The Brits – Paddy, Jimmy and I – were eating *aglio e oglio* (one of the few things I can cook) after our final rehearsal, and we all sensed that our work had taken on another dimension. *Iceman* is a ruthless dismantling of 'pipe-dreams' – it savages the delusions and fantasies that help people survive; although in the end, it says that when the only thing you have left is a dream, it is fatal to take it away. In America, we realised, the word dream effortlessly evokes the carrot that dangles over the continent – the American Dream. The play developed added, disturbing power.

And *did* people come to be disturbed?!! Jason Robards, the original Hickey – and the original Jamie in *A Long Day's Journey into Night* – turned up; Madeleine Albright, first woman Secretary of State, came; Bill Clinton himself – a friend of Kevin's. I could hardly believe my eyes when I saw Sidney Poitier at the stage door. It was rumoured that Woody Allen came, and lasted the First Act – an hour and 17 minutes. A critic once observed that you didn't buy a ticket for O'Neill, you enlisted! *If* Woody came, he did *not* enlist.

In July, when it was hot and humid, and we were nearing the end of the run, I climbed the stairs wearily to our communal dressing room – Kevin thought it was important for us to share, so he had them knock down a wall! We had reached the second interval, after Act Three, at a time of night when most other theatres were dark. I trudged upstairs in the company of Paul Giamatti. 'Only one more act to go,' I muttered. Paul, stifling an exhausted yawn, murmured, 'Yeah. Those awful words ... Act Four!' It was shattering, but a great experience and won me a Critics' Circle nomination.

27

FURTHER STEPS

Three other stepping stones between Compass and *King Charles III* were provided by Shakespeare. In 2001 I went to Stratford to do *Julius Caesar* for the third time, with Ed Hall. He had been at an impressionable age when I did Leontes for his dad, Peter, at the National Theatre. He had never forgotten it, and now asked me to play Cassius. We met and had a great chat; I really liked him. Like his father, he radiated ease and confidence.

Cutting was Ed's first wise decision. He cleverly removed some of the less interesting soldiery, like the poor man who runs on in Act Five shouting 'I am the son of Marcus Cato, ho!' At that stage of the evening, you want to kill him, not listen to him. 'Where are Brutus and Cassius?' and 'Where is Antony?' is all the audience care about. One of the difficulties with *Julius Caesar* is that the main characters the audience meet before the murder are human beings, more accessible than the soldiers they become in the second half. Taking out the interval was another skilled move towards a solution.

It was 2001. Fatal year. While we were playing *Julius Caesar*, the Twin Towers were hit. Occasionally, there are bits of Shakespeare that sound as though they were written just yesterday. Lines about the nature of revolutionary acts took on an eerie resonance. The conspirators are standing over Caesar's mutilated body, bathed in his blood:

> How many ages hence
> Shall this our lofty scene be acted o'er

In states unborn and accents yet unknown
     ... So oft as that shall be
So often shall the knot of us be called
The men that gave their country liberty!

The play was suddenly relevant. It was the best of the three productions I have been in.

I worked with director Ian Brown in 1999, on Shelagh Stephenson's beautiful play *Five Kinds of Silence*. This featured Linda Bassett, Gina McKee and Lizzy McInnerny. We played at the Lyric Hammersmith. It was originally written for radio, the true story of a man who had physically, sexually and mentally abused his wife and two daughters. When the eldest of the girls reached the age of 38, she shot her father. The girls were tried, and were let off on the grounds of mental cruelty. You may guess, in spite of a string of five-star reviews, why we played to thin houses. The piece itself was poetic, the staging was perfect; those who came loved it, but people stayed away in their droves. As a friend of ours once said, playing a feisty new play in old-fashioned Westcliff-on-Sea – 'They are dying of agoraphobia in the stalls!' But Ian achieved that rare thing – a perfect production: it could not have been done better.

Ian and I greatly enjoyed experimenting wildly in rehearsal, so we looked for opportunities to work together. He tried to lure me up to the West Yorkshire Playhouse, where he took over the artistic directorship, dangling the carrot of Ibsen's *The Master Builder* in front of me. Although I read two translations, there was one line, common to both, which struck me as terminal: I said to Ian, 'I don't think the theatre-going public of Leeds should pay good money to see me sitting on a sofa, saying to an attractive young woman, "There's a lot of the troll in you".' I greatly admire Ibsen, but it's rooted in an alien culture, and it has to be beyond first-rate to work. Even Sir Herbert Beerbohm Tree, an early champion of Ibsen, referred to 'the three Gs – gloom, goblins and gonorrhoea'!

Ian retaliated with a better carrot – *King Lear*. I could not say no, but I gave him two basic conditions – no rain, no nudity. I did once take my kit off onstage – in Caryl Churchill's play *Traps*, in the Upstairs Theatre at the Royal Court in 1976 – and I have no objection to it *per se*, but nudity can distract: on my way out of Ian Holm's and Ian McKellen's Lears, I heard audiences discussing the size of the royal penises! I am sure that is not what either of those great actors would have wanted. Likewise, rain can be distracting: I have seen *Lear* storm scenes which have all but drowned the actors, and all you think about is how wet they must be. I have seen the rain directed into one corner of the stage, while the actors, bone-dry, play elsewhere: all you think about is – where is all that water going? Water is real; nudity is real; they cross some line of convention. You need to be careful how you use them.

Ian and I spent well over a year preparing the script. There are two quarto versions of the play and the First Folio, which does not contain the 'mock trial scene'. Some scholars contend that the First Folio represents Shakespeare's final decision on the text of his plays, so they make the point – without any real supportive evidence – that Shakespeare himself took the mock trial out of *Lear*, concluding that he removed it because it does not advance the action of the play. It is undeniably true that the action stalls, but this feels to me like an academic judgement. I cannot imagine any actor wanting to take on Lear without playing that scene, partly because it shows his growing madness in a comedic light. It's not a long scene. Its pain and violence are shocking. It shows that Lear is being ruthlessly pursued by his enemies; that he is being hidden and moved about for his own safety. It shows what he is thinking, what the causes of his madness are, and how far he has deteriorated. It shows Kent and Gloucester caring for him, and his other self, the Fool, who *should* be tending his master, humouring him, before deserting him. It may not push the action forward, but you can't say nothing happens! We trimmed it a bit.

I like working on text, and, as I had less to do than Ian, I would offer the first – often brutal – cuts to him, one act at a time, then he adjusted it. We took out 700 lines in all – again using fundamental comprehensibility as the first pair of scissors, then thinking about the story, its shape and needs. We cut a lot of Poor Tom's madness, and restructured some of the better 'raving', trying always to give the audience a line through it they could follow. The accessibility of our text really helped – you could feel audiences settle because they could follow it.

Ian worked with Ruari Murchison on the design, and produced an extraordinary, off-kilter room for the first half. After a really impressive opening eclipse – taken from a hint in the text about how the natural world predicts man-made tragedy – this strange room was suddenly resplendent in gold and red. We wanted to start with as much panoply, wealth, power and kingship as possible. Running from upstage to downstage centre, where it reached my throne, was a strip of scarlet carpet, and in the middle of that stood a large sword. I sat with my back to the house – getting up whenever needed to illustrate the division of the kingdom, or to confront Cordelia – and the girls came formally to the sword for their opening speeches, where, addressing me, they were able to talk directly to the house. It was simple and real. Crucially, it established Lear's power, giving me somewhere mighty to fall from.

Looking at the model with Ian and Ruari one day, I said, 'How are we going to do the storm?' After various suggestions, I asked Ruari if he could get me to the top of the set. Because the upstage wall of the room was at an angle, he said he could run a ladder up the back of it. When the lights came up on me for 'Blow winds...' I was 30 feet above the stage! Ruari had intended to use a revolve to denote changes of scene, but when we embraced this idea of how to do the storm he changed his mind and said, 'We should save the revolve for the storm.' Ian added two thunder-sheets, visible on each side of the stage, carefully orchestrated with the text, and operated live by the cast. So with me up high, thunder thundering its bellyful, and lightning flashing, a third of the way into the scene, the set began slowly to turn, bringing me round to down stage centre, way above the audience. I was able to play the end of the scene as I came down the ladder. It looked much more

King Lear, with Bernard Lloyd as Gloucester, West Yorkshire Playhouse, 2011

dangerous than it was, and although it had the one disadvantage of my not being physically close to the Fool, it was very impressive and really helped capture the elemental power of that very difficult scene. *No rain.* One hell of a storm.

For the second half, Ruari took us to a bare stage, which at West Yorkshire Playhouse is an enormous space, with a sloping back. It was a fantastic contrast with the first half, and gave the sense of a harsh, unyielding universe, over which the moon hung low. Playing the great scene at the end of Act Four, on this fabulous open heath, when the mad King meets the blind Duke, with my lifelong friend Bernie Lloyd as Gloucester, was simply unforgettable. 'When we are born, we cry that we are come to this great stage of fools.' If there is a greater stretch of drama in any play anywhere than the last act and a half of *Lear*, I don't know it.

I didn't want to have help carrying Cordelia on – the relationship with her is so personal and heart-breaking. Olivia Morgan, who was a very fine Cordelia, is a slip of a thing, and I managed to bring her on, on my back, like a tortoise. I was able to lower her, unaided, to the ground. She lay in my lap, the rope that hanged her, trailing over the stage. As I died, the moon sank from sight. I was very proud of the work we achieved and will be eternally grateful to Ian for giving me a realistic crack at that mountain of a play. The *Observer* cited it as one of the top ten theatrical events of the year. The 'King' muscles I exercised on this play were unconscious preparation for King Charles.

Over the years I have done a lot of work at the Theatre Royal, Bath, but it was a particular thrill to get a call from Adrian Noble, whom I had known since his early days at Bristol Old Vic in the late seventies, but never worked for, asking me to play Prospero for the Bath Summer Festival, 2012. After Lear, it seemed like the only big Shakespearean role left for me!

The Tempest is a complex play, its disparate storylines seemingly disconnected from the main thread. Its centrepiece is a Masque staged by Prospero for his daughter and her fiancé, and this is where most productions of the play falter. The Masque was a Court entertainment which developed in the early Jacobean period.

Lavishly funded by the king, it provided the superficial pleasures of theatrical spectacle – being roughly 30 times more expensive to stage than a play. It must have been as thrilling as seeing *Ben-Hur* at the Coliseum Theatre – the chariot horses, chained to the back wall of the theatre, galloping directly at the audience on a revolving drum! Ben Jonson was in charge of Court Masques for a while, and they figure in other plays of the period – most notably Thomas Middleton's *Women Beware Women*, where its use is stunning but melodramatic.

Shakespeare uses the Masque in *The Tempest* to create magical imagery. Prospero describes it as 'some vanity of mine art', and it is acted out by his 'spirits'. When he panics, and dismisses them, the whole scene, and all the performers, vanish. In the ensuing great speech, 'Our revels now are ended', Prospero is given one of Shakespeare's most sublime theatrical metaphors:

> We are such stuff
> As dreams are made on, and our little life
> Is rounded with a sleep.

Like the vanished Masque, like being an actor, like being a human being, *everything* will dissolve. It's all a dream; me speaking, you watching; all of it.

With a simple visual notion, and very strong, minimalist, Japanese influence, Adrian Noble united the disparate elements of the play – even the Masque – aided by some rich music by Shaun Davy, and, although it took me a while to get a handle on Prospero, it was a delightful evening and the most complete version of that play that I have encountered.

After Lear, I had felt a little 'What on earth do I do now?' I asked my agent to find me something that would pay the bills and give me time to recover. Be careful what you wish for. I spent three months filming *Strikeback* in South Africa, where I had enough free time to learn Prospero's lines for the upcoming *Tempest*. But when we started rehearsing, I had no idea of how to play him. Still lost, in rehearsal week three of four, the thought occurred to me that this play – famously regarded as Shakespeare's 'Farewell' – only really worked if the person saying farewell spoke the lines. I became convinced that it was a farewell from the actor. If it's the actor saying goodbye to his public, it develops real potency and poignancy. I quickly discovered that Richard Burbage, Shakespeare's leading man, was acting till 1619, seven years after *The Tempest* was written, so it clearly wasn't written for Burbage. For the moment my theory got me nowhere.

I had grown a beard for the part, and at a costume fitting Clancy, our designer, said to me, 'Why not make it a courtly beard?' I didn't much like the notion: Prospero has been on his island for 15 years. But the idea grew on me that he might dress his beard especially for the arrival of his enemies. The thought then came to me that I might wear a beard like Shakespeare's in one of the famous portraits. And then it occurred to me that if Shakespeare *began* his professional life as an actor, perhaps that was how he *ended* it! If he himself played Prospero, the play, and many of the lines really were the farewell I was looking for: the great writer took to acting again, assuming the role of the magician-creator, specifically to say his own, real adieu, in person, to his theatre, his company and his audience.

There is a sort of actor's myth, handed down – like Garrick's Hamlet sword – that the way to play Prospero is as if you know you do not have long to live. I was told this by Barry Stanton, who got it from Ian Richardson. And it makes sense in acting terms. But it makes even more sense, *if* ... Shakespeare himself played the part. The year was 1612. Will was not in good health. He sensed the end was nigh.

Shakespeare was to live for four more years – longer, maybe, than he expected. Imagine the potency of Shakespeare himself telling the world he was retiring, and that 'every third step will be my grave'. It helps to explain the sudden premonition of death, so breathtakingly expressed after the masque: like every play that ever was, the world will dissolve too, one day! The old boy was a prophet.

Prospero in The Tempest, *Bath Theatre Royal, 2012*

If Shakespeare really did play Prospero, *The Tempest* would have been special to his Company, and that might explain why, although it was his *last* play, it appears *first* in the listed plays of the First Folio of 1623 – something that has always caused surprise. All speculation, of course.

James Shapiro the Shakespeare scholar observes acutely that although we cannot draw any firm conclusions from the plays about Shakespeare's actual relationships with his two daughters, we can state for certain that the father/daughter relationship is a powerful axis within his creativity. Lear, Pericles, Miranda, Viola ... 'I am all the daughters of my father's house'. Shakespeare/Prospero is an old man dying; he uses his fading powers to provide his daughter with a secure future. Doesn't feel too far-fetched, does it? Thinking I was Shakespeare was something I did not mention to anyone, but from the moment it came into my mind the part fell into place. The creative imagination responds to strange stimuli.

28

A King on Broadway

In 2007, when my agent John Grant told me Peter Hall wanted me for Shaw's *Pygmalion*, I thought he might be offering me Colonel Pickering, but to my pleasure and surprise it was Henry Higgins he wished me to tackle. Peter had worked with Pam in *Animal Farm* way back, and he asked her to play Freddy Eynsford-Hill's mother. Bath Festival and nine weeks on the road. Together. Lovely.

Before rehearsal, Peter told me he saw it as quite a dark play: I am sure that was why he had thought of me – Ronald Merrick casts a long shadow! As I learnt the part, I developed, quite early on, a sense of the man. Shaw loves taking the Mickey out of the Brits, and Higgins and Pickering are two upper-class cronies who perform a heartless experiment. They take a guttersnipe, Eliza Doolittle, turn her into a lady then abandon her. This social engineering also destroys Eliza's father's life. Pickering has some sense of the damage done, but Higgins seems unaffected, in an almost autistic way, until it is too late. Suddenly he realises that Eliza is in love with him, that she is a girl in a million and he has let her go.

The more I read the play, and the more I thought about Higgins's relationship with his mother, exquisitely played in our production by Barbara Jefford, the more he seemed like a man who had never grown free of her; he was a schoolboy, with unique professional skills, but no interest in, or much understanding of, other people, and none *whatsoever* of women. This would make him a perfect target for Shaw. I made Higgins as ridiculous as I

With my wife, Pam

could, but someone who also took himself very seriously. Peter gave us a wonderfully dark context, in which the more seriously we played it, the funnier, and ghastlier, it got. He coaxed out of Michelle Dockery, in her first major stage role, an absolute gem of a performance as Eliza.

We opened in Bath to terrific audience response, and did good business on the road. It was obvious that this was West End material. With Peter's name and experience, and Danny Moar who runs Bath, at the helm, I felt we would probably get to London with this one, but in the event there was no theatre free. We were waiting for the musical *Bad Girls* to fail. It did, but not in time for us.

On the road, Pam kept on at me about taking the play to the Old Vic. My old friend Kevin Spacey was up and running there, and I kept saying to Pam, 'He doesn't bring shows in!' Eventually, more to shut her up than anything, I sent Kevin an email explaining our plight. Kevin can be elusive and I did not expect a reply. But Fate played a card. The very day he got my email, a huge project he had been nursing fell through, and he had a three-month hole in his programme. He replied almost immediately. He came to see the play, loved it, and the following summer we were at the Old Vic, a perfect home for Shaw's great play. Pam was right again.

An old friend of mine who saw it at the Vic said to me, 'It's perfect entertainment – the story is mythic, the language is stunning, it's very funny, it's moving, it's thought-provoking, it's political, it's got everything!' Leslie Howard, in the film, plays Higgins fairly straight, and that was the way I had seen it done before. People didn't seem to notice that Peter and I had reinterpreted Higgins – at least I had never seen it played as a peacock mummy's boy whose failure to notice Eliza bordered on the tragic – but it was a great success. I took on the play thinking it was something I *had* to do, rather than something I *wanted* to do, ended up having a ball, and, to my great surprise, found a freedom within it that I had not known hitherto.

My last stepping stone to *King Charles III* was *Enron*, my first show with Rupert Goold. Our son Tom went to the same school as Rupert and his brother, Toby, and their charming parents, our neighbours, shared with us the rigours of the morning run. Rupert was always quiet, observant, politic, extremely bright, concisely articulate and cool. In the summer holidays before he went to Cambridge he asked if he could watch our *Amadeus* rehearsals. He always knew where he was going.

Pam and I saw early productions of his in pubs and small theatres; he clearly had talent. We went to Northampton, when he ran the theatre there, to see a phenomenal, updated *Dr Faustus*. A little surprisingly, given his rather proper background, Rupert was a visionary, an experimenter and innovator, applying unlikely modern cinematic images to old plays, breathing new life into them. Although I had done workshops with Rupert, this was the first time we had worked together properly.

Enron was a colourful, Texas-based energy company that had risen rapidly to heady heights before collapsing like a pack of cards, revealing corrupt financial practices for which the main perpetrators were imprisoned. *Enron* explored the way the world of high finance was open to corruption, using and abusing ordinary people's savings. It was written by Lucy Prebble, a talented writer who came through the Royal Court Young Writers' programme: her fascinating work *The Sugar Syndrome* had attracted real attention. Although she and Rupert were developing *Enron*, it was not ready when Rupert felt that, in the wake of the economic crash of 2008, the time was ripe to mount a production. He and Lucy whipped it into good enough shape for us to go into rehearsal, and with the remarkable back-up skills of Adam Cork composing, Scott Ambler doing the movement, and a multi-talented company led by Amanda Drew, with Sam West and Tom Goodman-Hill as Skilling and Fastow, we started learning the lines, the songs and the routines. It was great fun but it felt a bit of a mess – here a song, there a number, here and there a scene-scene. What sort of a play were we in? No one seemed quite sure.

Rupert, Lucy and the splendid Ben Power, who worked with Rupert at Headlong and is now an associate director at the

National Theatre, calmly weeded and moulded. During previews Rupert courageously took out one entire sequence, gaining us 11 minutes, restoring momentum and giving us shape. The play was fun to do but we did not know whether it was any good until we got an audience on it, and then it rapidly became evident that it was more than good enough – it was … on the money! Rupert had sniffed the right moment – people were mustard-keen to see a show about how their money had been gambled away. We came into the West End at the Coward after a run at Chichester's Minerva and three months at the Royal Court, and it was a huge hit.

I was playing Ken Lay, boss of Enron, the man who stood by and watched as the company grew exponentially, not questioning methods or ethics – the *éminence grise*. There is an interesting documentary about Enron, called *The Smartest Guys in the Room*, and I watched that to get a handle on Ken Lay. It didn't help. This was a man who didn't give anything away: he was *so* nondescript as to be almost invisible. You occasionally meet people in showbiz who just want to stand next to someone famous. Sad. Ken Lay looked to me like just such a hollow man, so I decided immediately that there was no way I could play him how he really was – unless I wanted to disappear! My acting challenge was – how do you play a great big nothing? The scenes were short and pithy, interwoven with song and dance, so you had to make your impact fast – there was an element of cartoon about it. I read newspaper clippings, I looked at bits of film, but I could not find *any* useful acting information. I even met some ex-Enron employees who had actually known Lay, but even they could not help.

I am not a bad mimic, and for years, whenever I was telling stories about my time on *Escape to Victory*, I did a reasonable John Huston. One day, going through Lay's lines I reminded myself of Huston. And, basically, that is what I did – fleshed out my 30-year-old memory of Huston – there is no way *he* could be described as nothing. This seemed to meet the needs of the play. Above all, it was fun – I relished pushing my lips out, almost doing a Cagney with the hands and shoulders, and *eversho shlightly* shlushing my s's. Rupert and Lucy seemed happy, and my Ken Lay earned me an Olivier nomination for Best Supporting Actor. My expectations of winning were low – up against Eddie Redmayne in John Logan's *Red* – but if I had won, in my acceptance speech I could have said, 'Thank you. I now know ... I really am the Best Lay in the West End.'

Enron was a completely original, typical, Rupert production. The innovative aspect of his work proving both a hallmark and, to a degree, an albatross. When he brought me *King Charles III*, by Mike Bartlett, it seemed to be another one-off! Rupert gave it to me with the slightly apologetic warning that it was in blank verse, but, of course, that appealed to me. I was more concerned, as I sat down to read it, that after ten minutes of fun and pastiche at the expense of the royals there would be nothing worth getting your teeth into. There were certainly some funny lines early on – Kate Middleton says to Charles, speaking of the Queen's death, 'I never thought I'd see her pass away'. (Astute readers will observe a perfect blank verse line.) Charles's deadly serious reply is 'I felt the same'. Funny. Charles's first scene with the Prime Minister begins with the offer of tea, and the glorious line, 'Shall I be mother?' But a couple of laughs do not a play make.

However, in that scene with the Prime Minister, about 15 minutes into the play, Charles voices his concerns over a Bill for which the PM seeks royal assent, and that Bill is an attack on the freedom of the press. This intriguing development of the plot does three things: it sets up the central issue of the play, it cleverly brings the audience onside with Charles – depicted as a man of principle, nobly defending freedom of speech – and thirdly, crucially, it makes it clear that the author is taking the monarchy seriously. So ... not just a few laughs, but the smell of a proper play.

The interval achieves a theatrical coup. Charles – in full regalia – uses the royal prerogative to dissolve parliament. The second half spins the country to the edge of civil war, and with Kate pushing William hard, Charles's tragedy evolves. I have only met Prince Charles once, when he was very charming and easy to chat to. I have always had a soft spot for him, and I admire our constitutional monarchy, but Charles often comes across as eccentric, and he has a mixed press. However, Mike had drawn a sympathetic and seemingly accurate portrait of a man betrayed by time, trapped within the confines of his principled, stubborn character. The play itself was *so* good, and it didn't strike me as offensive, that in spite of a work overload I leapt at Rupert's offer.

The writing is peppered with references to Shakespeare. You don't need to recognise them, but they add to the fun. Civil war is familiar territory for Bardaholics, but there are many other allusions, to Lear, Macbeth, Prince Hal, and, centrally, Richard II – the man who is forced to give away his crown. Mike had achieved the unbelievable, how I will never know, a plausible, modern, Shakespearean tragical-historical saga, in which the audience watch people they know well, if superficially, just as Elizabethan audiences must have watched *Richard III*. The blank verse confirmed the play's place in this Shakespearean tradition; its heightened form validated the presence of the Ghost of Princess Diana, and to me it offered the potential for raising the emotional power of the piece to a level that would simply not have been possible had the play been written in prose. Importantly, the play rephrased a growing question in people's minds – what is the future of our monarchy, in the wake of the longest reign in our history?

Rehearsing the play, I found that Rupert had grown as a director, developing his skills with actors. He could always stage things impressively, but here, in Tom Scutt's superb minimal design, he gave himself little to work with but his cast. While still using his powerful sense of ritual and strong visual flair, he staged the play with Brechtian honesty, achieving a dazzling simplicity. Rupert was now running the Almeida, which is where we were to open.

To impersonate or not to impersonate ... for the five of us playing well-known royals, that was the question. Rupert was clear when he gave me the play that impersonation would kill it. Dead right. Nevertheless ... playing real people is a responsibility, even people from the distant past, and these were people in the public eye. When I first read the play, I was working with Jon Glover, who was the voice of Michael Caine (and many others) in *Spitting Image* – a brilliant mimic. I asked him what character-istics he would use for Prince Charles. He immediately suggested the habit of holding his signet ring in one hand and twisting his little finger within it, and the way he pulls his lips down, and to one side, when speaking. I did not impersonate Charles, but I made judicious use of these recognisable traits, adding another, for my own pleasure. Looking at a film clip, I noticed that his hands sometimes hover outside his jacket pockets, but rarely go in – giving him an air of indecisiveness.

We did five weeks' immensely concentrated work. There were songs to learn: the play began with a *Requiem for the dead Queen* and ended with a Coronation anthem. Jocelyn Pook had also written a *Lacrimosa*, big stuff, for the interval. The House of Commons had to be realised, a riot had to be achieved, and the evolving text was cut and altered almost daily – something most new plays have in common. We honed and shaped Mike's play and were in pretty good shape by the time we left the rehearsal room, but the big shock, when we first met the audience, was how funny the play was. Our rather dry run-throughs in the rehearsal room, while suggesting we *might* have a decent evening on our hands, had not even begun to hint at the extent of the comedy. Mike said nothing, but I suspect he knew, as he penned his important, relevant – state of the nation – play, that when Prince Harry comes on, and Camilla simply says, 'Ah, Harry!' – that it would bring the place in. But none of *us* had anticipated the level of raucous comedy that greeted us. The laughs at the first preview were so colossal they literally blew me off centre, and before the first soliloquy I had to take quite a long moment to recover from a laugh-induced dry, to refocus the play in my head: I had got it very wrong! The Almeida sold out, and we moved to Wyndham's, one of the most beautiful of London's theatres. When we were successfully installed in the West End, a couple of the cast confided to me that, halfway through rehearsals at the

Almeida, they'd agreed we were on a hiding to nothing. Their point in telling me this was that the joke was on them. Our play was not just a hit, it was a big hit!! You never know.

I have been asked many times if Charles saw the play. He did not. However, when we were at the Almeida, a note arrived from Buckingham Palace pointing out that Charles did not wear a wedding ring. I must simply have forgotten at one performance, when Palace spies were in, to remove my own wedding ring, and slip on Charles's signet ring. But the Palace could have said Charles parts his hair on the other side. So what does this mean? It suggests to me we were being informed that the Palace knew exactly what was going on, but they were not concerned enough to take action. It was like a royal yellow card. We are incredibly lucky to work in a country where we are free to put on such a play.

In the summer of 2015, between our extended run at Wyndham's and opening on Broadway, our hurricane of a London producer, Sonia Friedman, had the idea of flying me to New York for the last night of Helen Mirren's reign as Elizabeth II on Broadway, in *The Audience*: Sonia's idea was that Helen, once *her* show was over, would hand *me* the crown! It didn't happen, but it serves to illustrate the difference between the West End and the glitz of transatlantic showbiz – in England such an idea would have no legs at all.

In preview in New York, Mike and Rupert adjusted the text very slightly to clarify English things for our American audience: the passage of a Bill through the Commons, the Lords, to royal assent, needed pinning in for America in a way that had not been necessary in England. But after ten days, Stuart Thompson, our wise producer, who had made his money from *The Book of Mormon*, sent them home. There is pressure to fiddle about in preview, but Stuart was smart. The play had reached a point at which it was what it was, and any further tampering might have damaged it.

For our opening night we had lots of Broadway pizazz – a red carpet outside the theatre, two sentries with busbies and a crazed party at the Bryant Park Brasserie! I had caught a bug on the plane on the way over, which I found hard to shake off, but I was at about 90 per cent on press night. Pam was working, so Tom flew over and after the performance he shepherded our close New York friends into a stretch limo I had hired to take them to the party. It was a hoot. It was good to be with old mates, but I spent much of my time at the do being interviewed. I persuaded Tom to walk me home early. Self-preservation. More voices are damaged yelling at first-night parties than are ever lost in theatres. Tom left at five the next morning, by which time we knew the press was favourable, and I settled into the run of the play. Pam came over for Christmas, which was perfect. After that, with one month left, it was downhill. On our last Saturday but one, we lost two shows when Governor Cuomo closed the city. I was in my apartment when the blizzard arrived, driving fine snow almost horizontally past my fortieth-floor window for eight or nine hours. It left 27 inches of snow in Central Park, and delivered 24 hours of calm. The only time Manhattan is quiet is when it's snowbound.

My spell as a king on Broadway was very different from earlier times in New York. In 1974, playing in *Sherlock Holmes*, Pam and I devoured the city. This time I was, frustratingly, a good deal older – even than I had been on *Iceman* in 1999. I had to take things easy, or I simply could not play Charles. I never sleep that well in New York, and, with throbbing sinuses, rehearsals and previews were vile. Playing with a head full of custard and a sore throat is no fun at any time, but the bizarre thing is that when you get onstage, you don't feel so ill, and unless you actually tell other people they don't notice that you are in a muck sweat, cannot speak clearly, that you have to breathe at the end of every line because you have no lung power, and that when you get into the wings you heave and cough like a miner. It's called *Doctor Theatre*, or *Doctor Floorboards*. I have tried applying this technique to daily life, mind over matter, and, frustratingly, it does not work. All the world is not a stage.

Our stage for *King Charles III* was the Music Box, one of Broadway's most beautiful theatres, built by Irving Berlin in 1921.

King Charles III, *backstage at Wyndham's Theatre, 2015*

Decorated with roundel paintings, and other antiques of European provenance, it had cost Berlin a fortune. People said he would have to play to full houses there for the rest of his life, just to cover his costs. It seemed the right time to read Moss Hart's autobiography *Act One*, a lot of which takes place in the Music Box. It's a fabulous read.

Broadway suffered that season from the impact of a murder in San Bernardino, California, when a radicalised Muslim couple went on the rampage, killing 13 people and ending up dead themselves. In the wake of yet another shooting, which called to mind the dreadful Columbine massacre that had occurred during the run of *Iceman*, Isis issued an old video threatening civil disturbance and showing a brief clip of Times Square. The effect was felt across the theatre world. *Hamilton*, the hip-hop musical, was the only show that did not suffer. Our houses were very good without being spectacular, and we were consistently the third best-selling play on Broadway. Number One was just across the street from us – Al Pacino in Mamet's *China Doll*. Number Two – down Shubert Alley at our old *Sherlock Holmes* theatre, the Broadhurst – was Bruce Willis in *Misery*. Then us. It was said that both Willis and Pacino had earpieces to help them with the lines, and that Pacino, who we forget is 77, had TV screens in the wings as well! Up the street the other way, the mighty James Earl Jones was performing *The Gin Game* with Cicely Tyson. He is 84, She is 93. They too had earpieces. We had the distinction – if any of this is true – of being the only actors on our block who actually knew their lines.

At the Almeida, Joan Rivers saw the play and asked – as is the American way – if she could meet the company. She was huge fun. Sadly, not long after, she died in some kind of a botched operation. In New York, lots of people came to the stage door asking to meet me. Trudi Styler, a friend of Margot Leicester's (playing Camilla), whom I knew a little, came backstage with Sting; the remarkable 90-year-old Angela Lansbury bounded up the stairs to my dressing room!! What a joy to meet this great lady. But the moment of sheer and utter bliss which eclipsed all others was when Tim on the stage door called up to say Meryl Streep wanted to say hello. I found it hard to speak at first. But she turned out to be the most straightforward, the most natural person in the world. She has the reputation of being completely approachable at work, which cannot be said of all American stars, and here she was, this goddess, having just watched our play, chatting like an old friend. Sandy, my ace dresser, pointed out to me, when Meryl left, that with her had been the director Bob Andrews. I shan't be working for him any time soon – I barely noticed him!

Somewhat surprisingly, audience reaction to the play was almost the same in New York as it had been in London. There were some very English details that were lost on them, but substantially the response was identical. And when it was clear that we were a hit, Americans acted with their characteristic generosity. The Broadway audience for the first two months is about the sharpest you will play to anywhere. They read the *New York Times*. They read the latest books. They go to art galleries and the latest exhibitions. They are smart. After that, when the 'bridge and tunnel' set arrive, audience quality changes.

Audiences, in general, are both predictable and surprising. Ralph Richardson once said, 'Acting is the art of stopping a large group of people coughing.' As if that was easy! Musicians say English audiences save their coughing for the quiet bits. When I worked with George Cole (Arthur Daly in *Minder*), he told me he simply ignored the audience. 'They'll laugh if they want to' was his view. Brought up and taught by the genius Alastair Sim, George knew a thing or two about comedy, but I find that somewhat naive. There is a famous story about an actor who got a laugh on a line, simply asking for a cup of tea. During the run, the laugh disappeared, and he wondered why. The director explained, 'You are asking for the laugh, not the cup of tea!' The one sure-fire way to kill a laugh is to ask for it.

But surely our job as actors is to lead the audience in the direction we want them to go, not just let them take us where they fancy – which will always be towards being easily entertained! Margot Leicester, as Camilla, controlled the tone of the opening of *King Charles III*, and if she played it dead straight it took audiences too long to pick up on the comedy; this was particularly true on Broadway, where they needed a tonal nudge to tell them they were allowed to laugh at the royals.

King Charles III remains the only play I have been in where the audience could laugh *at* you, without losing interest in the fate of the characters. In the last act of a Shakespeare, it is not difficult to get unsuitable reactions. In *Titus Andronicus*, when Tamara is eating the pie with her own sons cooked in it, there are tricky laughs. You bet. Inappropriate laughter at that stage in a play makes it very hard to lead the audience to a satisfactory emotional conclusion, because when they are laughing *at* you, they are no longer *with* you. In *Charles*, this was not the case. I think, although even after 350-odd performances I am not dead certain, that they were laughing at our public personas, but were able to separate that from, and still go along with what we, as actors, were doing. In spite of some surprising laughs, I was able to carry the audience through to a sense of pain and loss at Charles's fate. The abdication always took place in tangible silence, except on two occasions, when some members of the audience called out, 'Don't sign!'

It is fascinating, given that audiences really do differ, how they characterise themselves within the first few seconds. The actor learns almost instantly what kind of a house it is: this can sometimes be a question of which night it is – some plays go really well on Thursdays, some on Fridays! Tony Hancock had a theory that all West End audiences met up before their shows, in Piccadilly Circus, and decided how they were going to react. There are 'easy laughers' who laugh at anything for ten minutes, but get bored if the play turns serious; intelligent laughers who will also listen and quiet listeners who hardly laugh at all. I like an audience to listen; their attention is more valuable to me than their laughter. If they are listening, you can take them places. Matinee audiences tend to be of a listening nature – quieter, readily attentive. This may be because they are often made up of older people. Another of my maxims is 'Nobody goes to a matinee who doesn't want to see a play'. The contrary is also true: with evening audiences, you often feel that quite large sections of the house have been dragged along against their will. Saturday night audiences are usually looking for a laugh. Some audiences perk up after an interval drink and laugh at anything. You can have thick, humourless audiences who don't laugh at all, even at the regular big jokes. You can have coughers, talkers, sweet-eaters and, of course, mobile-phone users.

Mobile phones became a nuisance towards the end of the nineties. I first became aware of them as a consistent problem during *The Iceman Cometh*, which was four and half hours long: I was onstage the whole time. In those days, before official mobile-phone reminders became commonplace, we put up a label at the entrance to the Almeida, saying, *Forty-three mobile phones have gone off during this play so far!* We updated it every day, and topped 50 in three months. One Saturday night, a phone interrupted a big scene I had with Kevin in the Third Act. This was at about 21.00. I reacted angrily.

In my defence, on Saturdays I went onstage at 13.50. Lights up was 14.00, curtain down 18.20. We were given something to eat, had time to rest for a few minutes and then – at 18.50 – went back onstage again. So by the time the phone that enraged me went off, I had been onstage for some seven hours. It takes a lot for me to get really carried away, but on *Iceman* matinee days I was not in the Almeida, I was in a bar in 1911 downtown New York! This phone wrenched me back into the real world and I swore violently at the audience. When I got offstage, the words *Brring-Brring!* had been written on my dressing-room mirror. I had acted on instinct. I will never do it again.

One night at the Old Vic a phone went off just after Kevin's first entrance. He used to hold a longish pause when he saw a stranger in the bar. The phone went off slap bang in the middle of this tense silence. Kevin turned to the house, quipped, 'Tell 'em we're busy!', and simply carried on. He is a cool bastard.

It actually amazes me that audiences themselves are so tolerant of mobiles. In the Dissolution scene in *King Charles III* on

Broadway, the same phone went off twice. In one speech! As the house lights go down in any theatre now you can see reflected light on people sending their last texts, and, one prays, turning off their phones. These people rush out at the interval to see if they have messages, and forget to switch their mobiles off for the second half.

Quite the worst mobile-phone story I know was told me by Elizabeth Franz. She was playing the wife in *Death of a Salesman* on Broadway in 1999. One of the last scenes is Willy's funeral. In the play he boasts that this will be a mighty affair, with all the salesmen from the eastern seaboard in attendance. In the event, the only people there are his neglected wife, his disaffected sons and a neighbour. Elizabeth used to play her final speech lying on the stage, talking to the buried Willy. It was heartbreaking. During this speech, one matinee, a little old lady in the second row got her phone out. She switched it on. It gets worse. She dialled a number. Can you believe this? She spoke. Audibly! And this is what she said: 'Hello-o? Hello. You can bring the car round now. It's nearly over. She's having a breakdown.'

Tony Quayle once said to me, 'I don't know why we do it, Tim. They don't really want us.'

29

Do You Know Who I Am?

Since setting out as an actor, my body and mind have been rented out to hundreds of characters, and sometimes I look in the mirror and wonder where they have all gone, and who the person left looking out at me really is. 'Do you know who I am?' is a good question; because I am not quite sure that I do...

I didn't ask to be driven in the way I am. I wish I didn't take acting as seriously as I do, or love the theatre so much that these things dominate my life. We are what we are. But I have reached a point in my life when I think that I have lived to work, and that I would have been a better human being, and probably a better actor, if I had worked to live. I have had the stabilising benefit of a long marriage, an incomparable wife, whom I admire as an actress, a fine son, and now a delightful daughter-in-law and two adorable grandchildren. But try as I do to achieve equilibrium in my life, acting dominates.

In 2003, James Watson spoke to a convocation of scientists at a dinner in celebration of the fiftieth anniversary of the discovery of DNA. Because of *Life Story*, Alan Howard and I were invited. On the way home together we expressed our envy of the scientific community's freedom to take itself seriously. On similar occasions, actors are expected, and perhaps feel obliged, to entertain! Writing about something as relatively unimportant as acting (unimportant in relation to the structure of DNA) carries with it the danger of pretentiousness, but as I have spent over 50 years thinking about it, bear with me ... firstly, why do we do it?

Tom with his wife Rachel, on their wedding day, 2011

Our friend Patrick Godfrey relates that when he was eight he was involved in an event organised by his father, the local vicar, in the village hall, and Pads was showing off. His father took him to one side and reprimanded him. Pads, close to tears, said, 'I just wanted to make the little girls laugh.' So yes, of course ... we like to entertain.

I know people who like the fear. I don't; it knots me up and I can't function. I deal with pressure, on and off the stage, by pretending it is not there: when my mother died, suppression of my grief made me ill.

It is fatal to think of acting as escapism or therapy. It just won't work. Nevertheless, I think a lot of us act as a partial compensation for something conscious or subconscious that is missing in our real lives. It goes back to my question – which parent are you acting for?

I sometimes think I do it to prove to myself that I actually exist; the heightened reality of the theatre is undeniable. Acting has always been one way for me to feel properly alive, proving to myself that I am *someone* – not someone important, just someone, someone *alive* – even if that someone is not me!

I sometimes wonder if I act because it gives me a momentary illusion that I have control over the chaos of living. One's inner life is turmoil at the best of times, but when you are doing a play for a brief period of time it is possible to feel you are in charge, that you have pinned the demon down.

Some people act out of vanity, but that is fatal. John Wood was always at his best early on; after a while, his performances became a mutual celebration, between him and his audience, of his brilliance, and this vanity marred his acting. He also looked for control, but something very different from what I mean: he wanted control over other actors, asking them to do what he wanted, so it was easier for *him* to do what *he* wanted. That is egotism, but of course actors *need* ego; without it, you would not leave the wings. It's a question of balance.

Any attempt to analyse acting is *made* complex because we are locked in ourselves. What do I sound like? What do I look like?

My parents, 1937

Am I achieving what I have in my head? How can I know? Being an actor is more like being a competitive runner than any other sort of creative artist – a musician has an instrument, a painter has a brush and oils, a sculptor has a chisel: Ralph Richardson described acting as *sculpting against time*. But when you *are* the chisel, it's hard to determine the truth. A sprinter, running the hundred metres, can analyse the length of stride he needs to achieve the perfect race. He *then* has to run it – that's the mystery. You can analyse acting, too, as I have done on occasion, by creating emotional and psychological graphs. You can define what ingredients are necessary to get a scene to work, but such tools can be too precise, too coldly diagnostic, to light a creative flame. The contradiction is that you can get everything exactly where it should be, but not find the spark that ignites it: it's a mystery.

I knew an actor who understudied Rex Harrison in *My Fair Lady*. At one point Sexy Rexy used to enter, and, kneeling, he got a round. My friend had to go on for him, and, try as he might, he could not get that round. One day he was a moment late. The audience clapped. It's a mystery. If you take the mystery out of it, it will always be dead.

I think I act for that mystery – when a play happens, either on the rehearsal-room floor or in front of an audience, it is a beautiful experience. For me, those wonderful nights are when I myself have hardly been present; the play has moved through me and the cast, and there has been a powerful sense that the total of the evening is far greater than the sum of its parts.

And I believe that is the Holy Grail that the theatre actor aspires to; we are trying to capture the smoke, to enable, and experience the mystery.

If that is the elusive *why*, how do you go about it? The director Terry Hands observed that the actor must be a combination of the madman and the monk. You need monk-like dedication and commitment, but you have to have the madman's ability to let go and embrace uncertainty. I express it as needing to use all the tools in your craft box to lay the ground accurately, and then trust, perhaps pray, that in letting go, the spark will come, and you will find the freedom to play. It's an act of faith. And there is always the infuriating contradiction that, when it happens, it is easy, simple and effortless.

What, then, are the tools? First is instinct – you have to react to your material, but then your first weapon is voice – be easily heard; that is personal work, and plays are communal things, so … what I want from a director, and the first thing I try to provide *as* a director, is a sense of the world of the new play we are creating together. What is the picture? Is it naturalistic or stylised? Is the paint boldly applied in oil, or do we have a gently detailed watercolour? Is this a world picture in a massive, ornate frame? Is there *no* frame?

Research is a vital tool. It provides food for thought, but it rarely sets the creative juices running.

Character can be liberating. You will say a line, a phrase, make some small gesture, move in a certain way, and your instinct will tell you, you are not you – you have sensed the different person you are looking for. This can engage the imagination, and you are on the way.

For me, the fundamental tool is the text – the text is sacrosanct, and that is where you find the first spark. When I learn lines I try to learn more than lines – I learn 'the play', but the question people always ask actors is, how *do* you learn the lines? Well, learning is hard work, but I try to learn thoughts, feelings, mood and tone, and if I have these elements right they lead inexorably to the right words.

One of the things you develop as an actor as you get older is your own approach; my approach has changed radically in one important aspect. Since *Pygmalion*, in 2007, I have learnt my lines before rehearsal, based on the very simple theory that the more times I have spoken them aloud before the play opens, the more likely they will seem to come out of *my* mouth! I like to go through the lines three times before rehearsals. One: spadework. Two: struggle through. Three – hopefully – breeze through. As young actors we were told not to do this, because, in learning, you might fix your performance and that was considered rude to

310

the other actors. This is not true: the way you learn the lines does not have to be the way you perform them.

There are some bits of some parts you cannot learn at all unless you develop an idea of what you want to do, so when learning you can fix things, but nothing is set in stone. To know it is the crucial thing: every day I spend on the rehearsal room floor with the book in my hand is a day wasted. There is real value in a cast sitting round a table and dissecting a knotty bit of text before standing it on its feet, but once you know what the lines mean the easiest way to find out how the play works, and at the same time instil confidence in the actor, is to place the play on the stage.

The proof of the pudding is in the eating. If your private work is accurate, it convinces in rehearsal, and draws other people along; they like it and contribute to it. If it doesn't quite work, people question, comment, make suggestions, the director tweaks and you develop it. If it doesn't work at all, you have to go back to the drawing board – look for another spark. This work is your main tool.

Blocking is vital: being in the wrong place on the stage can terminally damage a speech. Some years ago, when Tom Morris ran the Battersea Arts Centre, he asked three critics to direct a play each: he thought it might give them some insight into the challenges of the craft they spend their lives criticising. One of the actresses in the cast assembled by their director/critic told me that after the read-through, he said to his very august trio, 'Thank you. I will go away now, and come back when you have done the moves.' This man had been a critic for at least 20 years, but he did not even know that blocking the play is something absolutely central to the director's work.

Lines and moves are interwoven: when you go round the table you ask her if she would like a cup of coffee; when you get down-stage left and say you feel tired, you turn and see the ghost; when the Gravedigger throws the skull at you, you catch it and say 'Alas, poor Yorick'. Moves and actions embed the lines in the actor's system.

I first heard the phrase 'in the system' from Itzhak Rashkovsky, Tom's violin teacher at the Royal College of Music. One term, Tom won the Concerto Competition. His prize was to play the concerto that had won him that opportunity, with the full college orchestra. Tom played the Delius. Unable to attend the evening performance, I went to the morning dress run. I was overwhelmed. Talking to Itzhak afterwards, I asked him if the experience of standing in front of a big orchestra for the first time, looking at a packed concert hall, would be too much for Tom. Itzhak replied calmly, 'He'll be fine. It's in his system.' It's the same with lines. If you are trying to remember them, you won't. If they're in your system, you don't have to remember them, they just happen: it's a reflex.

There won't be much spark until they're *in your system*.

There are certain other, basic, shaping tools available to the director, and they are to do with igniting and uniting the collective imagination. With *Royal Hunt of the Sun*, I created a company by letting Frankie Armstrong loose on the group with her tribal chants. Very early on, with *Mary Stuart* (NT, 1995), Howard Davies brought in Jane Gibson, an expert in historical dance, to teach us some rudimentary Elizabethan court dance, in order to convey the *feeling* of the world he wanted to create, a world with a different sense of time and, vitally, a different social order. The first thing you learn, as your leg muscles begin to tremble, is that you have to be strong to do this stuff: these people were more physical than us – they rode, they fought, they had real stamina. Then you develop a growing awareness of others, which is not something that people experience readily in *modern* dance: instead of a room full of people jigging up and down on their own, we became one, performing the same, small but precise, rise and fall, exactly together. Then you realise that the shape of the dance, and your position in it, honours its most important member – the Queen. Within two hours of such work, our imaginations, our systems, were fed new and valuable data that informed us about the world we were building together.

Always, there is the play. When working a play on the rehearsal room floor, Howard will often say something like, 'When you say that line, I think you need to invest more in it to justify the reply you get.' Howard crafts his productions so that one line leads inevitably to the next, because their emotional and psychological content has been considered. Nothing happens arbitrarily and you are woven into the tapestry of the play. What that means is that when you get in front of an audience, you feel secure. Ready. Free.

When we were working on *The Iceman Cometh*, I was playing the old 'phoolosopher': Larry spends the whole play keeping a young man, who makes unwanted filial demands of him, at arm's length. In their final encounter, it is clear that the youngster means to commit suicide. Towards the end of rehearsals, I was beginning to feel that, having spent the play rejecting him, I wanted him to go to his death with my blessing. We were working this scene, and I was thinking, 'Dare I put my arms round him?' when Howard said, 'Put your arms round him.' He had read my mind. Maybe he had led me to that point.

Good acting always looks easy. But how you achieve it can be weird, and there are more ways than one, as they say, to kill a cat. Daniel Day-Lewis takes preparation to extremes: on *In the Name of the Father*, a powerful IRA story, he spent the night before an important scene *in* the prison cell they were shooting in the next day; he asked to be woken up every time he looked like falling asleep. If that had been me, I would have been too tired to work next day. But look at the staggering results Dan gets!

I am very tolerant of other people's work methods – whatever it takes – but for me the imagination either works or it doesn't; you can't force it. If the creative imagination is not engaged, nothing will work. Once I have the lines in my system, have found out about the piece, and have the key to my character, what I look for is the spark. Monk-like work prepares the ground for the possibility of that mad spark.

There is a story about Olivier who, playing Othello one night, was on fire. Word got round, and the company gathered in the wings to watch. Afterwards, he stomped off and locked himself in his dressing room. People could not understand why. When the company manager was finally allowed in, and told Olivier he had been out of this world, he replied, 'I know! I don't know *why*.' The French, who are sympathetic to the notion of the inspired artist, say, *les dieux sont venus ce soir* – the gods came tonight.

In *The Man Who Mistook his Wife for a Hat*, a stage production based on the work of Oliver Sacks, Peter Brook explored different kinds of unusual mental conditions: one man, given a glove, could not understand its purpose; all he saw was five, connected tubes. The most affecting scene for me was the man who thought he only had one side to his face. Seated at a table was the great Japanese actor Yoshi Oshida. A video camera provided huge close-ups on two large upstage screens. After an attendant had prepared his face with soap, the man was asked to shave himself. Meticulously, he shaved one side of his face, and put the razor down. In order to explain to the patient the strangeness of his condition, it was pointed out that he had only shaved one half of his face, and he was asked to look again in the mirror. This, Oshida did, holding a long silence. The look on his face was astounding: mystified, pained, completely at a loss. At a Q and A, Oshida was asked how on earth he had achieved this stunning moment. He was reluctant to explain his thinking, but eventually he was prevailed upon to reveal – 'I count very slowly from one to five.'

So there can be mystery, even when there is no mystery. It's smoke.

Eisenstein made three short films, one happy, one sad, one mundane. At the centre of each film sits the same close-up of the main actor. The audience read into that same shot, the emotions suggested by its context.

When confronted with a young actor who said that the scene they were doing didn't feel real, Dame Peg said, 'You don't need to feel real. You need to remember what it was like when it did feel real.'

It's a mystery.

What is the actor?

A poor player?

A rogue and vagabond?

A mere conduit for the writer's words and intentions?

A blank canvas for directors to paint on?

A puppet for the designer to manipulate?

An interpreter?

The harsh and ultimate truth is that part of the mystery comes with the audience, and in the end it is the audience that counts. It is not our job to *be* or to *feel*, but to *appear* to be or feel, realistically enough to affect the audience. Gielgud, who could produce tears at the drop of a hat, said that if the actor was crying, the audience would probably not be. You are faking the truth. It's smoke. It's a mystery.

Judi Dench told me that Ralph Richardson, talking to her husband Michael Williams about acting, had said, 'Funny thing acting. One day it's there. The next ... nowhere to be found.'

Do you know who I am? Do I know who I am? Is it any surprise that I am not sure?

Acting is the most minor of gifts. After all,
Shirley Temple could do it when she was four.

Katherine Hepburn

INDEX

A
A Fish Called Wanda
  (film) 124–5
A Midsummer Night's
  Dream (W.
  Shakespeare) 64
A Passage to India (film)
  193–4
A Winter's Tale (W.
  Shakespeare) 33,
  218, 221–2
Aces High (film) 101–2
Actors' Company 235
Alderson, John 247
Aldwych Theatre,
  London 26, 36,
  47–8, 69, 71, 75
Alexander (film) 102,
  273
Allen, Sheila 193
All's Well That Ends Well
  (W. Shakespeare)
  194–5
Almeida Theatre, London
  102–3, 275, 276,
  295, 296, 297
Amadeus (P. Shaffer)
  197, 259–60, 264
amateur productions,
  mother in 4, 6
Amnesty International
  195
Anderson, Jim 114
Anderson shelter,
  grandfather's 3
Anglia TV 255
Antony and Cleopatra
  (W. Shakespeare)
  66, 68, 69, 71, 213,
  214–16, 225–6

Armstrong, Frankie 250,
  312
Art of Coarse Acting (M.
  Green) 16–17
Arts Council 223, 235,
  236–7, 238, 245,
  253, 254, 255–6,
  259, 260, 263,
  264–5
As You Like It (W.
  Shakespeare) 53
Ashcroft, Dame Peggy
  14, 21–2, 28, 41,
  42, 47–8, 182, 187,
  189–92, 193–7,
  225, 314
Atkins, Eileen 222
Atkins, Robert 18–19
Attenborough, David 10
Australia 179–80
Ayot, William 202–3,
  207, 208

B
baby boom 1
Bacall, Lauren 179–80
BAFTAs 104, 180–1, 213
Baring Foundation 244,
  259
Bartlett, Mike 294, 295,
  296, 297
Barton, John 20, 86–8,
  214
Bates, Alan 262
Bax, Martin 79, 259
Baxendale, Helen 260
Bayliss, Lilian 192–3
BBC (British
  Broadcasting
  Corporation) 3,

110, 112, 124,
  127–8, 132, 134,
  136, 150, 155, 182,
  184–5, 211, 213
Benefactors (M. Frayn)
  182–3, 185, 204,
  253
Bengal Lancer (F. Yeats-
  Brown) 201
Bengal Lancer (W. Ayot
  play adaptation)
  205–9
Berliner Ensemble 189
Berry, Cicely 67
Best, Eve 273
Birt, John 124
Blackett, Mr 236, 256,
  258
Blakely, Colin 76
Blakemore, Michael 71,
  182, 183, 251, 252
Bogarde, Dirk 262–3
Boswell, Ruth 247
Boycott, Geoffrey 183–4
Branagh, Kenneth 236
Brando, Marlon 146
Brandt, George 33
Brecht, Bertolt 189, 192
Brenner, Nat 35–7, 39,
  42, 48–9, 51, 69
Brett, Jeremy 99
Bristol Old Vic 36–7,
  51–3, 69, 117, 204,
  264
Bristol Old Vic Theatre
  School 35–9, 41–2,
  48–9, 51–2
Bristol University drama
  department 24, 25,
  29, 31, 33–5

British Film Institute (BFI) 119
Broadhurst Theater, New York 93
Broadway, TPS on 92, 93–6, 228, 267, 276, 297–8, 300–1, 304
Brook, Faith 57–8
Brook, Peter 15, 26, 64, 79–80, 314
Brown, Ian 280–2
Budapest 137, 148
Burton, Richard 104
Byron, John 54–5

C
Cadell, Gill 43, 44
Cadell, Jean 42, 44
Cadell, Simon 42–4, 47–8, 52, 54, 117, 235
Caine, Jeffrey 247, 255
Caine, Michael 144, 145–7
Cairncross, Jimmy 57, 58, 59, 60
Cambridge Theatre, London 60, 61
cameramen, BBC 114
Camp III, Dr and Mrs 91–2
Carteret, Anna 155–6
cartoons, Evening Standard 183–4
Caucasian Chalk Circle (B. Brecht) 11, 64
censorship 46–7
Chain Reaction (film) 204–5
Chandler, Raymond 123–4
The Changeling (T. Middleton and W. Rowley) 255
Chastleton House, Moreton-in-Marsh 128

Chetak (horse in Jewel in the Crown) 168–9
Chetwyn, Bob 56, 61
The Chief (ITV) 247–9, 255, 259
choirs 9, 11
Church, Tony 18, 21
Clare, Rob 244, 259
Clark, Brian 124
Clash of the Titans (film) 118–23, 233
Cleese, John 124–5
Clutton-Brocks, Lord and Lady 128
Clwyd Theatr Cymru 251–2
Codron, Michael 182, 183
Cogo-Fawcett, Robert 208, 245, 262
Cole, George 301
Collins, John 25–6, 28
Comedians (T. Griffiths) 244, 249
Comedy of Errors (W. Shakespeare) 67
Coming in to Land (S. Poliakoff) 213–14
community outreach projects, Compass 244–5, 249, 254, 258, 259–60
Company (S. Beckett) 241
Compass Theatre Company 197, 235, 236, 237–45, 249–54, 255–6, 258–60, 262, 263–5
Conscious Lovers (R. Steele) 35, 36
Conway, Jeremy 156–7
Cooney, Ray 45
Coriolanus (W. Shakespeare) 66, 68–9, 71, 73–4
Cornwell, Charlotte 69–70

Cottesloe Theatre, London 183, 218, 222
Crichton, Charles 124
Curry, Julian 58, 60, 137, 143, 144–5, 241
Cymbeline (W. Shakespeare) 86–8, 218, 221, 222

D
Dance, Charles 161–2, 185, 225
Dare, Zena 7
Davenport, Tiv 96, 97
David, John 56
Davies, Howard 273–6, 312, 313
Davis, Desmond 107–12, 114, 115, 118, 119, 120, 123–4, 259
Davis Jr, Sammy 95–6
The Day Christ Died (TV movie) 127
Day-Lewis, Daniel 313
Day, Nick 275
deaf, theatre outreach for the 244–5, 259, 260
Dear Octopus (D. Smith) 44–6
Dench, Jeffrey 88
Dench, Judi 14, 213, 216, 218, 225–30, 249, 315
Dexter, John 54
digs, theatrical 18
Dockery, Michelle 291
Donat, Robert 169
Douglas, Kirk 97
Drake, Fabia 194
Dray, Michael 244–5, 259, 260
The Dresser (R. Harwood) 68
Duggan project 124
Dunlop, Frank 81–2, 94
dynamation, Ray Harryhausen's 118–19

E
Early English Stages (G. Wickham) 33
Edgar Flower Reading Prize 21, 22
educational projects, Compass 244, 258, 259–60
Eisenhower Theatre, Washington DC 88
Eisenstein, Sergei 314
Elgar, David 216, 218
Elstree Studios 69
Engels, Johann 259
English Shakespeare Company 235–6
Enron (L. Prebble) 291–4
Entertaining Strangers (D. Edgar and A. Jellicoe) 216–18
Equity 51, 223, 249, 260, 276
Escape to Victory (film) 136–41, 143–5
Eustace and Hilda (BBC television film trilogy) 110–12
Evening Standard 183–4, 185
Everyman 41–2

F
Falklands War 148, 150
Fame Is the Spur (BBC) 150, 153, 169
Farrell, Nicholas 38
Fenton, George 180–1, 204
Fields, Freddie 136, 140–1, 143, 144, 145
films
  Aces High 101–2
  Alexander 102, 273
  Chain Reaction 204–5
  The Challenge 179
  Clash of the Titans 118–23

The Day Christ Died 127
Escape to Victory 136–41, 143–5
A Fish Called Wanda 124–5
The Hunchback of Notre Dame 157–8
Joseph Andrews 128
Life Story 211–13
No Mama No 127
Quantum of Solace 229–30
The Shipping News 227, 228–9
Thirty-Nine Steps 193
'Tis Pity She's a Whore 127, 128
Five Kinds of Silence (S. Stephenson) 280
Fleetwood, Sue 57, 61, 64, 86, 111
flamenco dancing 121
forgetting lines 102–3
Forman, Sir Denis 169, 176, 185
Forrester, Julian 238, 239, 241, 250, 251, 253, 254, 255–6
Forster, Mark 229–30
Foster, Barry 263–4
Franz, Elizabeth 304
Frayn, Michael 182, 183
Frears, Stephen 211
Friedman, Sonia 297

G
Gaiety Theatre, Manchester 15
Ghosts (H. Ibsen) 41, 47–8
ghosts, theatre 117, 193
Gibson, Ken 270
Gielgud, John 14, 22, 120, 192, 234, 268, 315
Giles, David 150
Gill, Peter 63

Gillette, William 81
The Girl with Green Eyes (film) 107, 109, 112
Glittering Prizes, The (BBC mini-series) 130
Glover, Jon 296
Glover, Julian 118, 241
Godfrey, Patrick 241, 275, 307
Gold, Jack 101
Goldblum, Jeff 211, 213
Goldman, Milton 100
Goodbody, Buzz 76, 78–9, 80, 81
Goodman, Ada (T.P.S.'s maternal grandmother) 6–7
Goodman, Eddie (T.P.S.'s maternal grandfather) 1, 3, 6
Goold, Rupert 267, 291–3, 294, 295–6, 297
Grace, Nick 57
Granada 120–1
Granada Studios 157, 169, 172, 175

H
H Street, Washington DC 91
the Half theatre term 58–9
Hall, Ed 189, 279
Hall, Peter 15, 20, 26, 27–8, 30, 63, 189, 213, 214–15, 216, 221, 222, 267–8, 279, 289, 291
Hall, Sir Ernest 258, 265
Hamlet (W. Shakespeare) 34–5, 37, 56–62, 80, 222–3, 267–73
Hancock, Tony 302
Hands, Terry 75
Hannah (TV mini-series) 132

Hardy, Robert 14, 262
Harryhausen, Ray 118–19
Hartley, Basil 18
Harwood, Ronald 67–8
Hayman, Ronald 262
Haymarket, Leicester 190, 204
Hazeldine, James 273
Heffer, Richard 155
Henry IV (i) (W. Shakespeare) 132, 134–6, 233
Hernon, Paul 241–2, 244, 249–50, 251
Heston, Charlton 15
Hirsch, Dr Leonard 5
Hogg, Ian 68–9
Hoggart, Richard and Simon 11
Holm, Ian 20, 274
Holy Trinity Church, Stratford-upon-Avon 18–19
Hopkins, Anthony 157, 213, 216
Horniman, Miss Annie 15
Howard, Alan 64, 213
Howard, Trevor 101
The Hunchback of Notre Dame (TV movie) 157–8
Huppert, Isabelle 273
Huston, John 136, 137, 138–9, 140–1, 293–4

I
The Iceman Cometh (E. O'Neill) 227, 228, 274–8, 303, 313
India, filming in 167, 171–4
Irons, Jeremy 52–3

J
Jackson, Barry 64, 190
Jackson, Mick 31, 211

Jackson, Sir Barry 64, 234
James, Clive 115
Jane Eyre (C. Brontë) 37
Jellicoe, Ann 45, 216, 218
The Jewel in the Crown (TV mini-series) 153, 155–7, 158–63, 165–76, 177–80, 183–4, 185–7, 194, 225
Joffe, Roland 127–8
Johnson, Richard 65, 101, 104
Joseph Andrews (film) 128
Joyce, Michael 204, 256, 258–9, 267
Julius Caesar (W. Shakespeare) 15, 65, 66, 67, 189, 255–6, 258–9, 279

K
Karlin, Miriam 223
Keith, Penelope 74, 99
King Charles III (M. Bartlett) 102–3, 185, 187, 294–302, 303–4
King Edward VI School 14, 21, 22, 24–5, 66
King Lear (W. Shakespeare) 15, 34, 51–2, 64, 75, 80, 280–4
Klaff, Jack 245, 251, 253
Krapp's Last Tape (S. Beckett) 46, 204, 241
Kruger, Rolf 101, 103–4
Kulukundis, Sir Eddie 265
L
Lacey, Horace 10
Lansbury, Angela 300
laughter in theatre 301–3

Lean, David 109, 193–4
Lee, Jennie 63–4
Leicester Cathedral choir 9
Leicester, Margot 301–2
Leicester Mercury 9, 10, 190
Leigh-Hunt, Barbara 51, 262
Lewis, Damian 268
Lewis, Ronald 56–7
Life Story (TV movie) 211–13
Little Round House, Stratford-upon-Avon 79
Littlewood, Joan 78
Livingstone, Sid 83
Lloyd, Marie 47
Locke, Philip 81, 96
Longdon, Terence 256, 259
Look Back in Anger (J. Osborne) 15, 44–5, 109, 238
Lord Chamberlain 46
Love's Labour's Lost (W. Shakespeare) 42–3
Luther (J. Osborne) 53–4

M
M & B penicillin 4
Macbeth (W. Shakespeare) 53, 117–18, 235, 249
MacGowran, Jack 191
Madách Theatre, Budapest 148
Major Barbara (G.B. Shaw) 52–3
makeup and latex 150, 153, 165, 167
Malta 121–2, 233
The Man Who Mistook his Wife for a Hat (based on work of O. Sacks) 314

Manoel Theatre, Malta 122
Marat-Sade (P. Weiss) 26
Martin, Trevor 252
Mary Stuart (F. Schiller) 228, 273, 312
Mason, Brewster 87
Massey, Anna 273
Massey, Dan 137, 139, 143, 144–5, 147
The Master Builder (H. Ibsen) 280
McCabe, Richard 259
McCallin, Tanya 267, 268, 270
McCann, Liz 93, 95
McKellen, Ian 56, 61, 62, 85–6, 235, 281
McWhinnie, Donald 46
Measure for Measure (W. Shakespeare) 112–15
Memorial Theatre, Stratford-upon-Avon 13–15, 18–19, 190–2, 234
memorials, actors' 39, 96, 197
Merchant of Venice (W. Shakespeare) 190, 191
Meredith, Burgess 'Buzz' 120–1
Merman, Ethel 94–5
Messina, Cedric 112
Miles, Connie 65–6
Miles, Pamela 78, 100, 156, 180, 263
   in *Animal Farm* 183
   Australia visit 179
   birth of son 107
   doubts about Compass 238, 241, 249, 265
   in *A Fish Called Wanda* 124–5
   in *Hamlet* 268
   Highgate house 43
   in *Julius Caesar* 256

meets TPS 55, 56
move to Greenwich 97–8, 155
move to Stratford-upon-Avon 65–7
play visits 80
proposal and wedding 65–6
in *Pygmalion* 289, 291
recital of *Out of India Anthology* 195–6
in *Sherlock Holmes* 85, 95
Welsh National Theatre 74–5
Miller, Max 46–7
mini-series, demise of the British 184–5
Mirren, Helen 273, 274, 297
mobile phones in theatres 303–4
Moore, Bobby 140
Moore, Ted 118
Morahan, Christopher 155–7, 158, 161, 171, 173, 174, 175, 176, 184, 185
Morgan, Wendy 161
Morris, Tom 51–2
Mourning Becomes Electra (E. O'Neill) 273
Much Ado About Nothing (W. Shakespeare) 54, 55–6, 148, 234
Murchison, Ruari 282, 284
Music Box Theatre, New York 185–6, 298, 300
Music of Time (TV mini-series) 184

N
Nairobi 3–4
National Service 108

National Theatre 15, 63, 68, 70, 183, 213, 216–18, 221–2, 225–6, 234, 235, 253, 262, 273–4, 279
National Union of Students Drama Festival 78
Nelligan, Kate 69–70
Neville, John 54, 55, 64
New York City 92, 93–6, 99–100, 178, 298
   see *also* Broadway, TPS on
New York Times 94
Next Time I'll Sing to You (J. Saunders) 79
Nicholas Nickleby (C. Dickens) 144
No, Mama, No (BBC Playhouse) 127
Noble, Adrian 31, 96, 284, 285
Novello, Ivor 18
Nugent, Nell 93, 95
Nunn, Trevor 63, 64–5, 69, 74, 75, 78, 81, 194–5, 239

O
Observer 115, 208
O'Brien, Jim 158, 161, 171, 173, 174, 175, 176
Old Vic Theatre, London 18, 31, 68, 81, 192–3, 225, 235, 256, 276, 291, 303
Olivier, Laurence 15, 68, 71, 76, 96–7, 104, 120, 134, 146, 234, 256, 313–14
Olivier Theatre 216, 222, 262
'Ombra mai fu' (Handel) 38–9

Open Air Theatre,
    Regent's Park 18,
    267–8, 272
Ormond, Julia 263–4
Oshida, Yoshi 314
O'Sullivan, Maureen 99
O'Toole, Peter 14, 36–7,
    104, 190–1, 192,
    235
Oxley, John 38–9

P
paint-shop, RSC 25–9
Parfitt, Judy 161, 180,
    182
parties, show-business
    94–6, 100, 298
*Passages to India/Out
    of India* anthology
    195–6
Peck, Gregory 147
Pelé 136, 139, 140
Peter, John 253–4
Phipps, Jack 255, 260
Pigott-Smith, Harry
    (TPS's father) 3, 6,
    9, 14, 29, 67, 190
Pigott-Smith, Margaret
    (TPS's mother) 1,
    3–4, 5, 6, 7, 29,
    65, 66
Pigott-Smith, Tim
    acting fears/forgetting
        lines 101–3
    acting roles
        in *Aces High* 101
        in *Alexander* 102,
            273
        in *Antony and
            Cleopatra* 69, 78,
            213, 214–16, 225–6
        in *Aspects of a Hero*
            148–50
        in *Benefactors* 182–3,
            253
        in *Bengal Lancer*
            205–9

in *Chain Reaction*
    204–5
in *The Chief* 247–9,
    255, 259
in *Coming in to Land*
    213–14
as Coriolanus 73–4
in *Cymbeline* 86–8,
    218, 221, 222
in *The Day Christ
    Died* 127
in *Enron* 292–4
in *Entertaining
    Strangers* 216, 218
in *Eustace and Hilda*
    (BBC) 110–12
in *Fame is the Spur*
    (BBC) 150, 153, 169
in *Five Kinds of
    Silence* 280
in *Hamlet* 56–62
in *Hannah* 132
in *Henry IV(i)* 132,
    134–6, 233
in *The Hunchback of
    Notre Dame* (BBC)
    157–8
in *The Iceman
    Cometh* 227, 228,
    274–6, 303, 313
in *The Jewel in the
    Crown* 153, 155–7,
    158–63, 165–76
in *Joseph Andrews*
    128
in *Julius Caesar* 279
as King Charles
    III 102–3, 267,
    294–302, 303–4
as King Lear 280–4
in *Life Story* 211–13
in *Macbeth* 117–18
making *Clash of the
    Titans* 118–23, 233
making *Escape to
    Victory* 136–41,
    143–5

in *Mary Stuart* 228,
    273, 312
in *Measure for
    Measure* 112–15
in *Mourning
    Becomes Electra*
    273–4
in *No Mama No* 127
in *Pygmalion* 289,
    291
in *Quantum of
    Solace* 229–30
in repertory theatre
    17, 18, 51, 52–3
in the RSC 63, 65,
    67, 68–9, 71, 73–4,
    75–6, 78–9, 81–3,
    86–92, 93–6, 99,
    189, 279–80
in *School Play* 130–1
in school plays 11–13
in *Sexual Perversity
    in Chicago* 204
in *Sherlock Holmes*
    81–3, 88–92, 93–6,
    99, 298
in *The Tempest* 218,
    221, 222, 284–8
in *'Tis Pity She's a
    Whore* 128–30
in *Titus Andronicus*
    75–6
in *Wings* 109–10
in *A Winter's Tale*
    218, 221–2
Arts Council withdraw
    funding from
    Compass 264–5
auditions 9, 11, 53–4,
    63
birth of son 107
Bristol Old Vic Theatre
    School 35–9, 41–2,
    48–9
Bristol University drama
    department 24–5,
    29, 31, 33–5, 36

on Broadway 92,
93–6, 228, 267,
276, 297–8, 300–1,
304
charity performances
with Dame Peggy
Ashcroft 195, 197
choirs 9, 11
commissions *Bengal
Lancer* 201–2, 204
Compass production
of *Amadeus*
259–60, 264
Compass production
of *Julius Caesar*
256, 258–9
Compass production
of *Playing the Wife*
263
Compass Theatre
Company 197,
235, 236, 237–45,
249–54, 255–60,
262, 263–5
creates Duggan
character 124
Dame Peggy Ashcroft's
80th birthday
celebrations 225
dealing with fame
199–201
directing
Hamlet 267–73
Krapp's Last Tape
and *Company* 241
*Next Time I'll Sing to
You* 79
*Royal Hunt of the
Sun* 241–4, 245,
249–54, 312
early childhood 1,
3–6, 9
Edgar Flower Reading
Prize 21, 22
finances 97–8, 155,
249
health 4–6, 48, 174

horse in *Jewel in the
Crown* 167–8
job at the RSC paint-
shop 25–9
Judi Dench and the
'black glove' game
225–30
A levels 25, 29
Michael Caine in LA
145–7
moves to Greenwich
97–8, 155
on the nature of acting
305, 307, 309–15
near-death experience 5
proposal and wedding
65–6
Prospect Theatre
company 54–6
responses to *Jewel in
the Crown* 177–80,
183–4, 185–7
Saki recitals with Dirk
Bogarde 262
schools 9, 10–13, 14,
24–5
theatre visits in
Stratford-upon-
Avon 13–15, 190–1
US tour of *Sherlock
Holmes* 88–92,
93–6, 99
voiceovers 103–4, 237
West End debut 60–2
yoga 201–2
Pigott-Smith, Tom 107,
112, 125, 179,
291–2, 298, 312
Pinewood Studios 120,
157–8
Pingle, Ollie 18
Pinter, Harold 24–5
Platform Theatre
Company 262
Playing the Wife (R.
Hayman) 263–4
Plunder (B. Travers) 36–7

Porter, Eric 14, 161
Power, Ben 292–3
Powergen 262
Pratt, Stephen 22, 24–5
Prebble, Lucy 292–3, 294
prison performances,
Compass 244, 249,
258, 259, 260
Private Eye 184
Prospect Theatre
company 54–6, 235
Prudential Building
Society 256
Puddephat, Mr 66
Pursey, Elizabeth 162–3
Puttnam, David 255, 262
Pygmalion (G.B. Shaw)
289, 291

Q
Quantum of Solace (film)
229–30
Quayle, Anthony 132,
134, 190, 233–5,
236, 237–8, 250–1,
256–7, 262, 304
Quem quaeritis tropes 33
Quick, Diana 69–70
Quilley, Denis 96, 239,
241, 251–2, 253, 254

R
radio 3, 17, 97, 262
Raison, Jeremy 262
Raj Quartet (P. Scott)
155, 156
Raphael, Frederick 130
Rayner, Ed 11, 13
Redgrave, Sir Michael
100, 134
regional theatre, 1960s
64–5
The Rehearsal
(J. Anouilh) 14
Reid, Major Pat 138
religion and acting 9–10,
33

Renaissance Theatre
Company 236
repertory theatre 15–19,
51, 52–3, 234
resurrection theme in
theatre 33–4, 222
Revenger's Tragedy (T.
Middleton) 64
Richard of Bordeaux (G.
Daviot) 22
Richardson, Ian 64, 86
Richardson, Ralph 301,
309, 315
Richardson, Tony 109
Righter, Anne 86, 88
Ring Round the Moon (J.
Anouilh) 53
Rivers, Joan 300
Robertson, Toby 54, 55
Robeson, Paul 192
Robinson, Annie 256
Rock-me-Amadeus
Roadshow 259–60
Rodway, Norman 64
Rome 5, 136
Romeo and Juliet (W.
Shakespeare) 34
The Room (H. Pinter) 25
Rose Theatre, discovery
of the 197
Rosemont, Norman 157
Round the Horne (radio
series) 17
Rowell, George 33
Royal Court Theatre,
London 47, 109,
180, 281
Royal Hunt of the Sun
(P. Shaffer) 238–44,
245, 249–54, 312
Royal Shakespeare
Company (RSC)
15, 18, 26–8, 183,
222–3, 235
*All's Well That Ends
Well* 194–5
Cymbeline 86–8

Dame Peggy Ashcroft
189–90
Julius Caesar 189
Nicholas Nickleby 144
The Other Place (TOP)
79–81
Romans cycle 65, 67,
68–9, 71, 73–4,
75–6, 78–9, 81
Sherlock Holmes 81–3,
85, 86, 88–92,
93–6, 99
TPS in 63, 65, 67,
68–9, 71, 73–4,
75–6, 78–9, 81–3,
86–92, 93–6, 99,
189, 279–80
Trevor Nunn 63, 64–5,
74, 75, 78
Wars of the Roses cycle
19–20, 29–30
Royal Shakespeare
Theatre 26–8
Rudman, Michael 63
Runswick, Daryl 11
rushes, viewing 143–4,
172

S
Saki (H.H. Munro) 262
Sardi's restaurant, NYC
94–5
Schneer, Charles H. 118,
119–20
School for Scandal (R.B.
Sheridan) 11, 13, 53
School Play (F. Raphael)
130–1
Scofield, Paul 15, 104–5
The Screens (J. Genet) 69
Second World War 1, 3,
4, 108–9
Şerban, Andrei 239–40
Sewell, Rufus 249, 254
*Sexual Perversity in
Chicago* (D. Mamet)
204

Shaffer, Peter 45, 193,
238, 239–40, 241,
254, 259, 260
Shakespeare, John 66
Shakespeare, William 14,
19, 33–4, 53, 286–7
see also Royal
Shakespeare
Company (RSC);
individual plays by
name
Shaw, Rose Tobias 136
Shaw, Tommy 140–1
Sheen, Martin 204
Shelley, Rudi 37–8
Sherlock Holmes
(W. Gillette) 81–3,
85, 86, 88–92,
93–6, 99
The Shipping News (film)
227, 228–9
Show of Hands Theatre
Company 244
Siddons, Sarah 117
Small, Colin 249, 251
Smith, Maggie 14, 127,
213, 214, 254
Solti, Georg 145
Spacey, Kevin 83, 227–9,
275, 291, 303
Spector, Maude 100–1
Spence, Paul 263
St John the Baptist Junior
School 10
St Paul's Church, Covent
Garden 96
Stafford, Kathleen 38
Stallone, Sylvester 139,
143, 145
Stewart, Greg 161
Stewart, Patrick 68–9,
75–6, 274
Stratford-upon-Avon
13–14
see also Memorial
Theatre, Stratford-
upon-Avon; Royal

Shakespeare
Company (RSC)
*Stratford-upon-Avon
Herald* 14
Streep, Meryl 211, 301
Such Rotten Luck (radio)
262
Sunday Times 253–4
superstitions, acting
117–18
Swan Theatre, Stratford-
upon-Avon 189
Symons, Vic 172, 175

T
The Talking Cure (C.
Hamptons) 273
Tamás 148
The Taming of the Shrew
(W. Shakespeare)
190–1
Taylor, Ken 157, 158,
173, 180, 194
television
1970s studios
112, 114
Antony and Cleopatra
69
Aspects of a Hero
148–50
The Chief 247–9, 255,
259
Eustace and Hilda
110–12
Fame is the Spur 150,
153, 169
Hannah 132
Henry IV 132, 134–6
*Hunchback of Notre
Dame* (BBC) 157
Jewel in the Crown
153, 155–7,
158–64, 165–76,
177–80, 183–4,
185–7, 194
Measure for Measure
112–15

School Play 130
Wings 109–10, 202
The Tempest (W.
Shakespeare) 218,
221, 222, 284–8
Thatcher, Margaret
184–5, 223, 247
The Other Place (TOP)
79–81
Theater an der Wien,
Vienna 56, 57–60
Theatre Royal, Bath 242,
254, 262, 284–5
Theatre Royal, Bristol
39, 69, 117
see also Bristol Old Vic
Thirty-Nine Steps (film)
193
Thompson, Stuart 297
Thorson, Linda 178
Timon of Athens (W.
Shakespeare) 104–5
'Tis Pity She's a Whore
(J. Ford) 127,
128–30
Titus Andronicus (W.
Shakespeare) 66,
68, 71, 75–6, 234,
302
Todd, Richard 44
touring theatre 234–6,
242, 244
see also Compass
Theatre Company
Tushingham, Rita 107–8,
112
Two Monsoons (T.
Wilkinson) 205,
207
Tynan, Kenneth
45, 46
Tyzack, Maggie 73, 107,
162, 254
U
United States of America
see Broadway, TPS
on; Caine, Michael;

Iceman Cometh
(E. O'Neill); *King
Charles III* (M.
Bartlett); New
York City; *Sherlock
Holmes* (W. Gillette)

V
Vaudeville Theatre,
London 183, 185
voice and accents 38,
45, 67, 85, 104–5,
159–60, 161, 162–3
voiceovers 103–4, 237
von Sydow, Max 138,
139

W
Waller, David 64
Wallingford,
Hughie 17
Wanamaker, Zoë 262
Warner, David 20
Warren, Roger 267–8
Watergate scandal 88
Waye, Tony 119–20
Weissberger, Arnold
99–100, 101
Welles, Orson 100
Welsh National Theatre
74–5
West End 45, 182–3,
245, 254, 260
TPS's debut 60–2
see also individual
theatres by name
West, Tim 55–6
West Yorkshire
Playhouse 280, 284
Westminster Cathedral
Choir School 9
The White Devil (J.
Webster) 38
Whitehall Theatre,
London 45
Whyman, Erica 81
Wickham, Hesel 33

Wickham, Professor
    Glynne 24, 25, 31,
    33–5
Willcox, Toyah 259
Williams, Emlyn 13, 190
Williamson, Nicol 71,
    73, 74
Wilson, Stuart 60
Wings (TV series)
    109–10, 202
Winterbottom, Michael 31

Wolfit, Donald 67–8
Wood, John 75, 76,
    81–2, 96–7, 307
Woodfall films 107–8,
    109
World Trade Center
    terror attacks
    279–80
Wyggeston Boys grammar
    school 10–13

Y
Yeats-Brown, Francis
    201–2, 207, 208,
    209
Yentob, Alan 124
yoga 201–2
Young Vic 'Cycle
    Factory' 81

ABOUT THE AUTHOR

Tim Pigott-Smith OBE was a British actor who trained at the Bristol Old Vic before beginning a career in theatre, television and film including *King Lear, King Charles III, The Jewel in the Crown, Enron, Pygmalion, Sherlock Holmes, The Chief, Miranda, Escape to Victory, Quantum of Solace, Clash of the Titans* and *V for Vendetta*. He died shortly before this book was published, in April 2017.

A NOTE ON THE TYPE

The text of this book is set in Linotype Sabon, a typeface named after the type founder, Jacques Sabon. It was designed by Jan Tschichold and jointly developed by Linotype, Monotype and Stempel in response to a need for a typeface to be available in identical form for mechanical hot metal composition and hand composition using foundry type.

Tschichold based his design for Sabon roman on a font engraved by Garamond, and Sabon italic on a font by Granjon. It was first used in 1966 and has proved an enduring modern classic.